Austrian Identities

Twentieth-Century Short Fiction

Studies in Austrian Literature, Culture and Thought
Translation Series

General Editors:

Jorun B. Johns
Richard H. Lawson

Austrian Identities
Twentieth-Century Short Fiction

Edited by
Craig Decker

ARIADNE PRESS
Riverside, California

Ariadne Press would like to express its appreciation to the Bundes-kanzleramt - Sektion Kunst, Vienna for assistance in publishing this book.

.KUNST

Library of Congress Cataloging-in-Publication Data

Austrian identities : twentieth-century short fiction / edited by
   Craig Decker.
      p.   cm. -- (Studies in Austrian literature, culture and
   thought. Translation series)
   Includes bibliographical references.
            Contents: Austrian identities in a twentieth-century land-
scape of historical change / Kathy Brzovic — Sightseeing in an old city /
Ingeborg Bachmann — The tale of the 672nd night / Hugo von
Hofmannsthal — Lieutenant Gustl / Arthur Schnitzler — The bust of
the emperor / Joseph Roth — The blackbird / Robert Musil — Crossing
the border / Ödön von Horváth — Youth in an Austrian town ; Among
murderers and madmen / Ingeborg Bachmann — The Italian ; Crimes of
an Innsbruck merchant's son / Thomas Bernhard -- Oh, my dear
Augustin ; A neighbor of mine and Musil's / Barbara Frischmuth —
Baronkarl / Peter Henisch — Inventory / Felix Mitterer — The Sunday
roast ; How far is Mauthausen? / Elisabeth Reichart — The right nose /
Doron Rabinovici.
ISBN 1-57241-129-5
   1. Austrian fiction--20th century--Translations into English. 2. Short
stories, Austrian--Translations into English. 3. Austria--In literature. I.
Decker, Craig, 1956- II. Series.
PT3826.F5A97 2004
833'.010832436--dc22

                                                      2004057365

Cover Design:
Art Director, Designer: George McGinnis

Copyright ©2004
by Ariadne Press
270 Goins Court
Riverside, CA 92507

for Grace—
    who has taught me
    the joys of reading
    anew

Contents

Acknowledgments

An anthology of this sort presupposes as many people to thank as it does individual authors. At Ariadne Press, I thank Jorun Johns for inviting me to edit a collection of short stories and for seeing this particular compilation through to completion. Along the way, this volume and its editor benefited greatly from the knowledge and generosity of many individuals. I especially wish to thank Kathy Brzovic´ for introducing the stories so expertly, for getting me to revisit the punctuation in the Anichstrasse, and for shaping my understanding of Austrian literature and history so profoundly; Georgette Dumais for her scanning wizardry; A. Holmes Fetherolf for bringing his sense of style to the project; Peter Henisch and Eva Schobel for accompanying me through Favoriten and introducing me to the wonders of Tiroler Steinöl; Gerda Neu-Sokol for being the only one who knew what a "Wechsel" was; Martina Preis for cheerfully confirming all sorts of German formulations; Renate Schmid for guiding me through Vienna's often murky waters so intrepidly; Jeffrey Schneider for pointing me in the direction of the AUSTROBUS; and Waltraud and Werner Zirngast for walking me through Tyrolean interiors. As always, I owe my deepest gratitude to Susanne Fetherolf, who has contributed to this volume in far more ways that I could enumerate.

C.D.

Permissions

Ariadne Press would like to express its appreciation to the following publishers and individuals for permission to use their material:

Ingeborg Bachmann, "Sightseeing in an Old City," from Ingeborg Bachmann and Christa Wolf, *Selected Prose and Drama*, edited by Patricia A. Herminghouse © *The German Library*: volume 94, 1998. Reprinted by permission of The Continuum International Publishing Company, New York.
"Youth in an Austrian Town," and "Among Murderers and Madmen," from *The Thirtieth Year: Stories* by Ingeborg Bachmann, Holmes & Meier, New York. English-language translation © 1964 by André Deutsch Ltd., London.

Thomas Bernhard, "The Italian," reprinted from *Relationships: An Anthology of Contemporary Austrian Prose*, Edited by Adolf Opel, ©Ariadne Press, Riverside, CA, 1991.
"Crimes of an Innsbruck Merchant's Son," translated from "Das Verbrechen eines Innsbrucker Kaufmannssohns" from Thomas Bernhard, *Die Erzählungen* © Suhrkamp Verlag, Frankfurt am Main, 1979.

Barbara Frischmuth, "Oh, My Dear Augustine" and "A Neighbor of Mine and Musil's," translated from "O du lieber Augustin" and "Mein und Musils Nachbar" from *Traumgrenze* © Residenz Verlag, 1983. Printed by permission of Residenz Verlag, Salzburg.

Peter Henisch, "Baronkarl," translated from "Baronkarl" from *Vagabundengeschichten* © Peter Henisch.

Hugo von Hofmannsthal, "The Tale of the 672nd Night," from *German Literary Fairy Tales*, edited by Frank G. Ryder and Robert M. Browning © *The German Library*: volume 30, 1992. Reprinted by permission of The Continuum International Publishing Company, New York.

Ödön von Horváth, "Crossing the Border," translated from "Der Grenzübertritt" from *Der ewige Spießer* ["Vorarbeiten"] © Suhrkamp Verlag, Frankfurt am Main, 1987.

Felix Mitterer, "Inventory," translated from "Inventur" from *An den Rand des Dorfes* © Jugend & Volk, 1981.

Robert Musil, "The Blackbird," from *Robert Musil, Selected Writings*, edited by Burton Pike © *The German Library*: volume 72, 1995. Reprinted by permission of The Continuum International Publishing Company, New York.

In Austria, where philosophy and poetry (mathematical-musical) are a mausoleum, *we* look at history vertically. That's terrifying on the one hand, progressive on the other, in a word: In Austria, in contrast to other countries, philosophy and art exist not in the consciousness of its people but in the consciousness of its culture of philosophy and poetry . . .

—Thomas Bernhard

Kathy Brzović

Austrian Identities in a Twentieth-Century Landscape of Historical Change

When Arthur Schnitzler was born in Vienna in 1862, the lands under the Habsburg crown extended from beyond Prague in the north, Dubrovnik in the south, Lake Constance in the west, and Czernowitz in the east, covering a landmass of more than 260,000 square miles and embracing a population of 53 million people speaking some 15 languages. By the 1961 birth date of Doron Rabinovici, the youngest author represented in this collection of twentieth-century short stories, Austria had become a rump state of 32,374 square miles with a population of approximately 8 million largely German-speaking people. How Austro-German fiction marks the passage from a semi-feudal-agrarian, multi-ethnic empire of Germans, Czechs, Slovaks, Poles, Ruthenians, Slovenes, Serbs, Croats, Italians, Rumanians, and Magyars – through two tumultuous world wars – to a modern, industrialized Austro-German republic is the subject of this introduction.

The short story, concise by definition, and thus constrained by the genre itself to focus primarily on a single or singular event, idea, character, mood, state of mind, or simply on a single overriding emotion, would appear an unlikely form for the exploration of such epic events as those that led to the violent collapse in World War I of a dynastic house that had played a central role in European history for six hundred years, the establishment of an unstable republic, the rise of fascism, Hitler's triumphant annexation, the barbarism of World War II, defeat and occupation by foreign powers, and the formation of an ostensibly neutral republic in the crucible of the Cold War. And yet, the short story is particularly well suited to the modern sensibility for individual psychology, to the portrayal of private life and personal concerns, to the expression of private thoughts and private feelings. The grand historical event is sketched in the short story only as a landscape against which life in the small plays itself out. The requirement of compactness may limit the length of the story, but it does not necessarily limit the depth of expression, the intensity of an impression, or the emotional impact of a transformative moment. A few short pages suffice for Washington Irving to capture the emotional shock of a Rip Van Winkle falling asleep as one of King George's colonial subjects in a picturesque Dutch village on the banks of the Hudson and awakening twenty years later "a free citizen of the United States."

When history delivers a shock to the social system, the storyteller goes to work depicting the point of impact on the human psyche as it seeks to fathom it, to banish it, to neutralize it, to overcome it, or, in some instances, to welcome it. To be sure, as indicated by the series of cataclysmic events outlined above, there is little to welcome in twentieth-century Austrian history. And, therefore, it should not surprise the reader to find that mournful tales and sad stories in this volume far outnumber those of a lighter cast. Of course, if history did not impinge so dreadfully on one's life experience, if it could be *passed off* as someone else's heritage, that might be an attitudinal asset bearing greater happiness than that which accrues to those shackled by history to the past. Indeed, the comic premise of Ingeborg Bachmann's "Sightseeing in an Old City" is that it is possible for Austrians to experience history as a lark, "to see the Vienna we've never seen before" by posing as American tourists on the AUSTROBUS.

The two impostors, Mr. and Mrs. Malina, are treated to a topsy-turvy world of sights and sounds, from a welter of grand historical monuments commemorating Habsburg dynastic rule to the wine-garden pleasures provided by a set of stock fictional characters who have traded the theatrical stage for the stage of life. The master of ceremonies – a buffoon of a tour guide with a mask of the German-born composer Beethoven hanging from his neck – issues frequent malapropisms derived from a too literal translation of German words into English. Under his direction, history is all a jumble and the distinction between fiction and reality a blur. The "last medieval ruler," Maximilian I, defeats Napoleon at the Battle of Aspern in 1804, and the Field Marshall, Archduke Charles, becomes the protagonist in a popular legend whereby an angel – in response to the fervent prayers of the people – is said to have appeared in the form of a peasant lad to lead their entrapped emperor from the rocky heights of the Tyrolean cliffs to safety below.

There is only one discernibly logical chronology the tour guide obeys, as must we all. The fountains, with which the tour begins, and the Capuchins' Crypt, where it ends, symbolize the eternal cycle of life and death. What comes to an end here is not only the Habsburg family dynasty but also the mythical allure of an ancient culture that in its medieval religious mysticism would bury the remains of 12 emperors, 16 empresses, and more than 100 archdukes in the crypt while consigning their hearts to 55 urns in the Church of the Augustinians and their intestines and other internal organs to the catacombs of St. Stephen's Cathedral. The vomiting American purges the scene of the dead weight of the past, thus freeing the traveling Austrian duo to walk into the sunrise of a new day.

Although time may heal all wounds, as Bachmann's comic treatment indicates, the experience of the dissolution of the Empire as loss was very real for Hofmannsthal, Schnitzler, Roth, and Musil, four authors collectively representing the period between 1900 and 1938. Only those who, like Horváth, fully embraced republican principles were in a position to welcome the change and properly assess the emerging threat of National Socialism.

While in March of 1898 it was possible for a visiting American with a satirical bent and the pen name of Mark Twain to inform the readers of *Harper's New Monthly Magazine* that the Austrian parliament was "a ceaseless din and uproar" and the Austro-Hungarian Monarchy "a confusion of irreconcilable elements" existing in "a condition of incurable disunion" that only benefited the government, for Hugo von Hofmannsthal, a one-year volunteer in the 6th Dragoons in the year 1894/95, it was possible to view the discordant nationalities only as servants disloyal to a divine principle that invested the right of imperial rule in the House of Habsburg. "The Tale of the 672nd Night" portrays the death struggle of a bourgeois aesthete – a king in his own realm – who, having adopted a secularized form of mysticism, retreats from life to worship at the altar of art. His ambition is to complete an aesthetic palace comprised of splendid artifacts and beautiful relics that will bear witness to "a great heritage, the divine work of all the generations." Death will come peacefully and slowly when the palace is completed. However, he soon discovers that he cannot foreordain either the time or the place of his own death – that is determined by his servants, those angry and ungrateful nationalities who for some inexplicable reason reproach him with every glance for their lack of independence and fill his every waking hour with fear and dread and a terrible foreboding of death.

Hofmannsthal's telling of the tale, like Scheherazade's nightly stories to the aggrieved Sultan Schahriar in the *Arabian Nights*, is intended to stave off death so as "to live another day," to tell another tale, and, like all good myths, to deliver people from the terror of the unknown by naming it. And indeed, for the Empire death came slowly, although it did not come peacefully. On June 28, 1914, the Bosnian Serb Gavrilo Princip assassinated the heir apparent to the Habsburg throne, Archduke Franz Ferdinand, in Sarajevo. The Emperor Franz Joseph, having determined that it was "better to perish with honor," declared war on Serbia on July 28th. And what all Europe thought would be "a splendid little war" became the Great War that led to the final destruction of the Habsburg Empire and to the creation of the independent states of Czechoslovakia, Poland, Yugoslavia, Hungary, and a reluctant Austrian Republic that proclaimed in its constitution, "German-Austria is a constituent part of the German Republic."

That the code of honor the Emperor invoked in those fateful days was already a rusty relic of a bygone era is the theme of Arthur Schnitzler's turn-of-the-century story "Lieutenant Gustl." When an immature and impetuous young Lieutenant becomes the recipient of a sotto voce insult to his integrity at the hands of a common baker from whom, by the rules of engagement, he cannot seek satisfaction, he is forced into a night-long sojourn through the streets of Vienna in which he rehearses his all too brief life and the spectacle of his untimely death by suicide as the only means of restoring what his comrades in arms would surely see as his lost honor.

Gustl considers a number of possible exit strategies from his obligation to behave "like an officer and a gentleman," including exiting the stage on which traditional rites of honor are still performed: "If I only could run away from it all and go to America where nobody knows me. In America no one will know what happened here this evening. No one cares about such things there." Since Gustl cares about what people know and what they might say, what they may have seen or heard, and what they think about him, in the end, only a *deus ex machina* can rescue our protagonist from this personal and social drama by eliminating his antagonist for him. Chance intervenes in the form of a heart attack that strikes the baker dead shortly after he leaves the opera house. In a world where appearances do matter, the timely departure of the actor in and the audience to the outrage to one's honor makes for a happy ending.

It is the death of honor both as an individual character trait and as an inherent feature of the body politic that Joseph Roth laments in "The Bust of the Emperor." Published some sixteen years after the dissolution of the Empire into a multiplicity of nation-states, this prose meditation on exile from the imperial house of "many mansions" evokes the tradition of the pastoral elegy with its expression of tender sentiments for the beloved Emperor and for a golden age of pure and simple nobility in which the good shepherds of the realm once tended their flocks. If Emperor Franz Joseph (1848-1916) is the final worthy descendent of Rudolf I (remembered as the Ancestor because he was the first Habsburg to be crowned Holy Roman Emperor of the German Nation in 1273), Count Morstin is the spiritual descendent of Rudolf, who when still Count Habsburg was revered by the burghers of Zurich as the "pious count." When the cardinal virtues of faith and charity, upon which the House of Austria was founded, fall victim to the whore of modernity, to base individualism, and to vulgar nationalism through the sacrilegious defilement of St. Stephen's crown in the American bar in Zurich, the Count assembles a procession of mourners who provide a decent burial to that last relic of the honest paterfamilias, the emperor's bust.

Roth's story attests to the difficulty of letting go of the concrete forms of everyday life and of human relationships long defined by a feudal agrarian order that is quickly becoming part of a vanishing past. Yet for all its modern urbanity and metaphysical abstractness, Robert Musil's "The Blackbird" is no less a story about the difficulty of letting go of the old forms of life. A fractured existence in isomorphic apartments, trenches, and cages has replaced the borderless world of the old dynasty. The abandoned marriage bed, the seductive vision of death in war, and the caged blackbird, mother to one's childhood, are three epiphanies in a world without wise men who might unlock their deeper meaning. Aone and Atwo are merely signs in an equation that describes the uncertainty and fluidity of the modern, postwar period.

As Ödön von Horváth recognized, with the end of the Empire not only had new borders been created, but new and dangerous boundaries were being crossed. Fatal accidents were bound to happen as the fledgling republic's confused and disoriented citizenry – uncertain about which "rules of the road" to follow, which political course to steer – veered from right to left and back to the right again. Whichever vehicle, Communist, Social Democratic, Christian Socialist, or Nationalist party, conveys them to their destiny, the Wheel of Fortune will elevate some and crush others such that a man's presumed fortune may well be his misfortune, as in the case of the hapless truck driver who runs over a motorcyclist "because he wanted to pass on the wrong side of the road." Ultimately, "Crossing the Border" poses a series of prescient questions about the political train the Austrian people have boarded: Is the nation on a single track to destruction? Is it going through a dark tunnel from which it may never emerge? Will it occupy the dizzying mountain heights or find safety and tranquility in the plains below? Will Austrians and Germans alike be granted safe passage to cross borders only to be wounded in the end by an undesirable connection with a rotten wooden plank?

In historical hindsight, we know all too well the correctness of the satirist's prognosis that the Austrian nation would suffer from the wounds of its connection to a Greater Germany. As the political chaos intensified in tandem with the economic depression, so too overt anti-Semitism increased as a means of deflecting public discontent away from the government's inability to resolve the economic and political crisis in the country. In March of 1933 political infighting and party factionalism led to the dissolution of parliament, soon followed by severe restrictions on civil liberties, and then, in February 1934, by the use of the paramilitary Home Guard to crush all political opposition to Chancellor Engelbert Dollfuss's authoritarian Christian Social regime. The failed Nazi putsch of July 25, 1934, in which Dollfuss was assassinated, only served to move the government further in the direction of a dangerous endgame in which the Schuschnigg regime would seek to maintain Austria's precarious independence by continuing to play in midfield as an Austro-fascist state between Mussolini's Fascist Italy and Hitler's Nazi Germany. When Hitler finally marched into Austria in March of 1938, the independence game having played itself out and the political leadership having foreclosed the possibility of a "fratricidal war," he was greeted by millions of cheering Austrians from Braunau to Linz to Vienna. The union was sealed, and one year later the nation was at war.

If one generation of writers had metaphorically identified World War I with the eviction from the Garden of Eden, the next generation metaphorically identified World War II with the curse of original sin transmitted to the descendants by the fathers' dual sins of commission and omission. For not only had Austrians been full participants in the war effort and well represented in the Holocaust, but they also proclaimed their status as "first victim" of Nazi Germany in the 1955 State Treaty that returned full sovereignty to the Austrian Republic after ten years of Allied occupation. This kind of politically expedient reasoning, which makes a country the first victim of its own great crimes against humanity, is especially suited to that form of literary representation known as irony. And so we find that many of the stories written in the postwar period are peopled with sojourners and misfits, murderers and suicides, at once casualties of an unfathomable moral horror and of a rather banal, quotidian ethical muddle.

The muddle arises out of the simple fact that life goes on somehow – even amidst war and barbarism and even in its aftermath. At times, individuals may outwit successive social structures, as the title figure in Peter Henisch's playfully ironic "Baronkarl" does – or they may think they can – as Barbara Frischmuth portrays with double-edged irony in "Oh, My Dear Augustine." More typical, though, is the inevitable "going on" of the unexamined life that Felix Mitterer depicts in his prose still life, "Inventory," and that Elisabeth Reichart captures in all its bitter irony in "The Sunday Roast." Whatever ironic stance they may adopt in relation to the new social reality, from the tragic to the comic, the successor generation shares the uneasy realization that the reconstruction of the material conditions of life does not lead to a corresponding reconstruction of the moral basis for life as a progressive continuum in which human relations achieve ever higher forms of social, political, and ethical expression.

For the émigré in Bachmann's "Youth in an Austrian Town," who revisits the moments of childhood innocently played out in the small-town landscape of the 1930s and 1940s, all that remains of Lessing's Enlightenment vision of the progressive evolution of mankind are the shattered religious symbols of a failed moral education. Youth had been sacrificed to the leviathan, the fire-breathing dragon of war. The River of Life stood still and the Zigulln Castle, the symbol of Advent, did not rise in song to proclaim the coming of the Prince of Peace. To Christ's question, "Or what man is there of you, whom if his son ask bread, will he give him a stone? / Or if he ask a fish, will he give him a serpent?" (Matthew 7:9-10), the Austrian Catholic fathers did not respond unambiguously with "good gifts unto their children" (Matthew 7:11) but with "slices of dry bread and jam containing a stone." The burning bush that frames the story, albeit a thing of natural beauty and a source of the imagination, no longer glows with the fires of a lawgiving God promising deliverance and redemption. The time of moral education through revelation has passed both for the child and for mankind. From hereon in, one is dependent on oneself – on one's own moral imagination – to find one's way in the world, to depart for that New Jerusalem of individualism and self-reliance, America.

And, yet, Bachmann asks in "Among Murderers and Madmen," what might be the fate of a man of character with the moral imagination to recognize the murderous impulse in his own heart and to proclaim it publicly? If he were to find his way into that inner circle of literati and war veterans, who represent the Second Republic's ruling coalition of former Christian Socials, dusted-off Social Democrats, and integrated Nazis, on a leisurely evening when they might let slip the masks of their republican personas to revel in the glories of war, conquest, and brutality (fighting on the Russian front, occupying France, subjugating the Balkans by means of retributive massacres), he would become the ironic victim of his own criminal impulse to kill. For ethical authenticity in a world of moral duplicity is a provocation.

Consensus politics provided a method and a strategy for getting on with life without providing a public framework for a moral confrontation with the fact of genocide. As Friedl observes, *in private*, we didn't need new victims to teach us the moral lesson "that one should not kill. That's been known for two thousand years." History, no longer imbued with a teleological purpose, reverts to the ancient cycle of periods of calamity followed by periods of illumination that necessarily call for periodic ritualistic acts of purification. Friedl cleanses himself with water, the narrator with blood.

Provocation and paralytic fatalism play equally critical roles in Thomas Bernhard's exploration of persecution psychology in "Crimes of an Innsbruck Merchant's Son." The birth of a physically deformed son, of an only son who fails to exhibit the presumptive hereditary family trait of bourgeois uprightness, is a provocation that engenders a "perfidious solidarity" among family members bent on persecuting Georg to death. The animating principle in what Henry James would have called this "ugly little comedy" is the perfection of the art of animosity by means of a language of atrocity that consists, among other things, in naming Georg: an unsightly cripple of a son, a clump of flesh, a hideous stain, a criminal, unconstitutional, a crime against himself and a crime against his family. Overwhelmed by the "prodigious abundance of history" and epithets, Georg succumbs to the "madness of hopelessness" and submits to the tyranny of *being* in a constant state of internecine struggle by committing suicide. The persecuted thus fulfills the destiny marked out for him by the persecutors. In Bernhard's Austria, the family, the city, the very nation itself is existentially imprisoned in an instinctual unity of bellicose opposition and as such is forever condemned to reenact crimes against humanity and crimes against the soul.

That art and culture is constructed on the foundation of the graves of the dead is the basic premise of "The Italian." The *summer*house and the *slaughter*house invite the summer playgoers and the summer funeral goers to adopt the mood and don the costumes appropriate to the occasion. In principle, playgoers direct their attention to the staged action to discover what the outcome of human agency might be, whereas funeral goers observe the final outcome of the drama of life. Just as the stage unfolds a world, so the world unfolds as a stage on which present actions are narrowly prescribed by past events and actions, future expectations, customs, motives, and consequences. Bernhard's characters have decidedly clear religious and historical motives for directing attention away from the father's suicide as an abomination against God and away from the massacre of the Poles as an atrocity. Yet if the suicide is a consequence of having seen the massacre and hence is motivated by the desperate need to escape what one cannot overlook, then the son's role as an artist is to direct the funeral goers to become playgoers by placing them on the bridge overlooking the mass grave in the clearing and directing their attention to that very spot where they had stood only moments before on the hastily buried bodies of two dozen child soldiers. The humanist might well argue that art invites one to look at life from a distance in order to appreciate more fully the connection between one life and another. Perhaps it was in response to this view of art that the German Jewish émigré Theodor W. Adorno claimed it was barbaric to write poetry after the Holocaust. In acknowledgement of the horrible fact of genocide, Bernhard argues that post-Holocaust art forces one to look squarely at death in order to comprehend the connection between one premature death and another.

For youth, the moral lesson of death may have little resonance. A child's sense of time being immediate, death, if acknowledged at all, becomes at best a game one merely plays at and at worst a malicious taunt as demonstrated by the schoolboys in Reichart's "How Far is Mauthausen?" who for the sheer fun of it record the names of those they plan to lock up once they learn from their repeated field trips how to renew operations at Mauthausen. The narrator agonizes over the distance between past and present as measured in time, between seeing and not seeing as measured in space, and between feeling and not feeling as measured in attitude. Nevertheless, it is youth in Doron Rabinovici's "The Right Nose" that finds a spontaneous response for overcoming the mental and emotional distance created by difference. And here we land on the lighter side of irony – a good enough place to end. If anti-Semitism does rear its ugly head, we can always give it a good punch in the nose.

INGEBORG BACHMANN

| 9 7| Sightseeing in an Old City

Because Malina and I want to see the Vienna we've never seen
before, we take a tour with the AUSTROBUS. The tour guide hangs
a Beethoven mask around his neck, and while we experience a
whole new Vienna according to the views of a travel agency we
know nothing about, he concerns himself with speaking English for
the Americans, looking mistrustfully only at us, even though we
registered as Mr. and Mrs. Malina so we could travel with real
foreigners. The tour guide has probably traveled through Vienna
with all kinds of foreigners – Brazilians, Pakistanis, and Japanese
– because otherwise he couldn't allow himself these daring
digressions and stops at the strangest places. Because to begin
with, for example, the man only allows stops at a lot of fountains;
everyone may get off and drink from the Fountain of Geniuses, the
Danubius Fountain, and even from the Liberation of the Spring
Fountain in the City Park. The tour guide declares that everyone
has to have drunk Viennese mountain spring water, *the most
famous water in the world*, at least once. Without any stops, the
tour continues past many gray-green baroque domes, skipping the
Karlskirche, leaving out the National Library, and on the mountain
face of St. Martin's, Archduke Charles, the victor, the lion of
Aspern is mixed up with the Emperor Maximilian the First, whom
an angel saved from a Tyrolean mountain face after he lost his
bearings and whom the tour guide without hesitation set on a horse
to Vienna. To Malina's and my astonishment, the tour stops in
front of a confectionery shop in the inner city: the Americans have
five minutes to buy Mozartkugeln, the most famous Austrian
chocolates, ad gloriam and in memoriam *of the most famous
composer of all the times*, and while the Americans obediently bite
into a dried-out imitation of Mozartkugeln from Salzburg, we
circle the monument commemorating the plague, *to remember the
most famous and dreadful illness in the world which was stopped
with the Austrian forces and the prayers of Emperor Leopold I*. We
drive quickly past the State Opera House, *where are happening the
greatest singing successes and singing accidents in the world*, then
drive particularly fast past the Burgtheater, *where are happening*

every evening the old and most famous dramas and murderings in Europa. The tour guide runs out of breath in front of the university, hastily declaring it *the oldest museum of the world* and then, relieved, points to the Votive Church, *which was built to remember the salvation from the first turkish danger and the beaten turks left us the best coffee and the famous viennese breakfast* Kipfel, *to remember.* He whispers to the driver, with whom he's in cahoots, and out of the city we drive. Then because of the possibility of something collapsing we have to avoid the Stephansdom, the mammoth Pummerin Bell had just been loaned to America to be shown in a traveling exhibition, the giant ferris wheel is unfortunately under reconstruction at one of the big German firms, being made bigger for future, bigger and bigger demands. Our dear Lord is pointed to in passing; he has a peaceful bench in the Lainzer Tiergarten Park. At Schönbrunn Palace a rest stop is finally made, and everyone shyly admires the Doppelgänger of the emperor of peace, who, his seventieth anniversary of governing behind him, walks solitary and dignified through the park. He didn't want it. He was spared nothing. The tour guide leafs through his notes, finally finding the passage: "to my peoples!" Already suspecting, the tour guide looks at Malina and me for help, because he doesn't seem to know how to translate these three words. But Malina looks at him, unmoved. The tour guide asks: *is something wrong, Sir?* Malina smiles and answers in his best English: *Oh, no, it's extremely interesting, I'm interested in history, I love culture, I adore such old countries like yours.* The tour guide loses his suspicion, switches into another sentence: *Wednesday, July 29, 1914, the Emperor of the most famous Empire in the world spoke to his nineteen peoples and declared that in the most earnest hour of the greatest decision of our time before the Almighty, he is conscious.* A petite miss exclaims, "Gosh!" She doesn't want to believe that such a small country was once a big country; she was prepared for an operetta, for Grinzing, for the beautiful blue Danube. Our tour guide sets the pretty little American straight: *This was the biggest country which ever existed in the world and it gave a famous word, in the country the sun never goes down.* Malina says helpfully: "the sun never set."

But soon it's peaceful again, an anarchist killed Ms. Romy Schneider, in Korfu and in Miramar conference participants are in session at countless conferences, and Madeira is booming due to cruise trips. The tour guide turns tender-hearted, indulging himself in the dream of a waltz, the white lilacs are blooming again and in the Prater the trees are blooming again; Crown Prince Rudolf becomes acquainted with Madame Catherine Deneuve, who thank God is known to everyone in the AUSTROBUS. In Mayerling we stand around in the rain, the strictest order of nuns guards over a small wash stand that is permitted to be exhibited; there aren't any blood stains because the wing that contained this room was, by order of the Emperor, torn down a half century ago and replaced with a chapel. Only one nun is allowed to speak with us; all the other nuns pray for her, intercede for her. Night comes upon us suddenly. We haven't gotten everything for our money yet, "Vienna by night is still ahead." At the first tavern the gypsy barons and Csardas princesses appear and are enthusiastically applauded, there are two glasses of wine for everyone, in the second tavern the long-haired beggar-students are lounging around and the bird-peddlers go yodeling from table to table, there's a glass of German sparkling wine for everyone, the Americans are growing more and more spirited, we continue through the inner city from one land of smiles to another, an older American, overly enthusiastic, harasses the merry widow. At 5 A.M. we all sit before a goulash soup, including the driver from the AUSTROBUS. The tour guide offers the petite miss the Beethoven mask in a gesture of reconciliation, and everyone sings "Tales from the Vienna Woods," the tour guide and bus driver attempt "Vienna Life" alone. Finally it becomes apparent that only the driver really has a splendid voice, and everybody wants him to sing solo – there's no holding back for him. "Vienna, City of My Dreams!" Malina is exhausted, and I sense the feeling passing to me, he slides a tip to the driver who winks at me, the only one who has seen through me – he won't let me out of his sight, doesn't pay one bit of attention to the American girl, and sings to Malina: Give the laughing, charming women in Beauuutiful Vienna my greetings! *Your husband doesn't like music?* the tour guide asks with concern, and I, confused, tell him: *not so late, not so early in the morning.* Malina begins talking overanimatedly to the older American, he pretends to teach European history at a midwestern university, he's so surprised by his first stay in Vienna, there's so much to notice here that's never been noticed before, like how Western Civilization is being saved here in every place, here there is still this legendary tradition, movie theaters are dedicated to Apollo, Thalia, Eos, Urania, the Phoenix, yes indeed even to the cosmos, Eden is even a nightclub, a mild, filter cigarette for women advertises for Diana, Memphis is called to mind by the competition. I think about our apostolic emperors and whisper to Malina: I think the man just doesn't dare say that they've been baked into Kaiser rolls and shredded into Kaiserschmarrn. The American, who confesses to be a Missourian, toasts Malina, recognizing in him a *fine guy* who will take his observations and knowledge over the big pond into the wilderness.

Strengthened by the goulash soup and songs, the tour guide remembers that it's not yet time for bed, but that the tour continues unmercifully, because it's already bright outside.

Ladies and Gentlemen! Our trip will finish in the Kapuzinergruft. The Americans look at each other questioningly and disappointedly. Some would rather go to the Prater, but mornings there's no Prater and no wine taverns either, and we've already stopped in front of the Kapuziner Church and have to enter the crypt, fatigued and chilly. *Here you can see the most famous collection in the world, the hearts of all the Habsburgian emperors and empresses, archdukes and archduchesses.* A drunk old American woman starts laughing, the petite miss drops the Beethoven mask and shouts, *Gosh!* We all want to get out of the crypt, the older American who still liked the merry widow throws up. The tour guide is scandalized and curses, but no longer in English – foreigners are only out for a good time, are clueless about culture, show no respect, his job has to be the most thankless in the world, no pleasure whatsoever guiding these hordes of barbarians through Viennese days and nights. He drives his herd back into the bus. Malina and I don't board, we offer our thanks and claim to be only a few steps from our hotel, go silently, arm-in-arm, to the next taxi stand, pressing tightly against one another. We don't say a word in the taxi, Malina's about to fall asleep, and home in the Ungargasse I say: that was your idea after all. Malina says exhaustedly, I beg your pardon, that was once again your idea.

Translated by Margaret McCarthy

1895

HUGO VON HOFMANNSTHAL

The Tale of the 672nd Night

I

 . A merchant's son, who was young and handsome and whose father and mother were no longer living, found himself, shortly after his twenty-fifth year, tired of social life and entertaining. He closed off most of the rooms of his house and dismissed all of his servants with the exception of four, whose devotion and general demeanor pleased him. Since his friends were of no great importance to him and since he was not so captivated by the beauty of any woman as to imagine it desirable or even tolerable to have her always around him, he grew more and more accustomed to a rather solitary life, one which seemed most appropriate to his cast of mind. However, he was by no means averse to human contact; on the contrary, he enjoyed walking in the streets and public gardens and contemplating the faces of men and women. Nor did he neglect either the care of his body and his beautiful hands or the decorating of his apartments. Indeed, the beauty of carpets, tapestries, and silks, of panelled walls, candelabras, and metal bowls, of vessels of glass and earthenware became more important to him than he could ever have imagined. Gradually his eyes were opened to the fact that all the shapes and colors of the world were embodied in the things of his household. In the intertwining of decorative forms he came to recognize an enchanted image of the interlocking wonders of the world. He discovered the figures of beasts and flowers and the transition of flowers into animals; the dolphins, the lions, and the tulips, the pearls and the acanthus; he discovered the tension between the burden of pillars and the resistance of solid ground, and the will of all water to move upward and then downward again. He discovered the bliss of motion, the sublimity of rest, dancing, and being dead; he discovered the colors of flowers and leaves, the colors of the coats of wild beasts and of the faces of nations, the color of jewels, the color of the stormy sea and the quietly shining sea; yes, he discovered the moon and the stars, the mystic sphere, the mystic rings and firmly rooted upon them the wings of the seraphim. For a long time he was intoxicated by this great, profound beauty that belonged to him, and all his days moved more beautifully and less emptily in the company of these household things, which were no longer anything dead or commonplace but a great heritage, the divine work of all the generations.

Yet he felt the emptiness of all these things as well as their beauty. Never did the thought of death leave him for long; often it came over him when he was in the company of laughing, noisy people, often at night, often as he ate.

Since there was no sickness in him, however, the thought was not terrifying; it had about it, rather, something of solemnity, of splendor, and was at its most intense precisely when he was intoxicated with thinking of beauty, the beauty of his own youth and solitude. For the merchant's son often drew great pride from his mirror, from the verses of poets, from his wealth and intelligence, and dark maxims did not weigh on his soul. He said, "Wherever you are meant to die, there your feet will carry you," and he pictured himself, handsome, like a king lost on a hunt, walking in an unknown wood under strange trees toward an alien, wondrous fate. He said, "When the dwelling place is finished, death will come," and he saw death coming slowly, up over the bridge, the bridge borne on winged lions and leading to the palace, the finished dwelling, filled with the wonderful booty of life.

He thought he would now be living in solitude, but his four servants circled him like dogs, and although he spoke little with them he still felt somehow that they were incessantly thinking how best to serve him. For his part, too, he began to reflect now and then upon them.

The housekeeper was an old woman; her daughter, now dead, had been the nurse of the merchant's son; all her other children had also died. She was very quiet, and the chill of age emanated from her white face and her white hands. But he liked her because she had always been in the house and because she carried about with her the memory of his own mother's voice and of his childhood, which he loved with a great longing.

With his permission she had taken into the house a distant relative, a girl scarcely fifteen years old, extremely withdrawn. The girl was harsh with herself and hard to understand. Once in a sudden, dark impulse of her angry soul she threw herself out of a window and into the courtyard but fell with her childlike body into some garden soil that happened to be piled up there, so that all she broke was a collarbone, and that only because at this spot there had been a rock in the dirt. After she was put to bed the merchant's son sent his physician to see her. In the evening, however, he came himself and wanted to see how she was getting along. She kept her eyes closed; for the first time he looked at her long and quietly and was amazed at the strange and precocious charm of her face. Only her lips were very thin, and there was something disturbing and unattractive in this. Suddenly she opened her eyes, looked at him in icy hostility and, with her lips clenched in anger, overcoming her pain, turned toward the wall, so that she lay on her injured side. At this instant her deathly pale face turned color, becoming greenish white; she fainted and fell back into her former position, as if dead.

For a long time after her recovery the merchant's son did not speak to her when they met. Once or twice he asked the old lady whether the girl did not resent being in his house but she always denied it. The only servant whom he had decided to retain in his house was a man he had once come to know when he was dining with the ambassador assigned to this city by the king of Persia. This man had served him on that occasion and was so accommodating and circumspect and seemed at the same time to be so very retiring and modest that the merchant's son had discovered more pleasure in observing him than in listening to what the other guests were saying. His joy was all the greater, therefore, when many months later this servant stepped up to him on the street, greeted him with the same deep earnestness as on that previous evening, and, without a trace of importuning, offered him his services. The merchant's son recognized him immediately by his somber, mulberry-hued face and by his good breeding. He employed him instantly and dismissed two young servants whom he still had with him, and from that moment on would let himself be served at meals and other times only by this earnest and reserved person. The man had permission to leave the house during the evening hours but almost never took advantage of it. He displayed a rare attachment to his master, whose wishes he anticipated and whose likes and dislikes he sensed instinctively, so that the latter in turn took an ever greater liking to him.

Although he allowed only this person to serve him as he ate, there was still a maid who brought in the dishes with fruit and sweet pastries, a young girl but still two or three years older than the youngest. This girl was one of those who, seen from afar or stepping forth as dancers by the light of torches, would scarcely pass for very beautiful, because at such times the refinement of their features is lost. But seeing her close to him and every day, he was seized by the incomparable beauty of her eyelids and her lips;

and the languid, joyless movements of her beautiful body were to him the puzzling language of a self-enclosed and wondrous world.

It was a time when, in the city, the heat of summer was very great and its dull incandescence hovered along the line of houses, and in the sultry, heavy nights of the full moon, the wind drove white clouds of dust down the empty streets. At this time the merchant's son traveled with his four servants to a country house he owned in the mountains, in a narrow valley surrounded by dark hills, the site of many such country estates of the wealthy. From both sides waterfalls descended into the gorges, cooling the air. The moon was almost always hidden on the far side of the mountains, but great white clouds rose behind the black walls, floated solemnly across the darkly glowing sky, and disappeared on the other side. Here the merchant's son lived his accustomed life, in a house whose wooden walls were constantly penetrated by the cool fragrance of the gardens and the many waterfalls. In the afternoon, until the time when the sun fell beyond the hills, he sat in his garden, most often reading a book in which were recorded the wars of a very great king of the past. Sometimes, in the midst of a passage describing how thousands of cavalrymen of the enemy kings turned their horses, shouting, or how their chariots were dragged down the steep bank of a river, he was compelled to stop suddenly, for he felt, without looking up, that the eyes of his four servants were fixed on him. He knew, without lifting his head, that they were looking at him, each from a different room. He knew them so well. He felt them living, more strongly, more forcefully than he felt himself live. Concerning himself he sensed on occasion a slight shock of emotion or surprise, but also on this account a puzzling fear. He felt, with the clarity of a nightmare, how the two old people were moving along toward death, with every hour, with the inescapable, slow altering of their features and their gestures, which he knew so well; and how the two girls were making their way into that life, barren and airless, as it were. Like the terror and the mortal bitterness of a fearful dream, forgotten on awakening, the heavy weight of their lives, of which they themselves knew nothing, lay upon his limbs.

Sometimes he had to rise and walk about, lest he succumb to his anxiety. But while he gazed at the bright gravel before his feet and observed with great concentration how, from the cool fragrance of grass and earth, the fragrance of carnations welled up toward him in bright, sharp breaths and, intermittently, in warmish, excessively sweet clouds, the fragrance of heliotropes, he felt their eyes and could think of nothing else. Without raising his head, he knew that the old woman was sitting by her window, her bloodless hands on the sun-drenched sill, the bloodless mask of her face an ever more terrible setting for her helpless, black eyes, which could not die. Without raising his head he could sense when his servant stepped back from the window, for a matter only of minutes, to busy himself with one of the wardrobes; without looking up he waited in secret fear for the moment when he would return. While his two hands were letting supple branches close behind him, so that he might crawl away and disappear in the most overgrown corner of his garden, and while all his thoughts were bent on the beauty of the sky that fell from above through the dark net of branches and vines, in little gleaming bits of turquoise, the one thing that seized hold of his blood and all his thinking was that he knew the eyes of the two girls were fixed on him; those of the taller languid and sad, filled with a vague challenge that tormented him, those of the little one with an impatient, then again a mocking attentiveness that tormented him even more. And still he never had the idea that they were looking at him directly, in the act of his walking about with lowered head, or kneeling by a carnation to tie it with twine, or leaning down beneath boughs. Rather it seemed to him that they were contemplating his entire life, his deepest being, his secret human inadequacy.

A terrible oppression came over him, a mortal fear in face of the inescapability of life. More terrible than their incessantly watching him was the fact that they forced him to think of himself in such a fruitless and exhausting fashion. And the garden was much too small to permit his escaping them. However, when he was very close to them, his fear paled so completely that he almost forgot the past. Then he was capable of ignoring them totally, or of calmly observing their movements, which were so familiar that he felt an unceasing, as it were a physical sense of identification with their lives.

The little girl crossed his path only now and then, on the stairway or in the front part of the house. The three others, however, were frequently in the same room with him. Once he caught sight of the taller one in a slanting mirror; she was passing through an adjoining room set at a higher level; in the mirror, however, she approached him from below. She walked slowly and with effort but fully erect; she carried in each arm the heavy, gaunt figure, in dark bronze, of an Indian deity. The ornate feet of the figurines rested in the hollows of her hands; the dark goddesses reached from her hips to her temples, leaning their dead weight on her slender living shoulders, but their dark heads, with their angry serpents' mouths, their brows above three wild eyes apiece, the mysterious jewels in their cold, hard hair, moved alongside breathing cheeks and brushed her lovely temples in time with her measured steps. In fact, however, the true burden she bore with such solemnity seemed not so much the goddesses as the beauty of her own head with its heavy ornaments of dark and living gold, the hair curled in two great arching spirals at either side of her bright brow, like a queen at war. He was seized by her great beauty but at the same time realized clearly that to hold her in his arms would mean nothing to him. For he well knew that the beauty of his maidservant filled him with longing but not with desire; hence he did not rest his eyes long upon her but stepped out of the room, out to the street in fact, and walked on in strange unrest between the houses and gardens in the narrow shadows. Finally he passed along the banks of the river where the gardeners and flower sellers lived; there for a long while he sought – knowing that he would seek in vain – a flower whose form and fragrance, a spice whose fading breath could grant him for one moment of calm possession precisely that same sweet charm as lay, confusing and disconcerting, in the beauty of his maidservant. And as he peered about in the gloom of the greenhouses or bent over the long beds in the open air, with darkness already falling, his mind repeated, over and over, involuntarily, tormentedly and against his will, the words of the poet: "In the stems of carnations, swaying, in the smell of ripe grain you awakened my longing; but when I found you, you were not the one I was seeking, but the sisters of your soul."

II

During this time there came a letter that rather upset him. The letter was unsigned. In vague terms the writer accused the young man's servant of having committed, while he was in the household of his previous master, the Persian ambassador, some sort of repugnant crime. The unknown correspondent appeared to be consumed with violent hatred of the servant and accompanied his letter with a number of threats; in addressing the merchant's son himself he also assumed a discourteous, almost threatening, tone. But there was no way of guessing what crime was alluded to or what purpose this letter might serve for the writer, who neither gave his name nor demanded anything. The merchant's son read the letter several times and was forced to admit that the thought of losing his servant in such a disagreeable manner caused him a strong feeling of anxiety. The more he thought it over the more agitated he became and the less he could bear the idea of losing any one of these persons to whom he had grown so completely attached, through habit and through mysterious forces.

He paced up and down and became so heated in his angry agitation that he cast aside his cloak and his sash and kicked them with his feet. It seemed to him as if someone were insulting and threatening the things that were most deeply his, and were trying to force him to desert himself and to deny what was dear to him. He was sorry for himself and, as always at such moments, felt like a child. He pictured his four servants torn from his house and felt as if the whole content of his life were being drawn out of him, all the bittersweet memories, all the half-unconscious hopes, everything that transcended words, only to be cast out somewhere and declared worthless, like a bunch of seaweed. For the first time he understood something that had always irritated and angered him as a boy: the anxious love with which his father clung to what he had acquired, the riches of his vaulted warehouse, the lovely, unfeeling children of his hopes and fears, the mysterious progeny of the dimly apprehended, deepest wishes of his life. He came to understand that the great king of the past would surely have died if his lands had been taken from him, lands he had traversed and conquered, from the sea in the west to the sea in the east, and dreamed of ruling, yet lands of such boundless extent that he had no power over them and received no tribute from them, other than the thought that he had subjugated them, that no other than he was their king.

He determined to do everything he could to put to rest this thing that caused him such anxiety. Without saying a word to his servant about the letter, he set out and traveled to the city alone. There he determined first of all to seek out the house occupied by the ambassador of the king of Persia, for he had a vague hope of finding some kind of clue there.

When he arrived, however, it was late afternoon and no one was at home, neither the ambassador nor a single one of the young people of his entourage. Only the cook and a lowly old scribe were sitting in the gateway in the cool semi-darkness. But they were so ugly and answered him in such a short and sullen manner that he turned his back on them impatiently and decided to return the following day at a better time.

Since his own house was shut and locked – for he had left no servants back in town – he was compelled to think of some place to stay for the night. Curiously, like a stranger, he walked through the familiar streets and came at last to the banks of a little river, which at this time of year was virtually dry. From here, lost in thought, he followed a shabby street inhabited by a large number of prostitutes. Without paying much attention to where he was going, he then turned to the right and entered a completely deserted, deathly still cul-de-sac, which ended in a steep stairway almost as tall as a tower. On this stairway he stopped and looked back on the way he had taken. He could see into the yards of the little houses; here and there were red curtains and ugly, dried-out flowers; there was a deathly sadness about the broad, dry bed of the stream. He climbed higher and at the top entered a quarter of the city that he could not recall having seen before. Nonetheless, an intersection of low-lying streets suddenly struck him with dreamlike familiarity. He walked on and came to a jeweler's shop. It was a very shabby little shop, befitting this part of the city, and its show window was filled with the kind of worthless finery one can buy from pawnbrokers and receivers of stolen goods. The merchant's son, who was an expert in jewels, could scarcely find a halfway beautiful stone in the lot.

Suddenly his glance fell on an old-fashioned piece of jewelry, made of thin gold and embellished with a piece of beryl, reminding him somehow of the old woman. Probably he had once seen in her possession a similar piece obtained in her youth. Also, the pale, rather melancholy stone seemed in a strange way to fit in with her age and appearance; the old-fashioned setting had the same quality of sadness about it. So he stepped into the low ceilinged shop to buy the piece. The jeweler was greatly pleased to have such a well-dressed customer drop in, and wanted to show him his more valuable stones as well, those that he did not put in his window. Out of courtesy he let the old man show him a number of things but he had no desire to buy more, nor, given his solitary life, would he have had any use for such gifts. Finally he grew impatient and at the same time embarrassed, for he wanted to get away and yet not hurt the old man's feelings. He decided to buy something else, a trifle, and leave immediately thereafter. Absentmindedly, looking over the jeweler's shoulder, he gazed at a small silver hand mirror, half coated over. In an inner mirror an image came to him of the maid servant with the bronze goddesses at either side; he had a passing sense that a great deal of her charm lay in the way her neck and shoulders bore, in unassuming, childlike grace, the beauty of her head, the head of a young queen. And in passing he thought it pretty to see around this same neck a thin, gold chain, in many loops, childlike, yet reminiscent of armor. And he asked to see such chains. The old man opened a door and invited him to step into a second room, a low ceilinged parlor where numerous pieces of jewelry were on display, in glass cases and on open racks. Here he soon found a chain to his liking and asked the jeweler to tell him the price of the two ornaments. The jeweler asked him also to inspect the remarkable metalwork of some old saddles, set with semiprecious stones; he replied, however, that as the son of a merchant he never had anything to do with horses, in fact did not even know how to ride and found no pleasure in old saddles or in new. He took out a gold piece and some silver coins to pay for what he had bought, and gave some indication of being impatient to leave the store. The old man, without saying another word, picked out a piece of fine silk paper and wrapped the chain and the beryl, each separately; while he was doing so the merchant's son, by chance, stepped over to the low latticed window and looked out. He caught sight of a very well-kept vegetable garden, obviously belonging to the neighboring house, framed against a background of two glass greenhouses and a high wall. He was struck by an immediate desire to see these greenhouses and asked the jeweler if he could tell him how to get there. The jeweler handed him his two packages and led him through an adjoining room into the courtyard, which was connected to the neighboring garden by a lattice gate. Here the jeweler stopped and struck the gate with an iron clapper. Since, however, there was no sound from the garden and no sign of movement in the neighboring house, he urged the merchant's son simply to go ahead and inspect the forcing beds and, in the event that anyone should bother him, to say that he had his, the jeweler's, permission, for he was well acquainted with the owner. Then he opened the door for him by reaching through the bars of the latticework. The merchant's son immediately walked along the wall to the nearer of the two greenhouses, stepped in, and found such a profusion of rare and remarkable narcissus and anemones and such strange, leafy plants, quite unfamiliar to him, that he kept looking at them for a long time, never feeling he had seen enough. At last he looked up and saw that the sun had set behind the houses. It was not his wish to remain in a strange, unattended garden any longer but rather simply to cast a glance through the panes of the second forcing shed and then leave. As he walked slowly past this second shed, peeking in, he was suddenly struck with great fear and drew back. For someone had his face against the panes and was looking out at him. After a moment he calmed down and became aware that it was a child, a little girl of no more than four years, whose white dress and pale face were pressed to the windowpanes. But now when he looked more closely, he was again struck with fear, and felt in the back of his neck an unpleasant sensation of dread and a slight constriction in his throat and deeper down in his chest. For the child, who stared at him with a fixed and angry look, resembled in a way he could not fathom the fifteen-year-old girl he had in his own house. Everything was the same, the pale eyebrows, the fine, trembling nostrils, the thin lips; like her counterpart this child also held one of her shoulders a bit higher than the other. Everything was the same, except that in the child all of this resulted in an expression that was terrifying to him. He did not know what it was that caused him such nameless fright. He knew only that he would not be able to bear turning around, knowing that this face was staring at him through the glass.

In his fear he walked quickly up to the door of the greenhouse, in order to go in. The door was shut, bolted from the outside; in his haste he bent down to reach the bolt, which was very low, and shoved it back so violently that he painfully dislocated one of the joints of his little finger, and headed for the child, almost at a run. The child came toward him and, not saying a word, braced itself against his knees, trying with its weak little hands to push him out. It was hard for him to avoid stepping on her. But now that he was close, his fear abated. He bent down over the face of the child, who was very pale and whose eyes trembled with anger and hatred, while the little teeth of its lower jaw pressed with unnerving fury into its upper lip. His fear disappeared for a moment as he stroked the girl's short, fine hair. But instantly he was reminded of the girl who lived in his house and whose hair he had once touched as she lay in her bed, deathly pale, her eyes closed; and immediately a shiver ran down his spine and his hands drew back. She had given up trying to push him away. She stepped back a few paces and looked straight ahead. It grew almost unbearable to him, the sight of this frail doll-like body in its little white dress, this contemptuous, fearfully pale child's face. He was so filled with dread that he felt a twinge of pain in his temples and in his throat as his hand touched something cold in his pocket. It was a couple of silver coins. He took them out, bent down to the child, and gave them to her, because they shone and jingled. The child took them and let them drop in front of his feet, so that they disappeared in a crack of the floor where it rested on a grating of wood. Then she turned her back on him and walked slowly away. For a time he stood motionless, his heart pounding with fear lest she return and look at him from outside, through the panes. He would have preferred to leave immediately but it was better to let some time pass, so that the child might leave the garden. By now it was no longer fully light in the glasshouse and the shapes of the plants took on a strange appearance. Some distance away, black, absurdly threatening branches protruded disagreeably from the semidarkness, and behind them was a glimmer of white, as if the child were standing there. On a board stood a row of clay pots with wax flowers. To deaden the passage of a few moments he counted the blossoms, which, in their rigidity, bore little resemblance to living flowers and were rather like masks, treacherous masks with their eye sockets grown shut. When he had finished he went to the door, thinking to leave. The door did not budge; the child had bolted it from the outside. He wanted to scream but he was afraid of the sound of his own voice. He beat his fists against the panes. The garden and the house remained as still as death, except that behind him something was gliding through the shrubbery with a rustling sound. He told himself it was the sound of leaves that had loosened in the shattering of the sultry air and were falling to the ground. Still, he stopped his pounding and peered through the half-dark maze of trees and vines. Then he saw in the dusk of the far wall something that looked like a rectangle of dark lines. He crawled toward it, by now unconcerned that he was knocking over and breaking many of the clay flowerpots, that the tall, thin stalks and rustling fronds, as they fell, were closing over and behind him in a ghostly fashion. The rectangle of dark lines was the opening of a door; he pushed and it gave way. The open air passed over his face; behind him he heard the broken stalks and crushed leaves rise with a soft rustling sound as if after a storm.

He stood in a narrow walled passageway; above him the open sky looked down and the wall on either side was barely taller than a man. However, after a distance of fifteen paces, roughly speaking, the passage was walled up once more, and he started imagining himself a prisoner for the second time. Hesitantly he moved ahead; here on the right an opening in the wall had been broken through as wide as a man, and from this opening a board extended through empty space to a platform located opposite him; on the near side of it there was a low iron grating closing it off. On the other two sides were the backs of tall houses with people living in them. Where the board rested, like a gangplank, on the edge of the platform, the grating had a little door.

So very impatient was the merchant's son to escape the confines of his fear that he immediately set one foot, then the other, on the board and, keeping his glance firmly fixed on the opposite shore, started to cross over. Unfortunately, however, he became aware that he was suspended over a walled moat several stories deep; in the soles of his feet and the hollow of his knees he felt fear and helplessness, in the dizziness of his whole body the nearness of death. He knelt down and closed his eyes; then his arms, groping forward, encountered the bars of the grating. He clutched them; they gave way, and with a slow, soft rasping sound that cut through his body like the exhalation of death the door on which he was hanging opened toward him, toward the abyss. With a sense of his inner weariness and great despondency, he felt in anticipation how the smooth iron bars would slip from his fingers, which seemed to him like the fingers of a child, and how he would plunge downward and be dashed to bits along the wall. But the slow, soft opening of the door ceased before he lost his footing on the board, and with a swing he threw his trembling body in through the opening and onto the hard floor.

He was incapable of rejoicing; without looking around, with a dull feeling of something like hate for the absurdity of these torments, he walked into one of the houses and down the dilapidated staircase and stepped out again into an alleyway that was ugly and ordinary. But he was already very sad and tired and could not think of anything that seemed worth being happy about. In a strange way, everything had fallen away from him; empty and deserted by life itself he walked through this alley, and the next, and the next. He went along in a direction he knew would bring him back to the part of the city where the rich people lived and where he could look for lodging for the night. For he felt a great desire for a bed. With childlike longing he remembered the beauty of his own wide bed and he recalled, too, the beds that the great king of the past had erected for himself and his companions when they married the daughters of the kings they had conquered: a bed of gold for himself, of silver for the others, borne by griffins and winged bulls. Meantime he had come to the low-set houses where the soldiers lived. He paid no attention to them. At a latticed window sat a couple of soldiers with yellowish faces and sad eyes; they shouted something at him. He raised his head and breathed the musty smell that came from the room, a particularly oppressive smell. But he did not understand what they wanted of him. However, they had startled him out of his blank and aimless wandering, so now he looked into the courtyard as he passed the gate. The yard was very large and sad, and because the sun was just setting it seemed even larger and sadder. There were very few people in it and the houses that surrounded it were low and of a dirty yellow color. This made it even larger and more desolate. At one spot roughly twenty horses were tethered in a straight line; in front of each one there knelt a soldier in a stable smock of dirty twill, washing its hooves. Far in the distance, out of a gate, came many others in similar outfits of twill, two by two. They walked slowly, with dragging steps, and carried heavy sacks on their shoulders. Only when they came closer did he see that the open sacks they lugged along in silence had bread in them. He watched as they disappeared in a gateway, wandering on as if under the weight of some ugly, treacherous burden, carrying their bread in the same kind of sacks as clothed the sadness of their bodies.

Then he went over to the ones who were on their knees before their horses, washing their hooves. Here, too, each looked like the other and they all resembled the ones at the window and those who were carrying the bread. They must have come from neighboring villages. They too spoke hardly a word to one another. Since it was very hard for them to hold the horses' front feet, their heads swayed and their tired, yellowish faces moved up and down as if in a strong wind. The heads of most of the horses were ugly and had a look of malice about them, with their laid-back ears and their raised upper lips exposing the corner teeth of their upper jaws. For the most part they also had angry, rolling eyes and a strange way of expelling the air impatiently and contemptuously from curled-back nostrils. The last horse in line was particularly powerful and ugly. With its great teeth it tried to bite the shoulder of the man kneeling before it, drying its washed hoof. The man had such hollow cheeks and in his weary eyes such a deathly sad expression that the merchant's son was overcome by deep and bitter compassion. He wanted to give the wretched fellow a present, to cheer him up if only for a moment, and reached into his pocket for silver coins. He found none and remembered that he had tried to give the last ones to the child in the greenhouse, who had scattered them at his feet with such an angry look. He started to look for a gold coin, for he had put seven or eight into his pocket for his journey.

At that moment the horse turned its head and looked at him with ears treacherously laid back and rolling eyes that looked even more angry and wild because of a scar running straight across its ugly head just at the level of its eyes. At this ugly sight he was struck with a lightning-like memory of a long forgotten human face. However hard he might have tried, he would never have been capable of summoning up the features of this person's face; but now, there they were. However, the memory that came with the face was not so clear. He knew only that it came from the time when he was twelve years old, from a time the memory of which was associated somehow with the fragrance of sweet, warm, shelled almonds.

And he knew that it was the contorted face of an ugly poor man whom he had seen a single time in his father's store. And that his face was contorted with fear, because people were threatening him because he had a large gold piece and would not say where he had gotten it.

While the face dissolved again, his fingers searched the folds of his clothes; and when a sudden, vague thought restrained him, he drew out his hand hesitantly and in doing so cast the piece of jewelry with the beryl, wrapped in the silk paper, under the horse's feet. He bent down; the horse, kicking sideways with all its force, drove its hoof into his loins, and he fell over backward. He moaned aloud, his knees were drawn up, and he kept beating his heels on the ground. A couple of the soldiers rose and picked him up by the shoulders and under his knees. He sensed the smell of their clothes, the same musty, hopeless smell that earlier had come out of the room and onto the street, and he tried to recall where it was he had breathed it before, long, long ago; with this he lost consciousness. They carried him away over a low stairway, through a long, half-darkened passageway into one of their rooms, and laid him on a low iron bed. Then they searched his clothing, took the little chain and the seven gold pieces, and finally, taking pity on his incessant moaning, they went to get one of their surgeons.

After a time he opened his eyes and became conscious of his tormenting pain. What caused him even greater terror and fear, however, was to be alone in this desolate room. With effort he turned his eyes in their aching sockets, and, looking toward the wall, caught sight of three loaves of the kind of bread they had been carrying across the courtyard.

Otherwise there was nothing in the room but hard low beds and the smell of the dried rushes with which the beds were stuffed, and that other musty, desolate smell.

For a while the only things that occupied him were his pain and his suffocating, mortal fear, compared to which the pain was a relief. Then for a moment he was able to forget his mortal fear and wonder how all this had come to pass.

Then he felt another kind of fear, a piercing, less oppressive one, a fear he was not feeling for the first time; but now he felt it as something he had to overcome. And he clenched his fists and cursed his servants, who had driven him to his death, one to the city, the old woman into the jeweler's shop, the girl into the back room, the child, through the treacherous likeness of her counterpart, into the greenhouse, from which he saw himself reel dizzily over dreadful stairs and bridges, until he lay beneath the horse's hoof. Then he fell back into great, dull fear. He whimpered like a child, not from pain but from misery, and his teeth were chattering.

With a great feeling of bitterness he stared back into his life and denied everything that had been dear to him. He hated his premature death so much that he hated his life because it had led him there. This wild inner raging consumed his last strength. He was dizzy and for a time he slept a groggy, restless sleep. Then he awoke and felt like screaming because he was still alone, but his voice failed. Finally he vomited bile, then blood, and died with his features contorted, his lips so torn that his teeth and gums were laid bare, giving him an alien, threatening expression.

Translated by Frank G. Ryder

Retreat to solitude

ARTHUR SCHNITZLER

Lieutenant Gustl 1900

How much longer is this thing going to last? Let's see what time it is . . . perhaps I shouldn't look at my watch at a serious concert like this. But no one will see me. If anyone does, I'll know he's paying just as little attention as I am. In that case I certainly won't be embarrassed. . . . Only quarter to ten? . . . I feel as though I'd been here for hours. I'm just not used to going to concerts. . . . What's that they're playing? I'll have a look at the program. . . . Yes that's what it is: an oratorio. Thought it was a mass. That sort of thing belongs in church. Besides, the advantage that church has is that you can leave whenever you want to. – I wish I were sitting on the aisle! Steady, steady! Even oratorios end some time. Perhaps this one's very beautiful, and I'm just in the wrong mood. Well, why not? When I think that I came here for diversion . . . I should have given my ticket to Benedek. He likes this sort of thing. Plays violin. But in that case Kopetzky would have felt insulted. It was very nice of him; meant well, at least. He's a good fellow, Kopetzky! The only one I can really trust. . . . His sister is singing up there on the platform. There are at least a hundred women up there – all of them dressed in black. How am I to know which one is Kopetzky's sister? They gave him a ticket because she was singing in the chorus. . . . Why, then, didn't Kopetzky go? – They're singing rather nicely now. It's inspiring! Bravo! Bravo! . . . Yes, I'll applaud along with the rest of them. The fellow next to me is clapping as if he were crazy. Wonder if he really likes it as much as all that? – Pretty girl over there in the box! Is she looking at me or at the man with the blond beard? . . . Ah, here we have a solo! Who is it? ALTO: FRÄULEIN WALKER, SOPRANO: FRÄULEIN MICHALEK . . . that one is probably the soprano . . . I haven't been at the opera for an awfully long time. Opera always amuses me, even when it's dull. I could actually go again the day after tomorrow. They're playing *Traviata*. To think, day after tomorrow I might already be dead as a corpse! Oh, nonsense; I can't even believe that myself! Just wait, mister, you'll stop making remarks like that! I'll scrape the skin off the tip of your nose!

I wish I could see the girl in the box more clearly. I'd like to borrow an opera glass. But this fellow next to me would probably kill me if I broke in on his reveries. . . . Wonder in which section Kopetzky's sister is standing? Wonder if I'd recognize her? I've met her only two or three times, the last time at the Officer's Club. Wonder if they're all good girls, all hundred of them? Oh, Lord! . . . ASSISTED BY THE SINGER'S CLUB – Singer's Club . . . that's funny! I'd always imagined that members of a Singer's Club would be something like Vienna chorus girls; that is, I actually knew all along that it wasn't the same thing! Sweet memories! That time at the *Green Gate* . . . What was her name? And then she once sent me a postcard from Belgrade . . . that's also a nice place! Well, Kopetzky's in luck, he's been sitting in some bar, smoking a good cigar!

Why's that fellow staring at me all the time? I suppose he notices how bored I am and that I don't belong here. . . . I'll have you know that if you keep on looking fresh like that I'll meet you in the lobby later and settle with you! He's looking the other way already! They're all so afraid of my eyes. . . . "You have the most beautiful eyes I've ever seen!" Steffi said that the other day. . . . Oh Steffi, Steffi, Steffi! – It's Steffi's fault that I'm sitting here listening to them wail at me for hours. Oh, these letters from Steffi postponing engagements – they're getting on my nerves! What fun this evening might have been! I'd love to read Steffi's letter again. I've got it right here. But if I take it out of my pocket, I'll annoy the fellow next to me – Well, I know what it says . . . she can't come because she has to have dinner with "him." . . . That was funny a week ago when she was at the Gartenbau Café with him, and I was sitting opposite Kopetzky; she kept winking at me in the way we had arranged. He didn't notice a thing – why, it's amazing! He's probably a Jew. Sure, works in a bank. And his black mustache. . . . Supposed to be a lieutenant in the reserve as well! Well, he'd better not come to practice in our regiment! If they keep on commissioning so many Jews – then what's the point of all this anti-Semitism? The other day at the club, when the affair came up between the lawyer and the Mannheimers . . . they say the Mannheimers themselves are Jews, baptized, of course . . . they don't look it – especially Mrs. Mannheimer . . . blond, beautiful figure. . . . It was a good party, all in all. Great food, excellent cigars. . . . Well, the Jews are the ones with the money.

Bravo, bravo! Shouldn't it be over soon? Yes, the whole chorus is rising . . . looks fine – imposing! – Organ too! I like the organ. . . . Ah! that sounds good! Fine! It's really true, I ought to go to concerts more often. . . . I'll tell Kopetzky how beautiful it was.

. . . Wonder whether I'll meet him at the café today? – Oh Lord, I don't feel like going there; I was furious yesterday! Lost a hundred and sixty gulden in one round – how stupid! And who won all the money? Ballert. Ballert, who needed it least of all. . . . It's Ballert's fault that I had to go to this rotten concert. . . . Otherwise I might have played again today, and perhaps won back something. But I'm glad I gave myself my solemn word to stay away from cards for a whole month. . . . Mother'll make a face again when she gets my letter! – Ah, she ought to go and see Uncle. He's loaded; a couple of hundred gulden never made any difference to him. If I could only get him to send me a regular allowance . . . But, no, I've got to beg for every penny. Then he always says that crops were poor last year! . . . Wonder whether I ought to spend a two weeks' vacation there again this summer? I'll be bored to death there. . . . If the . . . What was her name? . . . Funny, I can't ever remember a name! Oh, yes: Etelka! . . . Couldn't understand a word of German . . . nor was it necessary. . . . I didn't need to say a thing! . . . Yes, it ought to be all right, fourteen days of country air and fourteen nights with Etelka or someone else. . . . But I ought to spend at least a week with Papa and Mama. She looked awful at Christmas. . . . Well, she'll have gotten over feeling insulted by now. If I were in her place I'd be happy that Papa's retired. – And Clara'll find a husband. Uncle will contribute something. . . . Twenty-eight isn't so old. . . . I'm sure Steffi's no younger. . . . It's really remarkable: the fast girls stay young much longer. Maretti, who played in *Sans Gêne* recently – she's thirty-seven, for sure, and looks . . . Well, I wouldn't have said no! Too bad she didn't ask me. . . .

Getting hot! Not over yet? Ah, I'm looking forward to the fresh air outside. I'll take a little walk around the Ring. . . . Today: early to bed, so as to be fresh for tomorrow afternoon! Funny, how little I think of it; it means nothing to me! The first time it worried me a bit. Not that I was afraid, but I was nervous the night before. . . . Lieutenant Bisanz was a tough opponent. – And still, nothing happened to me! . . . It's already a year and a half since then! Time sure flies! Well, if Bisanz didn't hurt me, the lawyer certainly won't! Still, these inexperienced fencers are often the most dangerous ones. Doschintzky's told me that on one occasion a fellow who had never had a sword in his hand before almost killed him; and today Doschintzky is the fencing instructor of the militia. – Though I wonder whether he was as good then as he is now? . . . Most important of all: keep cool. I don't feel the least angry now – and yet what an insult – unbelievable! He'd probably not have done it if he hadn't been drinking champagne. . . . Such insolence! He's probably a Socialist. All these shysters are Socialists these days. They're a gang. . . . They'd like to do away with the whole army; but they never think of who would help them out if the Chinese ever invaded the country. Fools! Every now and then you have to make an example of one of them. I was quite right. I'm really glad that I didn't let him get away with that remark. I'm furious whenever I think of it! But I behaved superbly. The colonel said I did exactly the right thing. I'll get something out of this affair. I know some who would have let him get away with it. Muller certainly would have taken an "objective" view of it, or something. This being "objective" makes anyone look foolish. "Lieutenant" – just the way in which he said "Lieutenant" was annoying. "You will have to admit – " . . . – How did the thing start? How did I ever get into conversation with a Socialist? . . . As I recall it, the brunette I was taking to the buffet was with us, and then this young fellow who paints hunting scenes – whatever is his name? . . . Good Lord, he's to blame for it all! He was talking about the maneuvers; and it was only then that the lawyer joined us and said something or other I didn't like – about playing at war – something like that – but I couldn't say anything just then. . . . Yes, that's it. . . . And then they were talking about the military school. . . . Yes, that's the way it was. . . . And I was telling them about a patriotic rally. . . . And then that lawyer said – not immediately, but it grew out of my talk about the rally – "Lieutenant, you'll admit, won't you, that not all your friends have gone into military service for the sole purpose of defending our Fatherland!" What nerve! How dare anyone say a thing like that to an officer! I wish I could remember exactly how I answered him – Oh, yes, something about "fools rushing in where angels fear to tread" . . . Yes, that was it. . . . And there was a fellow there who wanted to smooth over matters – an elderly man with a cold in the head – but I was too furious! The lawyer had said it in a way that meant me personally. The only thing he could have added was that they had expelled me from college, and for that reason I had to go into military service. . . . Those people don't understand our point of view. They're too dull-witted. . . . Not everyone can experience the thrill I did the first time I wore a uniform. . . . Last year at the maneuvers – I would have given a great deal if it had suddenly been in earnest. . . . Mirovic told me he felt exactly the same way. And then when His Highness rode up at the front and the colonel addressed us – only a cad wouldn't have felt proud. . . . And now a boor comes along who has been a penpusher all his life and has the gall to make a fresh remark. . . . Oh, just wait my dear. Unfit for battle – yes, that's what I'll make him!

Well, what's this? It ought to be over by now. . . . "Ye, his Angels, praise the Lord" – Surely, that's the final chorus. . . . Beautiful, there's no denying it, really beautiful! And here I've completely forgotten the girl in the box who was flirting with me before. . . . Where is she now? . . . Already gone. . . . That one over there seems rather nice. . . . Stupid of me – I left my opera glasses at home. Brunnthaler's smart, he always keeps his with the cashier at the café – you can't go wrong if you do that. I wish the cute little one over there would turn around. She sits there so properly. The one next to her is probably her mother. . . . I wonder whether I ought to consider marriage seriously? Willy was no older than I when he took the leap. There's something to be said for always having a pretty little wife home at your disposal. . . . Too bad that just today Steffi didn't have any time! If I only knew where she were. I'd sit down facing her again. That'd be a good one! If he'd ever catch me, he'd palm her off on me. When I think what Fliess's affair with that Winterfeld woman must cost him! – and even at that, she cheats on him right and left. One of these days the whole thing will end with a bang. . . . Bravo, bravo! Ah, it's over. . . . Oh, it feels good to get up and stretch. Well! How long is he going to take to put that opera glass into his pocket?

"Pardon me, won't you let me pass?"

What a crowd! Better let the people go by. . . . Gorgeous person. . . . Wonder whether they're genuine diamonds? . . . That one over there's rather attractive. . . . The way she's giving me the eye! . . . Why, yes, my lady, I'd be glad to! . . . Oh, what a nose! – Jewess. . . . Another one. It's amazing, half of them are Jews. One can't even hear an oratorio unmolested these days. . . . Now let's get into line. Why is that idiot back of me pushing so? I'll teach him better manners. . . . Oh, it's an elderly man! . . . Who's that bowing to me over there? . . . How do you do. Charmed! I haven't the slightest idea who he is. . . . I think I'll go right over to Leidinger's for a bite, or should I go to the Gartenbau? Maybe Steffi'll be there after all. Why didn't she write and let me know where she's going with him? She probably didn't know herself. Actually terrible, this dependency. . . . Poor thing – So, here's the exit. . . . Oh! that one's pretty as a picture! All alone? She's smiling at me. There's an idea – I'll follow her! . . . Now, down the steps. . . . Oh, a major – from the Ninety-fifth – very nice, the way he returned my salute. I'm not the only officer here after all. . . . Where did the pretty girl go? . . . There she is, standing by the

banister. . . . Now to the wardrobe. . . . Better not lose her. . . .
She's nabbed him already. What a brat! Having someone call for
her, and then laughing over at me! They're all worthless. . . . Good
Lord, what a mob there at the wardrobe. Better wait a little while.
Why doesn't the idiot take my coat check?

"Here, Number two hundred and twenty-four! It's hanging
there! What's the matter – are you blind? Hanging there! There! At
last. . . . Thank you." That fatso there is taking up most of the
wardrobe. . . . "If you please!" . . .

"Patience, patience."

What's the fellow saying?

"Just have a little patience."

I'll have to answer him in kind. "Why don't you allow some
room?"

"You'll get there in time." What's he saying? Did he say that
to me? That's rather strong! I won't swallow that. "Keep quiet!"

"What did you say?"

What a way to talk! That's the limit!

"Don't push!"

"Shut your mouth!" I shouldn't have said that. That was a bit
rough. . . . Well, I've done it now.

"Exactly what did you mean by that?"

Now he's turning around. Why I know him! – Heavens, it's the
baker, the one who always comes to the café. . . . What's he doing
here? He probably has a daughter or something in the chorus. Well,
what's this ? – What's he trying to do? It looks as though . . . Yes,
great Scott, he has the hilt of my sword in his hand! What's the
matter? Is the man crazy? . . . "You Sir! . . ."

"You, Lieutenant, hush your mouth."

What's he saying? For Heaven's sake, I hope no one's heard
it. No, he's talking very softly. . . . Well, why doesn't he let go of
my sword! Great God! Now I've got to get tough. I can't budge his
hand from the hilt. Let's not have a rumpus here! Isn't the major
behind me? Can anyone notice that he's holding the hilt of my
sword? Why, he's talking to me! What's he saying!

"Lieutenant, if you dare to make the slightest fuss, I'll pull
your sword out of the sheath, break it in two, and send the pieces
to your regimental commander. Do you understand me, you young
fathead?"

What did he say? Am I dreaming? Is he really talking to me?
How shall I answer him? But he's in earnest. He's really pulling
the sword out. Great God! he's doing it! . . . I can feel it! He's
already pulling it! What is he saying? For God's sake, no scandal!

– What's he forever saying?

"But I have no desire to ruin your career. . . . So just be a good boy. . . . Don't be scared. Nobody's heard it. . . . Everything's all right. . . . And so that no one will think we've been fighting I'll act most friendly toward you. . . . I am honored, Sir Lieutenant. It has been a pleasure – a real pleasure."

Good God, did I dream that? . . . Did he really say that? . . . Where is he? . . . There he goes. . . . I must draw my sword and run him through – Heavens, I hope nobody heard it. . . . No, he talked very softly – right in my ear. Why don't I go after him and crack open his skull? . . . No, it can't be done. It can't be done. . . . I should have done it at once. . . . Why didn't I do it immediately? . . . I couldn't. . . . He wouldn't let go of the hilt, and <u>he's ten times as strong as I am</u>. . . . If I had said another word, he <u>would actually have broken the</u> sword in two. I ought to be glad that he spoke no louder. If anyone had heard it, I'd have had to shoot myself on the spot. . . . Perhaps it was only a dream. Why is that man by the pillar looking at me like that? – Maybe he heard? . . . I'll ask him . . . ask him?! – Am I crazy? – How do I look? Does anyone notice? – I must be pale as a sheet – Where's the swine? I've got to kill him! . . . He's gone. . . . The whole place is empty. . . . Where's my coat? . . . Why, I'm already wearing it. . . . I didn't even notice it. . . . Who helped me on with it? . . . Oh, that one there. I'll have to tip him. . . . So. But what's it all about? Did it really happen? Did anyone really talk to me like that? Did anyone really call me a fathead? And I didn't cut him to pieces on the spot? . . . But I couldn't. . . . He had a fist like iron. I just stood there as though I were nailed to the floor. I think I must have lost my senses. Otherwise, I would have used my other hand. . . . But then he would have drawn out my sword, and broken it, and everything would have been over. . . . Over and done with! And afterward, when he walked away, it was too late. . . . I couldn't have run my sword through him from the back.

What, am I already on the street? How did I ever get here? – It's so cool. . . . Oh, the wind feels fine! . . . Who's that over there? Why are they looking over at me? I wonder whether they didn't hear something. . . . No, no one could have heard it. . . . I'm sure of it – I looked around immediately! No one paid any attention to me. No one heard a thing. . . . But he said it anyhow. Even if nobody heard it, he certainly said it. I just stood there and took it as if someone had knocked me silly. . . . But I couldn't say a word – couldn't do a thing. All I did was stand there – hush, hush your mouth! . . . It's awful; it's unbearable; I must kill him on the spot,

wherever I happen to meet him! . . . I let a swine like that get away
with it! And he knows me. . . . Great Heavens, he knows me –
knows who I am! . . . He can tell everybody just exactly what he
said to me! . . . No, he wouldn't do that. Otherwise, he wouldn't
have talked so quietly. . . . He just wanted me to hear it alone! . . .
But how do I know that he won't repeat it today or tomorrow, to
his wife, to his daughter, to his friends in the café – for God's sake,
I'll see him again tomorrow. As soon as I step into the café
tomorrow, I'll see him sitting there as he does every day, playing
Tarok with Schlesinger and the paper-flower merchant. No, that
can't happen. I won't allow it to. The moment I see him I'll run
him through. . . . No, I can't do that. . . . I should have done it right
then and there! . . . If only I could have! I'll go to the colonel and
tell him about the whole affair. . . . Yes, right to the colonel. . . .
The colonel is always friendly – and I'll say to him – Colonel, I
wish to report, Sir. He grasped the hilt of my sword and wouldn't
let go of it; it was just as though I were completely unarmed. . . .
What will the colonel say? – What will he say? There's just one
answer: dishonorable discharge! . . . Are those one-year volunteers
over there? Disgusting. At night they look like officers. . . . Yes,
they're saluting! – If they knew – if they only knew! . . . There's
the Hochleitner Café. Probably a couple of officers in my company
are there now. . . . Perhaps one or more whom I know. . . . Wonder
if it wouldn't be best to tell the first one I meet all about it – but
just as if it had happened to someone else? . . . I'm already going
a bit crazy. . . . Where the devil am I walking? What am I doing out
here in the street? – But where should I go? Wasn't I going to the
Leidinger Café? Haha! If I were to sit down in public, I'm sure
everyone would see what had happened to me. . . . Well, something
must happen. . . . But what? . . . Nothing, nothing at all – no one
heard it. No one knows a thing. At least for the time being. . . .
Perhaps I ought to visit him at his home and beg him to swear to
me that he'll never tell a soul. – Ah, better to put a bullet through
my head at once. That would be the smartest thing to do. The
smartest? The smartest? – there's just nothing else left for me –
nothing. If I were to ask the colonel or Kopetzky, or Blany, or
Friedmair: – they'd all tell me the same thing. How would it be if
I were to talk it over with Kopetzky? Yes, that seems the most
sensible thing to do. Not to mention because of tomorrow –
tomorrow – yes, that's right, tomorrow – at four o'clock, in the
armory, I'm to fight a duel. But I can't do it, I'm no longer
qualified for dueling. Nonsense, nonsense, not a soul knows it, not
a soul! – There are hundreds of people walking around to whom

worse things have happened. . . . What about all those stories I've
heard about Deckener – how he and Rederow fought with pistols.
. . . And the dueling committee decided that the duel could take
place at that. . . . But what would the committee decide about me?
– Fathead, fathead, and I just stood there and took it – ! Great
heavens, it makes no difference whether anyone knows it or not!
The main thing is: *I* know he said it! *I* feel as though I'm not the
same man I was an hour ago – *I* know that I'm not qualified for
dueling, and that I must shoot myself. I wouldn't have another calm
moment in my life. I'd always be afraid that someone might find
out about it in some way or another, and that some time someone
might tell me to my face what happened this evening! – What a
happy man I was an hour ago! . . . Just because Kopetzky gave me
a ticket, and just because Steffi canceled her date – destiny hangs
on things like that. . . . This afternoon, all was sailing smoothly,
and now I am a lost man about to shoot himself. . . . Why am I
running this way? No one is chasing me. What's the time? One,
two, three, four, five, six, seven, eight, nine, ten, eleven. . . .
Eleven, Eleven. . . . I ought to go and get something to eat. . . .
After all, I've got to go somewhere. I might go and sit down in
some little restaurant where no one would know me. – At any rate,
a man must eat even though he'll kill himself immediately
afterward. Haha! Death is no child's play. . . . Who said that
recently? – It makes no difference.

I wonder who'll be most upset, . . . Mama or Steffi? . . . Steffi,
Great God, Steffi! . . . She won't allow anyone to notice how she
feels. Otherwise "he" will throw her out. . . . Poor little thing! – At
my regiment. . . . No one would have the slightest idea why I did
it. They'd all wrack their brains. . . . Why did Gustl commit
suicide? But no one will guess that I had to shoot myself because
a miserable baker, a low person who just happened to have a strong
fist . . . It's too silly – too silly for words! – For that reason, a
fellow like myself, young and fit. . . . Well, afterward they're all
sure to say he didn't have to commit suicide for a silly reason like
that, what a pity! But if I were to ask anyone right now, they'd all
give me the same answer. . . . And if I were to ask myself. . . . Oh,
the devil, we're absolutely helpless against civilians. People think
that we're better off just because we carry swords, and if one of us
ever makes use of a weapon, the story goes around that we're all
born murderers. The paper will carry a story: "Young Officer's
Suicide" . . . How do they always put it? "Motive Concealed" . . .
Haha! . . . "Mourning at his Coffin." . . . – But it's true. I feel as if
I were forever telling myself a story. . . . It's true. . . . I must

commit suicide. There's nothing else left to do – I can't allow
Kopetzky and Blany to come tomorrow morning and say to me:
Sorry, we can't be your seconds. I'd be a cad if I expected them to
. . . what kind of guy am I, standing quietly by and letting myself
be called a fathead. . . . Tomorrow everyone will know it. Fancy
myself believing for a moment that a person like that won't repeat
it everywhere. . . . Why, his wife knows it already! Tomorrow
everyone in the café will know it. All the waiters will know it.
Schlesinger will know it – so will the cashier girl – And even if he
planned not to tell anybody, he'll certainly tell them the day after
tomorrow. . . . And if not then, in a week from now. . . . And even
if he had a stroke tonight, I'd know it. . . . I'd know it. And I could
no longer wear a cape and carry a sword if such a disgrace were on
me! . . . So, I've got to do it – I've got to do it – There's nothing to
it. – Tomorrow afternoon the lawyer might just as well run his
sword through me. . . . Things like this have happened before. . . .
And Bauer, poor fellow, got an inflammation of the brain and died
three days later. . . . And Brenitsch fell off his horse and broke his
neck. . . . And finally, there's nothing else to do, not for me
anyhow, certainly not for me! – There are men who would take it
more lightly. . . . But God, what sort of men are they! . . . a butcher
slapped Ringeimer's face when he caught him with his wife,
whereupon Ringeimer took his leave and is now somewhere out in
the country, married. . . . There are women, I suppose, who'll
marry people like that! . . . On my word, I'd never shake hands
with him if he came to Vienna! . . . Well, you've heard it, Gustl: –
life is over for you – finished, once and for all. Period! I know it
now, it's a simple story. . . . Well! I'm actually totally calm. . . .
I've always known it: if the occasion were ever to arise, I'd be
calm, completely calm. . . . But I would never have believed that it
would happen like this. . . . – That I'd have to kill myself just
because a . . . Perhaps I didn't understand him correctly after all.
. . . He was talking in an altogether different tone at the end. . . . I
was simply a little out of my mind on account of the singing and
the heat. . . . Perhaps I was momentarily demented, and it's all not
true. . . . Not true, haha! Not true! – I can still hear it. . . . It's still
ringing in my ears, and I can still feel in my fingers how I tried to
move his hand from the hilt of my sword. He's a husky brute. . . .
I'm no weakling myself. Franziski is the only man in the regiment
who's stronger than I.

Already at the Aspern bridge? . . . How far am I still going to
run? If I keep on this way I'll be in Kagran by midnight. . . . Haha!
. . . Good Lord, how happy we were last September when we

marched into Kagran. Only two more hours to Vienna! . . . I was dead tired when we got there. . . . I slept like a log all afternoon, and by evening we were already at the Ronacher. . . . Kopetzky and Ladinser. . . . Who else was along with us at the time? – Yes, that's right . . . that volunteer, the one who told us the Jewish stories while we were marching. Sometimes they're pleasant fellows, these one-year men. . . . But they all ought to be only substitutes. For what sense is there to it: all of us slave for ages, and a fellow like him serves a year and receives the same rank as we. . . . It's unfair! – But what's it to me? Why should I bother about such things? A private in the quartermaster corps counts for more than I do right now. . . . I no longer belong on the face of the earth. . . . It's all over with me. Honor lost – everything lost! . . . There's nothing else for me to do but load my revolver and . . . Gustl, Gustl, you still don't quite believe it? Come to your senses! . . . There's no way out. . . . No matter how you torture your brain, there's no way out! – The point is to behave properly at the end, like an officer and a gentleman so that the colonel will say: He was a good fellow, we'll always honor his memory! . . . How many companies attend the funeral of a lieutenant? . . . I really must know that. . . . Haha! Even if the whole battalion turns out, even if the whole garrison turns out, and they fire twenty salutes, it still won't wake me up! Last summer, after the army Steeplechase, I was sitting in front of this café here with Engel. . . . Funny, I've never seen the fellow since. . . . Why did he have his left eye bandaged? I always wanted to ask him, but it didn't seem proper. . . . There go two artillerymen. . . . They probably think I'm following that woman. . . . Actually I ought to have a look at her . . . . Oh, Lord! I wonder how that one can possibly earn a living. . . . I'd sooner . . . However, in time of need a person will do almost anything. . . . In Przemsyl – I was so horrified afterwards that I swore I'd never look at a woman again. . . . That was a ghastly time up there in Galicia. . . . Altogether a stroke of fortune that we came to Vienna. Bokorny is still in Sambor, and may stay another ten years, getting old and gray. . . . What happened to me today would never have happened if I'd remained there myself, and I'd far sooner grow old in Galicia than . . . Than what? Than what? – What is it? What is it? Am I crazy – the way I always forget? – Good God, I forget it every moment. . . . Has anyone ever heard of a man who within two hours of putting a bullet through his head digresses on all conceivable matters that no longer concern him? I feel as if I were drunk. Haha, drunk indeed! Dead drunk! Drunk with suicide! Ha, trying to be funny! Yes, I'm in a good mood –

must have been born with one. Certainly, if I ever told anybody they'd say I were lying. – I feel that if I had the revolver with me now . . . I'd pull the trigger – in a second all is over. . . . Not everyone is so lucky – others have to suffer for months. My poor cousin, on her back two years, couldn't move, had the most excruciating pains, what misery! Isn't it better when you take it in hand yourself? . . . Care is the only thing necessary; to aim well, so that nothing unfortunate happens, as it did to that cadet last year. . . . Poor devil, didn't die, but ended up blind. . . . Whatever happened to him? Wonder where he's living now. Terrible to run around the way he – that is, he can't run around, he's led. A chap like him – can't be more than twenty years old right now. He took better aim on his beloved. . . . She was dead at once. . . . Unbelievable, the reasons people have for killing. How can anyone be jealous? . . . I've never been jealous in my whole life. At this very moment Steffi is sitting comfortably at the Gartenbau; then she will go home with "him." . . . Doesn't mean a thing to me. . . . Not a thing. She has a nicely furnished place – a little bathroom with a red lamp – When she recently came in, in her green kimono. . . . I'll never see that green kimono again – Steffi, herself, I'll never see again – And I'll never go up the fine broad steps in Gusshausstrasse. Steffi will keep on amusing herself as if nothing had happened; she won't be allowed to tell a soul that her beloved Gustl committed suicide. But she'll weep – oh, yes, she'll weep. A great many people will weep. . . . Good God, Mama! – No, no, I can't think about it. Oh, no, I can't bear to. . . . You're not to think about home at all, Gustl, you understand? Not even with the faintest thought.

Not bad, I'm already at the Prater in the middle of the night. . . . That's another thing I didn't think of this morning, that tonight I'd be taking a walk in the Prater. . . . Wonder what the cop there thinks. . . . Well, I'll walk on. It's rather nice here. No point in eating; no fun in the café. The air is pleasant and it's quiet. . . . Indeed, I'll have a great deal of quiet – as much as I could possibly want. Haha! – But I'm altogether out of breath. I must have been running like crazy. . . . Slower, slower, Gustl, you won't miss anything, there's nothing more to do, nothing, absolutely nothing! What's this, am I getting a chill? – Probably on account of all the excitement, and then I haven't eaten a thing. What's that strange smell? . . . Are the blossoms out yet? – What's today? – The fourth of April. It's been raining a great deal the last few days, but the trees are still almost entirely bare . . . how dark it is! Hooh! Dark enough to give you the shivers. . . . That was really the only time in my whole life I was scared – when I was a little kid that time in the woods. . . . But I wasn't so little at that. . . . Fourteen or fifteen. . . . How long ago was it? – Nine years. . . . Sure – at eighteen I was a substitute; at twenty a lieutenant and next year I'll be . . . What'll I be next year? What do I mean: next year? What do I mean: next week? What do I mean: tomorrow? . . . What's this? Teeth chattering? Oh! – Well! let them chatter a while. Lieutenant, you are altogether alone right now and have no reason for showing off. . . . It's bitter, oh, it's bitter. . . .

I'll sit on that bench. . . . Ah. . . . How far have I come? – How dark it is! That behind me there, that must be the second café. . . . I was in there, too, last summer at the time our band gave a concert. . . . With Kopetzky and with Rüttner – there were a couple of others along . . . – Lord, I'm tired. . . . As tired as if I'd been marching for the last ten hours. . . . Yes, it would be fine to go to sleep now. – Ha, a lieutenant without shelter! . . . Yes, I really ought to go home. . . . What'll I do at home? – But what am I doing in the Prater? – Ah, it would be best never to get up at all – to sleep here and never wake up. . . . Yes, that would be comfortable! But, Lieutenant, things aren't going to be as comfortable as that for you. . . . What next? – Well I might really consider the whole affair in orderly sequence. . . . All things must be considered. . . . Life is like that. . . . Well, then, let's consider. . . . Consider what? . . . My God, doesn't the air feel good. . . . I ought to go to the Prater more often at night. . . . That should have occurred to me sooner. It's all a thing of the past – the Prater, the air, and taking walks. . . . Well, then, what next? – Off with my cap. It's pressing on my forehead. . . . I can't think properly. . . . Ah. . . . That's better! . . . Now, Gustl, collect your thoughts, make your final arrangements! Tomorrow morning will be the end. . . . Tomorrow morning at seven . . . seven o'clock is a beautiful hour. Haha! – At eight o'clock when school begins, all will be over. . . . Kopetzky won't be able to teach – he'll be too broken up. . . . But maybe he'll know nothing about it yet. . . . No need to hear about it. . . . They didn't find Max Lippay until the afternoon, and it was in the morning that he had shot himself, and not a soul heard it. . . . But why bother about whether Kopetzky will teach school tomorrow. . . . Ha! – Well, then, at seven o'clock – Yes. . . . Well, what next? . . . Nothing more to consider. I'll shoot myself in my room and then – basta! The funeral will be Monday. . . . I know one man who'll enjoy it: the lawyer. The duel can't take place on account of the suicide of one of the combatants. . . . Wonder what they'll say at Mannheimers? – Well, he won't make much of it. . . . But his wife, his pretty, blond . . . She did not seem disinclined. . . .

Oh, yes, I would have had a chance with her if I'd only pulled myself together a little. . . . Yes, with her it might have been something altogether different from that broad Steffi. . . . But the thing is, you can't be lazy: it's a question of courting in the proper way, sending flowers, making reasonable conversation . . . not: meet me tomorrow afternoon at the barracks! . . . Yes, a decent woman like her – that might have been something. The captain's wife at Przemysl wasn't respectable. . . . I could swear that Lubitzsky and Wermutek . . . and the shabby substitute – they all had her, too. . . . But Mannheimer's wife . . . Yes, that would have put me in a different social circle. That might almost have made me a different man – she might have given me more polish – or have given me more respect for myself – But always those easy types . . . and I began so young – I was only a boy that time on my first vacation when I was home with my parents in Graz. . . . Riedl was also along. . . . she was Bohemian. . . . Must have been twice as old as I – came home only the following morning. . . . The way Father looked at me . . . And Clara. I was most ashamed of all before Clara. . . . She was engaged at the time. . . . Wonder why the engagement never materialized. I didn't think much about it at the time. Poor thing, never had much luck – and now she's going to lose her only brother. . . . Yes, you'll never see me again, Clara – it's all over. You didn't foresee, little sister, did you, when you saw me at the station on New Year's Day, that you'd never see me again? – And Mother . . . Good God! Mother! . . . No, I can't allow myself to think of it. Ah, if I could only go home first. . . . When I think of that, I'm capable of doing something dishonorable. Say I have a day's leave. . . . See Papa, Mama, Clara again before it's all over. . . . Yes, I could take the first train at seven o'clock to Graz. I'd be there at one. . . . God bless you, Mama. . . . Hello, Clara! . . . How goes everything? . . . Well this *is* a surprise. . . . But they'll notice something. . . . If no one else, at least Clara will. . . . Clara for sure . . . Clara's such a smart girl. . . . She wrote me such a sweet letter the other day, and I still owe her an answer – and the good advice she always gives me. Such a wholeheartedly good creature. . . . Wonder whether everything wouldn't have turned out differently if I'd stayed at home. I might have studied agriculture and joined my uncle on his estate. . . . They all wanted me to do that when I was a kid. . . . By this time I'd be happily married to a nice, sweet girl. . . . Perhaps Anna – she used to like me a lot. . . . I just noticed it again the last time I was home – in spite of her husband and two children. . . . I could see it, just the way she looked at me. . . . And she still calls me "Gustl," just like she used to. . . . It will hit her hard when she finds out the way I ended up – but her husband will say: I might have known as much – a no-good like him! – They'll all think it was because I owed money. . . . It's not true. I've paid all my debts. . . . except the last hundred and sixty gulden – and they'll be here tomorrow. Well I must see to it that Ballert gets his hundred and sixty gulden – I must make a note of that before I shoot myself. . . . It's terrible, it's terrible! . . . If I only could run away from it all and go to America where nobody knows me. In America no one will know what happened here this evening. . . . No one cares about such things there. Just recently I read in the paper about some Count Runge, who had to leave because of some nasty story, and now he owns a hotel over there and doesn't give a hoot for the whole damn business. . . . And in a couple of years I could come back. . . . Not to Vienna, of course. . . . Nor to Graz . . . but I could go out to the estate. . . . And Mama and Papa and Clara would a dozen times rather have it that way – just so long as I stay alive. . . . And why worry about the other people at all? Who ever cares about me? – Kopetzky's the only one who'd ever miss me. . . . Kopetzky – just the one who gave me the ticket today . . . and the ticket's to blame for it all. If he hadn't given it to me, I wouldn't have gone to the concert, and all this would never have happened. . . . What did happen anyway? It's just as if a whole century had passed – and it's only two hours ago. Two hours ago someone called me a fathead and wanted to break my sword. Great God, I'm starting to shout here at midnight! Why did it all happen? Couldn't I have waited longer until the whole wardrobe had emptied out? And why did I ever tell him to shut up? How did it ever slip out of me? I'm generally polite. I'm usually not so rude, even to my orderly. . . . But of course I was nervous: all the things that happened just at the same time. . . . The tough luck in gambling and Steffi's eternal stalling – and the duel tomorrow afternoon – and I've been getting too little sleep lately, and all the drudgery in the barracks. . . . No one can stand that forever! . . . Before long I would have become ill – would have had to get a furlough. . . . Now it's no longer necessary. . . . I'll get a long furlough now – without pay – Haha! . . .

How long am I going to keep on sitting here? It must be after midnight. . . . Didn't I hear the clock strike midnight a while ago? – What's that there? A carriage driving by? At this hour? Rubber tires – I can already imagine . . . They're better off than I. Perhaps it's Ballert with his Bertha. . . . Why should it be Ballert, of all people? – Go ahead, right on! That was a good-looking carriage

His Highness had in Przemsyl. . . . He used to ride in it all the time on his way to the city to see the Rosenberg woman. He was a good mixer, His Highness – chummy with everyone, a good drinking companion. Those were good times. . . . Although . . . It was in a desolate part of the country, and the weather was hot enough in the summer to kill you. . . . One afternoon three men were overcome by the heat. . . . Even the corporal in my own company – a handy fellow he was. . . . During the afternoon we used to lie down naked on the bed. Once Wiesner came into the room suddenly; I must just have been <u>dreaming</u>. I stood up and drew my sword – it was lying next to me. . . . Must have looked funny! . . . Wiesner laughed himself sick. He's already been promoted to lieutenant colonel in the calvary – sorry I didn't go into the calvary myself. The old man didn't want me to – it would have been too expensive – but it makes no difference now. . . . Why? – Yes, I know: I must die, that's why it makes no difference – I must die. . . . How then? – Look here, Gustl, you came down here to the Prater in the middle of the night especially so that not a soul would bother you – now you can think everything over quietly. . . . That's all a lot of nonsense about America and quitting the service, and you haven't the brains to start on another career. And when you reach the age of a hundred and think back to the time that a fellow wanted to break your sword, and called you a fathead and you stood there and couldn't do a thing – no, there's nothing more to think about – what's happened has happened. – That's all nonsense about Mama and Clara – they'll get over it – <u>people get over everything</u>. . . . Oh, Lord, how Mama wept when her brother died – and after four weeks she hardly thought about it anymore. She used to ride out to the cemetery . . . first, every week, then every month, and now only on the day of his death. Tomorrow is the day of my death – April fifth. – Wonder whether they'll take my body to Graz – Haha! The worms in Graz will enjoy it! – But that's not my problem – I'll let others worry about that. . . . Well then, what actually *does* concern me? . . . Oh yes, the hundred and sixty gulden for Ballert – that's all – other than that I have no arrangements to make. – Are there letters to write? What for? To whom? . . . Taking my leave? The devil I will – it's clear enough that a man's gone after he's shot himself! Everyone will soon notice that he's taken his leave. . . . If people only knew how little the whole thing bothers me, they wouldn't feel sorry – No use pitying me. . . . What have I had out of life? – One thing I'd like to have experienced: being in war – but I would have had to wait a long time for that. . . . Outside of that I've experienced everything. Whether a broad's called Steffi or

Kunigunde makes no difference. . . . And I've heard all the best operettas – and I've been to see *Lohengrin* twelve times – and this evening I even heard an oratorio – and a baker called me a fathead. – Good God, I've had enough! I'm not in the least curious anymore. . . . Well then, I'll go home slowly, very slowly, there's really no hurry. – I'll rest for a few minutes on the bench here in the Prater, not a roof over my head. I'll never lie down in bed again. I'll have enough time to sleep. – This wonderful air! There'll be no more air. . . .

Well, what's this? – Hey there, Johann, bring me a glass of fresh water. . . . What's this? . . . Where? . . . Am I dreaming? My head. Oh, Good Lord . . . I can't get my eyes open! – I'm all dressed! – Where am I sitting? – Holy God, I've been sleeping! How could I have been sleeping? It's already growing light. How long have I been sleeping? – Must look at my watch – can't see a thing. . . . Where are my matches? Won't a single one of them light? . . . Three o'clock, and I'm to have my duel at four. – No, not a duel – a suicide! It has nothing to do with a duel; I must shoot myself because a baker called me a fathead. . . . What, did it actually happen? – My head feels so funny. . . . My throat's all clogged up – I can't move at all – my right foot's asleep. – Get up! Get up! . . . Ah, that's better! It's already growing light, and the air . . . Just like that morning when I was doing picket duty when we were camping in the woods. That was a different kind of waking up – that was a different sort of day ahead of me. . . . It seems as though I'm having trouble believing it. There's the street – gray, empty – just now I'm probably the only person in the Prater. I was here once at four o'clock in the morning with Pansinger. – We were riding. I was on Colonel Mirovic's horse, and Pansinger on his own nag. – That was May, a year ago – everything was in bloom – everything was green. Now the trees are still bare, but spring will soon be here – it will be here in just a few days. – Lilies-of-the-valley, violets – pity I'll never see them again. Every yokel will enjoy them, but I must die! Oh, it's miserable! And others will sit in the café eating, as if nothing had happened – just the way all of us sat in the café on the evening of the day they buried Lippay. . . . And they all liked Lippay so much. . . . He was more popular in the regiment than me. – Why shouldn't they sit in the Weingartl when I kick off? – It's quite warm – much warmer than yesterday and there's a fragrance in the air – the blossoms must be out. . . . Wonder whether Steffi will bring me flowers? –

It will never occur to her! She wouldn't dream of going to the funeral . . . Oh, if it were still Adele . . . Adele! I'm sure I haven't thought of her for the last two years. . . . As long as I lived I never saw a woman weep the way she did. . . . Come to think of it, that was the tenderest thing I ever lived through . . . she was so modest, so unassuming. – She loved me, I swear she did. – She was altogether different from Steffi. . . . I wonder why I ever gave her up. What a stupid thing! . . . It was too tame for me, yes, that was what it was. . . . Going out with the same person every evening . . . Then perhaps I was afraid that I'd never be able to get rid of her – she always whimpered so. – Well, Gustl, you could have postponed it . . . after all, she was the only one who really loved you. Wonder what she's doing now. Well, what would she be doing – probably has someone else now. This, with Steffi, is much more comfortable. When you're only together off and on – someone else has all the inconvenience – and I just have the pleasant part. . . . Well, in that case I certainly can't expect her to come to the cemetery. Wonder if there's anyone who'd go without feeling obliged to. Kopetzky, perhaps – and that's all! Oh, it's sad, not to have anyone. . . . Nonsense! There's Papa and Mama and Clara. It's because I'm a son and a brother. . . . What more is there to hold us together? They like me of course – but what do they know about me? – That I'm in the service, that I play cards, and that I run around with fast women. . . . Anything more? The fact I often get good and sick of myself – *that* I never wrote to them about – perhaps the reason is because I have never realized it myself. Well, Gustl, what sort of stuff are you muttering to yourself? It's just about time to start crying. . . . Disgusting! – Keep in step. . . . So! Whether a man goes to a rendezvous or on duty or to battle. . . . Who was it said that? . . . Oh yes, it was Major Lederer. When they were telling us that time at the canteen about Wingleder – the one who grew so pale before his first duel – and vomited. . . . Yes, a true officer will never betray by look or step whether he goes to a rendezvous or certain death! – Therefore, Gustl – remember the Major's words! Ha! – Always growing lighter. . . . Light enough to read, if you wanted to . . . What's that whistling there? – Oh yes, there's the North Railroad Station. . . . the Tegetthoff monument . . . It's never looked that tall before. . . . There are the carriages. Nobody except street cleaners around. They're the last street cleaners I'll ever see – Ha! I always have to laugh when I think of it. . . . I don't understand that at all . . . Wonder whether it's that way with everybody, once they're entirely sure. Three thirty by the clock at the North Railroad

Station.... The only question now is whether I'm to shoot myself at seven o'clock railroad time or Vienna time.... Seven o'clock ... Well, why exactly seven? ... As if it couldn't be any other time as well.... I'm hungry – Lord, I'm hungry – No wonder... . Since when haven't I eaten? ... Since – not since yesterday at six o'clock in the café! When Kopetzky handed me the ticket – café au lait and two croissants. – Wonder what the baker will say when he hears about it? ... Damned swine. He'll know – he'll catch on, he'll realize what it means to be an Austrian officer – a fellow like that can get in a fight in the open street and think nothing of it. But if an officer is insulted even in secret, he's as good as dead.... If a rascal like that could fight duels – but no, then at least he'd be much more careful – he wouldn't take a chance like that. The fellow keeps on living quietly and peacefully while I – croak! He's responsible for my death.... Do you realize, Gustl, it is he who is responsible for your death! But he won't get off as easily as that! – No, no, no! I'll send Kopetzky a letter telling him the whole story.... Better yet: I'll write to the colonel. He'll make a report to the military command.... Just like an official report.... Just wait – you think, do you, that a matter like this can remain secret! – That's where you're wrong. – It will be reported and remembered forever. After that I'd like to see whether you'll venture into the café! – Ha! – "I'd like to see" is good! There are lots of things I'd like to see which unfortunately I won't be able to – It's all over! –

Johann must be going into my room this very minute. And now he notices that the lieutenant hasn't slept at home. – Well he'll imagine all sorts of things. But that the lieutenant has spent the night in the Prater – that, on my word, will never occur to him... . Ah, there goes the Forty-fourth! They're marching out to target practice. Let them pass. – I'll remain right here.... A window is being opened up there. – Pretty creature. – Well I would at least put on a shawl or something when I go to an open window. Last Sunday was the last time. I'd never have dreamt that Steffi of all people would be the last. Oh God, that's the only real pleasure. Well, now the colonel will ride after them in two hours in his grand manner. These big fellows take life easy. – Yes, yes, eyes to the right! Very good. If you only knew how little I care about you all. Ah, that's not bad at all: there goes Katzer. Since when has he been transferred to the Forty-fourth? – How do you do, good morning! What sort of a face is he making? Why is he pointing at his head? – My dear fellow, your skull interests me not at all.... Oh, I see. No, my good chap, you're mistaken: I've just spent the night in the

Prater. . . . You will read about it in the evening paper. –
"Impossible!" he'll say, "Early this morning as we were marching
out to target practice I met him on the Praterstrasse" – Who'll be
put in command of my platoon? I wonder whether they'll give it to
Walterer. Well that'll be a good one! A fellow totally devoid of
pizzaz – should have gone into shoe repair. – What, the sun coming
up already! – This will be a beautiful day – a real spring day. The
devil – on a day like this! – Every cab driver will still be here at
eight o'clock this morning and I – well, what about me? Now
really, it would be funny if I lost my nerve at the last minute just
because of some cab drivers. . . . Why is my heart suddenly
pounding this way? – Not because of *that* . . . No, oh no, it's
because I haven't eaten in such a long time. But Gustl, be honest
with yourself: you're scared – scared because you have never tried
it before. . . . But that's no help to you. Being scared never helped
anybody. Everyone has to experience it once. Some sooner, some
later, and you just happen to have your turn sooner. As a matter of
fact you never were worth an awful lot, so the least you can do is
to behave decently at the very end, that I demand of you. I'll have
to figure it out – figure out what? . . . I'm always trying to figure
something out. . . . But it's so easy . . . It's lying in the drawer of
my night stand – loaded – all I have to do is pull the trigger –
certainly not very tricky!

That girl over there's already going to work . . . the poor girls!
. . . Adele also used to have to go to work – I went and picked her
up a few times in the evening. When they have a job they don't
play around so much with men. If Steffi belonged only to me, I
would have her sell hats or something. Wonder how she'll find out
about it? . . . In the newspaper! She'll be angry that I didn't write
to tell her. I believe I'm beginning to lose my mind. Why bother
about whether she'll be angry or not? How long has the whole
affair lasted? . . . Since January. . . . No, it must have begun before
Christmas. I brought her some candy from Graz, and she sent me
a note at New Year's. . . . Good Lord, that's right, I have her letters
at home. Are there any I should burn? . . . 'Mm, the one from
Fallsteiner. If that letter is found – the fellow will get into trouble.
Why should that concern me! – Well it wouldn't be much of an
exertion. . . . But I can't look through all that scrawl. . . . It would
be best to burn the whole bunch. . . . Who'll ever need them?
They're all junk. – My few books I could leave to Blany –
"Through Night and Ice" – too bad I'll never be able to finish it. .
. . . Didn't have much chance to read these last few months. . . .

Organ playing? In the church there. . . . Early mass – haven't been to one in an age. . . . Last time it was in February when the whole platoon was ordered to go. But that doesn't count. – I was watching my men to see if they were reverent and behaving properly. . . . I'd like to go to church . . . there might be something to it after all. . . . Well, after lunch I'll know all about it. Ah, "this afternoon" is good! – what shall I do – go in? I think it would be a comfort to Mother if she knew! . . . It wouldn't mean as much to Clara. . . . Well, in I go. It can't hurt! Organ playing – singing – hm! – what's the matter! I'm growing dizzy. . . . Oh God, Oh, God, Oh, God! I want somebody whom I can talk to before it happens! – How would it be – if I went to confession! The old cleric would certainly open his eyes wide if he heard me say at the end, "Pardon, Reverend Father; I am now going to shoot myself!" . . . Most of all I want to lie down there on the stone floor and cry my eyes out. . . . Oh no, I don't dare do that. But crying sometimes helps so much. . . . I'll sit down a moment, but I won't go to sleep again as I did in the Prater! . . . – People who have religion are much better off. . . . Well, now my hands are beginning to tremble! If it keeps on this way, I'll soon become so disgusted at myself that I'll commit suicide out of pure shame! That old woman there – What's she still got to pray for? . . . It would be a good idea to say to her: You, please include me too. . . . I never learned how to do it properly. Ha! It seems that dying makes one stupid! – Stand up! Where have I heard that melody before? – Holy God! Last night! – It's the melody from the oratorio! Out, out of here, I can't stand it any more. 'Pst! Not so much noise letting that sword drag – don't disturb the people in their prayers – so! – It's better in the open. . . . . Light. . . . The time's always growing shorter. Wish it were over already! – I should have done it at once in the Prater. . . . I should never go out without a revolver. . . . If I'd had one yesterday evening. . . . Good Lord Almighty! – I might take breakfast in the café. . . . I'm hungry. It always used to seem remarkable that people who were condemned to death drank their coffee and smoked their cigar in the morning. . . . Heavens, I haven't even smoked! I haven't even felt like smoking! – This is funny: I really feel like going to the café. . . . Yes, it's already open, and there's none of our crowd there right now . . . and if there were – it would be a magnificent sign of cool-headedness! "At six o'clock he was eating breakfast in the café and at seven he killed himself." . . . – I feel altogether calm again. Walking is so pleasant – and best of all, nobody is forcing me. If I wanted to I could still chuck the whole damn business. . . . America. . . . What do I mean, "whole damn business"? What "*damn* business"? I wonder whether I'm getting a sunstroke. Oho! – am I so quiet because I still imagine that I don't have to? . . . I do have to! I must! No, I will! Can you picture yourself, Gustl, taking off your uniform and beating it, and the damned swine laughing behind your back? And not even Kopetzky wanting to shake hands with you anymore? . . . I blush just to think of it. – The cop is saluting me. . . . I must acknowledge it. . . . "Good morning, sir!" There now, I've treated him like an equal! . . . It always pleases a poor devil like him. . . . Well, no one ever had to complain about me. . . . Off duty I was always pleasant. . . . When we were at the maneuvers I gave my NCOs Havana cigars. One time at drill I heard an enlisted man behind me say something about "the damned drudgery," and I didn't even report him. – I merely said to him, "See here, be careful – someone else might hear it, and then you'll be in hot water." . . . The palace yard . . . Wonder who's on guard today? – The Bosniacs – they look good. Just recently the lieutenant colonel said, "When we were down there in '78, no one would have believed that they'd ever stoop to us the way they have." Good God, that's a place I'd like to have been! Those fellows are all getting up from the bench. I'll salute. It's too bad I couldn't have been part of something like that – that would have been so much more wonderful – on the field of battle for the Fatherland, than . . . Yes, mister lawyer, you're getting off easy! . . . Wonder if someone couldn't take my place? Great God, there's an idea – I'll leave word for Kopetzky or Wymetal to take my place in the duel! . . . He shouldn't get off so easy as that! – Oh well, what difference does it make what happens later on? I'll never hear anything about it! – The trees are beginning to bud. . . . I once picked up a girl here at the Volksgarten – she was wearing a red dress – lived in the Strozzigasse – later Rochlitz took her off my hands. . . . I think he still keeps her, but he never says anything about it – probably ashamed of it. . . . Steffi's still sleeping, I suppose. . . . She looks so pretty when she's asleep – just as if she couldn't count to five! – Well, they all look alike when they're asleep! – I ought to drop her a line. . . . Why not? Everyone does it . . . writes letters just before – I also want to write Clara to console Papa and Mama and the sort of stuff that one writes! – And to Kopetzky. My Lord, I'll bet it would be much easier if one said good-bye to a few people . . . and the report to the officers of the regiment. – And the hundred and sixty gulden for Ballert. . . . Still lots of things to do. Well, nobody insists that I do it at seven. . . . There's still time enough after eight o'clock for being deceased! Deceased! That's the word – That's all there is to it.

Ringstrasse – I'll soon be at my café. . . . Funny, I'm actually looking forward to breakfast. . . . Unbelievable. – After breakfast I'll light a cigar, then I'll go home and write. . . . First of all I'll make my report to the military command; then the letter to Clara – then the one to Kopetzky – then the one to Steffi. What on earth am I going to write that hussy? . . . *My dear child, you should probably never have thought* . . . Lord, what nonsense! – *My dear child, I thank you ever so much* . . . – *My dear child, before I take my leave, I will not overlook the opportunity.* . . . – Well, letter writing was never my forte. . . . *My dear child, one last farewell from your Gustl.* . . . – What eyes she'll make! It's lucky I wasn't in love with her. . . . It must be sad if one loves a girl and then . . . Well, Gustl, let well enough alone: it's sad enough as it is. . . . Others would have come along after Steffi, and finally there would have been one who'd have been worth something – a young girl from a substantial family, with a good dowry – it might have been rather nice. . . . – I must write Clara a detailed letter explaining why I couldn't do otherwise. . . . *You must forgive me, my dear sister, and please console our dear parents. I know that I caused you all a good deal of worry and considerable pain; but believe me, I always loved all of you, and I hope that some time you will be happy, my dear Clara, and will not completely forget your unhappy brother.* . . . – Oh, I'd better not write to her at all! . . . No, it's too sad. I can already feel the tears in my eyes, when I think. . . . At least I'll write to Kopetzky. . . . A man-to-man farewell, and that he should let the others know. . . . – Already six o'clock – Oh no, half-past five – quarter to. – If that isn't a charming little face! – The little teenager, with her black eyes. I've met her so often in the Florianigasse! – Wonder what she'll say? – But she doesn't even know who I am – she'll only wonder why she doesn't see me any more. . . . Day before yesterday I made up my mind to speak to her the next time I met her. – She's been flirting plenty and in the end even a virgin. . . . She was so young – . . . . Yes, Gustl! Don't put off till tomorrow what you can do today. . . . That fellow over there probably hasn't slept all night either – Well, now he'll go home comfortably and lie down. – So will I! – Haha! This is getting serious, Gustl! Well if there weren't a little fear connected with it, there'd be nothing to it at all – and on the whole I must say on behalf of myself that I have been behaving very nobly. . . . Where'll I go now? There's my café. . . . They're still sweeping. . . . Well, I'll go in.

There's the table where they always play Tarok. . . . Remarkable, I can't imagine why that fellow who's always sitting next to the wall should be the same one who . . . – Nobody here yet. . . . Where's the waiter? . . . Ha! – There's one coming out of the kitchen. . . . Quickly putting on his apron . . . It's really no longer necessary! . . . Well, it is, for him. . . . He'll have to wait on other people today.

"Good morning, Lieutenant."

"Good morning."

"So early today, Lieutenant?"

"Oh that's all right – I haven't much time, I'll just sit here with my coat on."

"Your order, Sir?"

"A café au lait."

"Thank you – right away, Lieutenant."

Ah, there are the newspapers . . . are they out as early as this? Wonder what they say? Well, what? It's as though I wanted to see if they say I've committed suicide! . . . Haha! – Why am I still standing up? . . . Let's sit down by the window. . . . He's already brought in the coffee. There, I'll pull the curtain. I feel uncomfortable with people gaping in. Nobody's out yet. . . . Ah, this coffee tastes good – it wasn't a bad idea, this breakfast! . . . I feel like a new man. – The whole trouble was that I didn't eat anything last night. Why is the waiter back already? Oh, he's also brought some rolls. . . .

"Has the Lieutenant already heard?"

"Heard what?" For God's sake, does he know something about it already? . . . Nonsense, it's absolutely impossible!

"Herr Habetswallner – " What, what's that? That's the baker's name. . . . What's he going to say now? . . . Has he been here already? Was he here yesterday telling them the whole story? . . . Why doesn't he tell me more? . . . But he's talking right now. . . .

" – had a stroke last night at twelve o'clock."

"What?" . . . I mustn't shout this way. . . . No, I can't allow anybody to notice it. . . . But perhaps I'm dreaming. . . . I must ask him again. . . .

"Who did you say had a stroke?" – Rather good, that! – I said it quite innocently! –

"The baker, Lieutenant. You must know him. . . . Don't you remember the fat fellow who played Tarok at the table next to the officers' here every afternoon . . . with Herr Schlesinger and Herr Wasner – the one in the paper-flower business?!"

I'm completely awake – everything seems to check up – and still I just can't believe him. – I'll have to ask him again. . . . Altogether innocently. . . .

"You say that he was overcome by a stroke? . . . How did it happen? Who told you about it?"

"Who could know it sooner than we here, Lieutenant? – That roll you are eating there comes from Herr Habetswallner's own bakery. His delivery boy who comes here at half-past four in the morning told us about it."

Look out! I mustn't give myself away. . . . I feel like shouting. . . . I'll burst out laughing in a minute. In another second I'll kiss Rudolph. . . . But I must ask him something else! Having a stroke doesn't mean that he's dead. . . . I must ask him – if he's dead. . . . Altogether calmly – why should the baker concern me? – I must look in the paper while I'm asking the waiter.

"You say he's dead?"

"Why certainly, Lieutenant, he died immediately."

Wonderful, wonderful! . . . Maybe all because I went to church. . . .

"He went to the theater last night. On the way out he fell on the stairs – the janitor heard him fall. . . . Well, they carried him to his home, and he died long before the doctor ever arrived."

"That's sad – too bad. He was still in the prime of life." I said that marvelously – not a soul can tell. . . . And I have to do everything to keep from shouting my lungs out and jumping up on the billiard table. . . .

"Yes, Lieutenant, it is very sad. He was such a nice gentleman; he's been coming to this place for the last twenty years – he was a good friend of the boss. And his poor wife. . . ."

I don't think I've felt as happy as this as long as I've lived. He's dead – dead! Nobody knows about it, and nothing's happened! – What a brilliant piece of luck that I came into the café. . . . Otherwise I'd have shot myself for nothing – it's like a benediction from heaven. . . . Where did Rudolph go? Oh, he's talking to the furnace man. . . . – Well, he's dead – dead. I just can't seem to believe it! I'd better go and take a look at him myself. – He probably had a stroke out of anger – couldn't control himself. . . . Well, what difference does it make why it happened! The main thing is he's dead, and I can keep on living, and everything belongs to me again! . . . Funny, the way I keep on dunking the roll – the roll Habetswallner baked for me! It tastes very good too, Herr Habetswallner. Splendid! – Ah, now I'll light a cigar. . . .

"Rudolph! Hey, Rudolph! Don't argue so much with the furnace man."

"What is it, Lieutenant?"

"Bring me a cigar." . . . – I'm so happy, so happy! . . . What am I doing? . . . What am I doing? . . . Something's got to happen, or I'll be overcome by a stroke of joy! In a few minutes I'll wander over to the barracks and let Johann give me a cold rubdown. . . . At half-past seven we have drill and at half-past nine formation. – And I'll write Steffi to leave this evening open for me no matter what! And this afternoon at four. . . . Just wait, my boy, I'm in wonderful form. . . . I'll knock you to smithereens!

Translated by Richard L. Simon
and revised by Caroline Wellbery

Shame Requires public Knowledge

JOSEPH ROTH

The Bust of the Emperor   1935

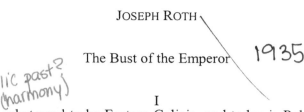

I

In what used to be Eastern Galicia, and today is Poland, far indeed from the solitary railway line which links Przemysl with Brody, lies the small village of Lopatyny, about which I intend to tell a remarkable tale.

Will readers be so kind as to forgive the narrator for prefacing the facts which he has to impart by a historico-political explanation. The unnatural moods which world history has recently exhibited compel him to this explanation, since younger readers may wish, perhaps need, to have it pointed out to them that a part of the eastern territories, which today belong to the Polish Republic, formed a part of the many Crown Lands of the old Austro-Hungarian monarchy until the end of the Great War which is now called the World War.

Thus, in the village of Lopatyny, there lived the Count Franz Xaver Morstin, the scion of an old Polish family, a family which (incidentally) originated in Italy and came to Poland in the sixteenth century. Count Morstin had, in his youth, served in the Ninth Dragoons. He thought of himself neither as a Polish aristocrat nor as an aristocrat of Italian origin. No: like so many of his peers in the former Crown Lands of the Austro-Hungarian monarchy, he was one of the noblest and purest sort of Austrian, plain and simple. That is, a man above nationality, and therefore of true nobility. Had anyone asked him, for example – but to whom would such a senseless question have occurred? – to which "nationality" or race he felt he belonged, the Count would have felt rather bewildered, baffled even, by his questioner, and probably bored and somewhat indignant. And on what indications might he have based his membership of this or that race? He spoke almost all European languages equally well, he was at home in almost all the countries of Europe. His friends and relations were scattered about the wide colorful world. Indeed the Imperial and Royal monarchy was itself a microcosm of this colorful world, and for this reason the Count's only home. One of his brothers-in-law was District Commandant in Sarajevo, another was Counselor to the

Governor in Prague; one of his brothers was serving as an Oberleutnant of artillery in Bosnia, one of his cousins was Counselor of Embassy in Paris, another was a landowner in the Hungarian Banat, a third was in the Italian diplomatic service, and a fourth, from sheer love of the Far East, had for years lived in Peking.

From time to time it was Franz Xaver's custom to visit his relations; more frequently, of course, those who lived within the monarchy. They were, as he used to say, his "tours of inspection." These tours were not only mindful of his relatives, but also of his friends, certain former pupils at the Theresianische Akademie who lived in Vienna. Here Count Morstin would settle twice a year, winter and summer (for a fortnight or longer).

As he traveled backwards and forwards and through the center of his many-faceted fatherland he would derive a quite particular pleasure from certain distinguishing marks which were to be picked out, unvarying but gay, on all the railway stations, kiosks, public buildings, schools, and churches of the old Crown Lands throughout the Empire. Everywhere the gendarmes wore the same cap with a feather or the same mud-colored helmet with a golden knob and the gleaming double eagle of the Habsburgs; everywhere the doors of the Imperial tobacco monopoly's shops were painted with black and yellow diagonal stripes; in every part of the country the revenue officers carried the same green (almost flowering) pommels above their naked swords; in every garrison town one saw the same blue uniform blouses and black formal trousers of the infantry officers sauntering down the Corso, the same coffee-colored jackets of the artillery, the same scarlet trousers of the cavalry; everywhere in that great and many-colored Empire, and at the same moment every evening, as the clocks in the church towers struck nine, the same retreat was sounded, consisting of cheerfully questioning calls and melancholy answers.

Everywhere were to be found the same coffeehouses, with their smoky vaulted ceilings and their dark alcoves where the chess players sat hunched like strange birds, with their sideboards heavy with colored bottles and shining glasses, presided over by golden-blond, full-bosomed cashiers. Almost everywhere, in all the coffeehouses of the Empire, there crept with a knee already a little shaky, feet turning outwards, a napkin across his arm, the whiskered waiter, the distant humble image of an old servitor of His Majesty, that mighty whiskered gentleman to whom all Crown Lands, gendarmes, revenue officers, tobacconists, turnpikes, railways, and all his peoples belonged.

And in each Crown Land different songs were sung; peasants wore different clothes; people spoke a different tongue or, in some instances, several different tongues. And what so pleased the Count was the solemn and yet cheerful black-and-yellow that shone with such familiar light amidst so many different colors; the equally solemn and happy "Gott erhalte," "God Save the Emperor," which was native among all the songs of all the peoples, and that particular, nasal, drawling, gentle German of the Austrians, reminding one of the Middle Ages which was always to be picked out again among the varying idioms and dialects of the peoples. Like every Austrian of his day, he loved what was permanent in the midst of constant change, what was familiar amid the unfamiliar. So that things which were alien became native to him without losing their color, and his native land had the eternal magic of the alien.

In his village of Lopatyny the Count was more powerful than any of the administrative branches known to, and feared by, the peasants and the Jews, more powerful than the circuit judge in the nearest small town, more so than the local town mayor himself and more so than any of the senior officers who commanded the troops at the annual maneuvers, requisitioning huts and houses for billets, and generally representing that warlike might which is so much more impressive than actual military power in wartime. It seemed to the people of Lopatyny that "Count" was not only a title of nobility but also quite a high position in local government. In practice they were not far wrong. Thanks to his generally accepted standing, Count Morstin was able to moderate taxes, relieve the sickly sons of Jews from military service, forward requests for favors, relieve punishments meted out to the innocent, reduce punishments which were unduly severe, obtain reductions in railway fares for poor people, secure just retribution for gendarmes, policemen and civil servants who overstepped their position, obtain assistant masterships at the *Gymnasium* for teaching candidates, find jobs as tobacconists, deliverers of registered letters, and telegraphists for time-expired NCOs, and find "bursaries" for the student sons of poor peasants and Jews.

How happy he was to attend to it all! In order to keep abreast of his duties, he employed two secretaries and three writers. On top of this, true to the tradition of his house, he practiced "seigneurial charity," as it was known in the village. For more than a century the tramps and beggars of the neighborhood had gathered every Friday beneath the balcony of the Morstin manor and received from the footmen copper coins in twists of paper. Usually, the

Count would appear on the balcony and greet the poor, and it was as if he were giving thanks to the beggars who thanked him: as if giver and receiver exchanged gifts.

Incidentally, it was not always goodness of heart which produced all these good works, but one of those unwritten laws common to so many families of the nobility. Their far distant forebears might indeed, centuries before, have practiced charity, help, and support of their people out of pure love. Gradually, though, as the blood altered, this goodness of heart had to some extent become frozen and petrified into duty and tradition. Furthermore, Count Morstin's busy willingness to be helpful formed his only activity and distraction. It lent to his somewhat idle life as a *grand seigneur* who, unlike his peers and neighbors, took no interest even in hunting, an object and an aim, a constantly beneficent confirmation of his power. If he had arranged a tobacconist's business for one person, a license for another, a job for a third, an interview for a fourth, he felt at ease not only in his conscience but in his pride. If, however, he proved unsuccessful in his good offices on behalf of one or another of his *protégés*, then his conscience was uneasy and his pride was wounded. And he never gave up; he invariably went to appeal, until his wish – that is, the wish of his *protégés* – had been fulfilled. For this reason the people loved and respected him. For ordinary folk have no real conception of the motives which induce a man of power to help the powerless and the unimportant. People just wish to see a "good master"; and people are often more magnanimous in their childlike trust in a powerful man than is the very man whose magnanimity they credulously assume. It is the deepest and noblest wish of ordinary folk to believe that the powerful must be just and noble.

This sort of consideration was certainly not present in Count Morstin's mind as he dispensed protection, beneficence, and justice. But these considerations, which may have led an ancestor here and an ancestor there to the practice of generosity, pity, and justice, were still alive and working, in the blood or, as they say today, the "subconscious" of this descendant. And just as he felt himself in duty bound to help those who were weaker than himself, so he exhibited duty, respect, and obedience towards those who were higher placed than himself. The person of His Royal and Imperial Majesty was to him forever a quite uniquely remarkable phenomenon. It would, for example, have been impossible for the Count to consider the Emperor simply as a person. Belief in the hereditary hierarchy was so deep-seated and so strong in Franz Xaver's soul that he loved the Emperor because of his Imperial, not his human, attributes. He severed all connection with friends, acquaintances or relations if they let fall what he considered a disrespectful word about the Emperor. Perhaps he sensed even then, long before the fall of the monarchy, that frivolous witticisms can be far more deadly than criminal attempts at assassination and the solemn speeches of ambitious and rebellious world reformers; in which case world history would have borne out Count Morstin's suspicions. For the old Austro-Hungarian monarchy died, not through the empty verbiage of its revolutionaries, but through the ironical disbelief of those who should have believed in, and supported, it.

II

One fine day – it was a couple of years before the Great War, which people now call the World War – Count Morstin was told in confidence that the next Imperial maneuvers were to take place in Lopatyny and the adjacent territory. The Emperor planned to spend a day or two, or a week, or longer in his house. And Morstin flew into a real taking, drove to the town mayor, dealt with the civil police authorities and the urban district council of the neighboring market town, arranged for the policemen and night watchmen of the entire district to have new uniforms and swords, spoke with the priests of all three confessions, Greek Catholics, Roman Catholics, and the Jewish Rabbi, wrote out a speech for the Ruthenian mayor of the town (which he could not read but had to learn by heart with the help of the schoolteacher), bought white dresses for the little girls of the village and alerted the commanding officers of every regiment in the area. All this so much "in confidence" that in early spring, long before the maneuvers, it was known far and wide in the neighborhood that the Emperor himself would be attending the maneuvers.

At that time Count Morstin was no longer young, but haggard and prematurely gray. He was a bachelor and a misogynist, considered somewhat peculiar by his more robust equals, a trifle "comic" and "from a different planet." Nobody in the district had seen a woman near him, nor had he ever made any attempt to marry. None had seen him drink, gamble or make love. His solitary passion was combating "the problem of nationalities." Indeed it was at this time that the so-called "problem of nationalities" began to arouse the passions. Everybody like himself – whether he wished to, or felt impelled to act as if he wished to – concerned himself with one or other of the many nations which occupied the territory of the old Monarchy. It had been discovered and brought to people's attention in the course of the nineteenth century that in order to possess individuality as a citizen every person must belong to a definite nationality or race. "From humanity, via nationalism to bestiality," the Austrian poet Grillparzer had said. It was just at this time that nationalism was beginning, the stage before the bestiality which we are experiencing today. One could see clearly then that national sentiment sprang from the vulgar turn of mind of all the people who derived from, and corresponded with, the most commonplace attitudes of a modern country. They were generally photographers with a sideline in the volunteer fire brigade, self-styled artists who for lack of talent had found no home in the art academy and in consequence had ended up as sign painters and paperhangers, discontented teachers in primary schools who would have liked to teach in secondary schools, apothecaries' assistants who wanted to be doctors, tooth pullers who could not become dentists, junior employees in the Post Office and the railways, bank clerks, woodmen and, generally speaking, anyone with any of the Austrian nationalities who had an unjustifiable claim to a limitless horizon within that bourgeois society. And all these people who had never been anything but Austrians, in Tarnopol, Sarajevo, Brünn, Prague, Czernowitz, Oderburg or Troppau; all these who had never been anything but Austrian, began in accordance with the "Spirit of the Age" to look upon themselves as members of the Polish, Czech, Ukrainian, German, Rumanian, Slovenian, and Croatian "nations," and so on and so forth.

At about this time "universal, secret, and direct suffrage" was introduced in the Monarchy. Count Morstin detested this as much as he did the concept of "nation."

He used to say to the Jewish publican Solomon Piniowsky, the only person for miles around in whose company he had some sort of confidence, "Listen to me, Solomon! This dreadful Darwin, who says men are descended from apes, seems to be right. It is no longer enough for people to be divided into races, far from it! They want to belong to particular nations. Nationalism; do you hear Solomon?! Even the apes never hit on an idea like that. Darwin's theory still seems to me incomplete. Perhaps the apes are descended from the nationalists since they are certainly a step forward. You know your Bible, Solomon, and you know that it is written there that on the sixth day God created man, not nationalist man. Isn't that so, Solomon?"

"Quite right, Herr Graf!" said the Jew, Solomon.

"But," the Count went on, "to change the subject: we are

expecting the Emperor this summer. I will give you some money. You will clean up and decorate this place and light up the window. You will dust off the Emperor's picture and put it in the window. I will make you a present of a black and yellow flag with the double eagle on it, and you will fly it from the roof. Is that understood?"

Indeed, the Jew Piniowsky understood, as, moreover, did everybody else with whom the Count had discussed the arrival of the Emperor.

III

That summer the Imperial maneuvers took place, and His Imperial, Royal, and Apostolic Majesty took up residence in Count Morstin's castle. The Emperor was to be seen every morning as he rode out to watch the exercises, and the peasants and Jewish merchants of the neighborhood would gather to see him, this old man who was their ruler. And as soon as he and his suite appeared they would shout "hoch" and "hurra" and "niech zyie," each in his own tongue. A few days after the Kaiser's departure, the son of a local peasant called upon Count Morstin. This young man, whose ambition was to become a sculptor, had prepared a bust of the Emperor in sandstone. Count Morstin was enchanted. He promised the young sculptor a free place at the Academy of Arts in Vienna.

He had the bust of the Emperor mounted at the entrance to his little castle.

Here it remained, year in, year out, until the outbreak of the Great War which became known as the World War.

Before he reported for duty as a volunteer, elderly, drawn, bald, and hollow-eyed as he had become with the passage of years, Count Morstin had the Emperor's bust taken down, packed in straw and hidden in the cellar.

And there it rested until the end of the war and of the Monarchy, until Count Morstin returned home, until the constitution of the new Polish Republic.

IV

Count Franz Xaver Morstin had thus come home. But could one call this a homecoming? Certainly, there were the same fields, the same woods, the same cottages, and the same sort of peasants – the same *sort*, let it be said advisedly – for many of the ones whom the Count had known had fallen in battle.

It was winter, and one could already feel Christmas approaching. As usual at this time of year, and as it had been in days long before the war, the Lopatinka was frozen, crows crouched motionless on the bare branches of the chestnut trees and the eternal leisurely wind of the Eastern winter blew across the fields onto which the western windows of the house gave.

As the result of the war, there were widows and orphans in the villages: enough material for the returning Count's beneficence to work upon. But instead of greeting his native Lopatyny as a home regained, Count Morstin began to indulge in problematical and unusual meditations on the question of home generally. Now, thought he, since this village belongs to Poland and not to Austria, is it still my home? What, in fact, is home? Is not the distinctive uniform of gendarmes and customs officers, familiar to us since childhood, just as much "home" as the fir and the pine, the pond and the meadow, the cloud and the brook? But if the gendarmes and customs officers are different and fir, pine, brook, and pond remain the same, is that still home? Was I not therefore at home in this spot – continued the Count inquiringly – only because it belonged to an overlord to whom there also belonged countless other places of different kinds, all of which I loved? No doubt about it! This unnatural whim of history has also destroyed my private pleasure in what I used to know as home. Nowadays they are talking hereabouts and everywhere else of this new fatherland. In their eyes I am a so-called Lackland. I have always been one. Ah! But there was once a fatherland, a real one, for the Lacklands, the only possible fatherland. That was the old Monarchy. Now I am homeless and have lost the true home of the eternal wanderer.

In the false hope that he could forget the situation if he were outside the country, the Count decided to go abroad. But he discovered to his astonishment that he needed a passport and a number of so-called visas before he could reach those countries which he had chosen for his journey. He was quite old enough to consider as fantastically childish and dreamlike such things as passports, visas, and all the formalities which the brazen laws of traffic between man and man had imposed after the war. However, since Fate had decreed that he was to spend the rest of his days in a desolate dream, and because he hoped to find abroad, in other countries, some part of that old reality in which he had lived before the war, he bowed to the requirements of this ghostly world, took a passport, procured visas, and proceeded first to Switzerland, the one country in which he believed he might find the old peace, simply because it had not been involved in the war.

He had known the city of Zurich for many years, but had not seen it for the better part of twelve. He supposed that it would make no particular impact on him, for better or for worse. His impression coincided with the not altogether unjustified opinion of the world, both rather more pampered and rather more adventurous, on the subject of the worthy cities of the worthy Swiss. What, after all, could be expected to happen there? Nevertheless, for a man who had come out of the war and out of the eastern marches of the former Austrian Monarchy, the peace of a city that even before that war had harbored refugees, was almost equivalent to an adventure. Franz Xaver Morstin gave himself up in those first days to the pursuit of long-lost peace. He ate, drank, and slept.

One day, however, there occurred a disgusting incident in a Zurich night club, as the result of which Count Morstin was forced to leave the country at once.

At that time there was often common gossip in the newspapers of every country about some wealthy banker who was supposed to have taken in pawn, against a loan to the Austrian royal family, not only the Habsburg Crown Jewels, but also the old Habsburg Crown itself. No doubt about it that these stories came from the tongues and pens of those irresponsible customers known as journalists and even if it were true that a certain portion of the Imperial family's heritage had found its way into the hands of some conscienceless banker, there was still no question of the old Habsburg crown coming into it, or so Franz Xaver Morstin felt that he knew.

So he arrived one night in one of the few bars, known only to the select, which are open at night in the moral city of Zurich where, as is well known, prostitution is illegal, immorality is taboo, the city in which to sin is as boring as it is costly. Not for a moment that the Count was seeking this out! Far from it: perfect peace had begun to bore him and to give him insomnia and he had decided to pass the nighttime away wherever he best could.

He began his drink. He was sitting in one of the few quiet corners of the establishment. It is true that he was put out by the newfangled American style of the little red table lamps, by the hygienic white of the barman's coat which reminded him of an assistant in an operating theater, and by the dyed blond hair of the waitress which awoke associations with apothecaries; but to what had he not already accustomed himself, this poor old Austrian? Even so, he was startled out of the peace which he had with some trouble arranged for himself in these surroundings by a harsh voice announcing: "And here, ladies and gentlemen, is the crown of the Habsburgs!"

Franz Xaver stood up. In the middle of the long bar he

observed a fairly large and animated party. His first glance informed him that every type of person he hated – although until then he had no close contact with them – was represented at that table: women with dyed blond hair in short dresses which shamelessly revealed ugly knees; slender, willowy young men of olive complexion, baring as they smiled sets of flawless teeth such as are to be seen in dental advertisements, disposable little dancing men, cowardly, elegant, watchful, looking like cunning hairdressers; elderly gentlemen who assiduously but vainly attempted to disguise their paunches and their bald pates, good-humored, lecherous, jovial, and bowlegged; in short a selection from that portion of humanity which was for the time being the inheritor of the vanished world, only to yield it a few years later, at a profit, to even more modern and murderous heirs.

One of the elderly gentlemen now rose from the table. First he twirled a crown in his hand, then placed it on his bald head, walked round the table, proceeded to the middle of the bar, danced a little jig, waggled his head and with it the crown, and sang a popular hit of the day, "The Sacred Crown is Worn Like This!"

At first Franz Xaver could not make head nor tail of this lamentable exhibition. It seemed to him that the party consisted of decaying old gentlemen with gray hair (made fools of by mannequins in short skirts); chambermaids celebrating their day off; female barflies who would share with the waitresses the profits from the sale of champagne and their own bodies; a lot of good-for-nothing pimps who dealt in women and foreign exchange, wore wide padded shoulders and wide flapping trousers that looked more like women's clothes; and dreadful-looking middlemen who dealt in houses, shops, citizenships, passports, concessions, good marriages, birth certificates, religious beliefs, titles of nobility, adoptions, brothels, and smuggled cigarettes. This was the section of society which was relentlessly committed, in every capital city of a Europe which had, as a whole continent, been defeated, to live off its corpse, slandering the past, exploiting the present, promoting the future, sated but insatiable. These were the Lords of Creation after the Great War. Count Morstin had the impression of being his own corpse, and that these people were dancing on his grave. Hundreds and thousands had died in agony to prepare the victory of people like these, and hundreds of thoroughly respectable moralists had prepared the collapse of the old Monarchy, had longed for its fall and for the liberation of the nation-states! And now, pray observe, over the grave of the old world and about the cradles of the newborn nations, there danced the specters of the night from American bars.

Morstin came closer, so as to have a better view. The shadowy nature of these well-covered, living specters aroused his interest. And upon the bald pate of this bowlegged, jigging man he recognized a facsimile – for facsimile it must surely be – of the crown of St. Stephen. The waiter, who was obsequious in drawing the attention of his customers to anything noteworthy, came to Franz Xaver and said, "That is Walakin the banker, a Russian. He claims to own the crowns of all the dethroned monarchies. He brings a different one here every evening. Last night it was the Tsars' crown; tonight it is the crown of St. Stephen."

Count Morstin felt his heart stop beating, just for a second. But during this one second – which seemed to him later to have lasted for at least an hour – he experienced a complete transformation of his own personality. It was as if an unknown, frightening, alien Morstin were growing within him, rising, growing, developing, and taking possession not only of his familiar body but, further, of the entire space occupied by the American bar. Never in his life, never since his childhood had Franz Xaver Morstin experienced a fury like this. He had a gentle disposition and the sanctuary which had been vouchsafed him by his position, his comfortable circumstances and the brilliance of his name had until then shielded him from the grossness of the world and from any contact with its meanness. Otherwise, no doubt, he would have learned anger sooner. It was as if he sensed, during that single second that changed him, that the world had changed long before. It was as if he now felt that the change in himself was in fact a necessary consequence of universal change. That much greater than this unknown anger, which now rose up in him, grew and overflowed the bounds of his personality, must have been the growth of meanness in this world, the growth of that baseness which had so long hidden behind the skirts of fawning "loyalty" and slavish servility. It seemed to him, who had always assumed without a second thought that everyone was by nature honorable, that at this instant he had discovered a lifetime of error, the error of any generous heart, that he had given credit, limitless credit. And this sudden recognition filled him with the honest shame which is sister to honest anger. An honest man is doubly shamed at the sight of meanness, first because the very existence of it is shameful, second because he sees at once that he has been deceived in his heart. He sees himself betrayed and his pride rebels against the fact that people have betrayed his heart.

It was no longer possible for him to weigh, to measure, to

consider. It seemed to him that hardly any kind of violence could be bestial enough to punish and wreak vengeance on the baseness of the man who danced with a crown on his bald whoremongering head; every night a different crown. A gramophone was blaring out the song from *Hans, Who Does Things With His Knee*; the barmaids were shrilling; the young men clapped their hands; the barman, white as a surgeon, rattled among his glasses, spoons, and bottles, shook and mixed, brewed and concocted in metal shakers the secret and magical potions of the modern age. He clinked and rattled, from time to time turning a benevolent but calculating eye on the banker's performance. The little red lamps trembled every time the bald man stamped. The light, the gramophone, the noise of the mixer, the cooing and giggling of the women drove Count Morstin into a marvelous rage. The unbelievable happened: for the first time in his life he became laughable and childish. He armed himself with a half-empty bottle of champagne and a blue soda-siphon, then approached the strangers. With his left hand he squirted soda water over the company at the table and with his right hand struck the dancer over the head with the bottle. The banker fell to the ground. The crown fell from his head. And as the Count stooped to pick it up, as it were to rescue the real crown and all that was associated with it, waiters, girls, and pimps all rushed at him. Numbed by the powerful scent of the women and the blows of the young men, Count Morstin was finally brought out into the street. There, at the door of the American bar, the obsequious waiter presented the bill, on a silver tray, under the wide heavens and, in a manner of speaking, in the presence of every distant and indifferent star; for it was a crisp winter night.

The next day Count Morstin returned to Lopatyny.

V

Why – said he to himself during the journey – should I not go back to Lopatyny? Since my world seems to have met with final defeat and I no longer have a proper home, it is better that I should seek out the wreckage of my old one!

He thought of the bust of the Emperor Franz Joseph which lay in his cellar, and he thought of this, his Emperor's corpse, which had long lain in the Kapuzinergruft.

I was always odd man out, thought he to himself, both in my village and in the neighborhood. I shall remain odd man out.

He sent a telegram to his steward announcing the day of his arrival.

And when he arrived they were waiting for him, as always, as in the old days, as if there had been no war, no dissolution of the Monarchy, no new Polish Republic.

For it is one of the greatest mistakes made by the new – or as they like to call themselves, modern – statesmen that the people (the "nation") share their own passionate interest in world politics. The people in no way lives by world politics, and is thereby agreeably distinguishable from politicians. The people lives by the land which it works, by the trade which it exercises, and by the craft which it understands. (It nevertheless votes at free elections, dies in wars, and pays taxes to the Ministry of Finance.) Anyway, this is the way things were in Count Morstin's village of Lopatyny, and the whole of the World War and the complete redrawing of the map of Europe had not altered the opinions of the people of Lopatyny. Why and how? The sound, human sense of the Jewish publicans and the Polish and Ruthenian peasants resented the incomprehensible whims of world history. These whims are abstract: but the likes and dislikes of the people are concrete.

The people of Lopatyny, for instance, had for years known the Counts Morstin, those representatives of the Emperor and the house of Habsburg. New gendarmes appeared, and a tax-levy is a tax-levy, and Count Morstin is Count Morstin. Under the rule of the Habsburgs the people of Lopatyny had been happy or unhappy – each according to the will of God. Independent of all the changes in world history, in spite of republics and monarchies, and what are known as national self-determination or suppression, their life was determined by a good or bad harvest, healthy or rotten fruit, productive or sickly cattle, rich pasture or thin, rain at the right or the wrong season, a sun to bring forth fruit or drought and disaster. The world of the Jewish merchant consisted of good or bad customers; for the publican in feeble or reliable drinkers, and for the craftsman it was important whether people did or did not require new roofs, new boots, new trousers, new stoves, new chimneys or new barrels. This was the case, at least in Lopatyny. And in our prejudiced view the whole wide world is not so different from the village of Lopatyny as popular leaders and politicians would like to believe. When they have read the newspapers, listened to speeches, elected officials, and talked over the doings of the world with their friends, these worthy peasants, craftsmen, and shopkeepers – and in big cities the workmen as well – go back to their houses and their places of work. And at home they find worry or happiness; healthy children or sick children, discontented or peaceable wives, customers who pay well or pay slowly, pressing or patient creditors, a good meal or a bad one, a

We are the world

clean or a dirty bed. It is our firm conviction that ordinary folk do not trouble their heads over world events, however much they may rant and rave about them on Sundays. But this may, of course, be a personal conviction. We have in fact only to report on the village of Lopatyny. These things were as we have described them.

No sooner was Count Morstin home than he repaired at once to Solomon Piniowsky, that Jew in whom innocence and shrewdness went hand in hand, as if they were brother and sister. And the Count asked the Jew, "Solomon, what do you count on in this world?"

"Herr Graf," said Piniowsky, "I no longer count on anything at all. The world has perished, there is no Emperor any more, people choose presidents, and that is the same thing as when I pick a clever lawyer for a lawsuit. So the whole people picks a lawyer to defend it. But, I ask myself, Herr Graf, before what tribunal? Just a tribunal of other lawyers. And supposing the people have no lawsuit and therefore no need to be defended, we all know just the same that the very existence of these lawyers will land us up to the neck in a lawsuit. And so there will be constant lawsuits. I still have the black and yellow flag, Herr Graf, which you gave me as a present. What am I to do with it? It is lying on the floor of my attic. I still have the picture of the old Emperor. What about that, now? I read the newspapers, I attend a bit to business, and a bit to the world. I know the stupid things that are being done. But our peasants have no idea. They simply believe that the old Emperor has introduced new uniforms and set Poland free, that he no longer has his Residence in Vienna, but in Warsaw."

"Let them go on thinking that," said Count Morstin.

And he went home and had the bust of the Emperor Franz Joseph brought up from the cellar. He stood it at the entrance to his house.

And from the following day forward, as though there had been no war and no Polish Republic; as though the old Emperor had not been long laid to rest in the Kapuzinergruft; as though this village still belonged to the territory of the old Monarchy; every peasant who passed by doffed his cap to the sandstone bust of the old Emperor and every Jew who passed by with his bundle murmured the prayer which a pious Jew will say on seeing an Emperor. And this improbable bust ⌐presented in cheap sandstone from the unaided hand of a peasant lad⌐ this bust in the uniform jacket of the dead Emperor, with stars and insignia and the Golden Fleece, all preserved in stone, just as the youthful eye of the lad had seen the Emperor and loved him – won with the passing of time a quite special and particular artistic merit, even in the eyes of Count Morstin. It was as if the passing of time ennobled and improved the work which represented this exalted subject. Wind and weather worked as if with artistic consciousness upon the simple stone. It was as if respect and remembrance also worked upon this portrait, as if every salute from a peasant, every prayer from a believing Jew, had ennobled the unconscious work of the young peasant's hands.

And so the bust stood for years outside Count Morstin's house, the only memorial which had ever existed in the village of Lopatyny and of which all its inhabitants were rightly proud.

The bust meant even more, however, to the Count, who in those days no longer left the village any more. It gave him the impression, whenever he left his house, that nothing had altered. Gradually, for he had aged prematurely, he would stumble upon quite foolish ideas. He would persuade himself for hours at a time, although he had fought through the whole of the greatest of all wars, that this had just been a bad dream, and that all the changes which had followed it were also bad dreams. This in spite of the fact that he saw almost every week how his appeals to officials and judges no longer helped his *protégés* and that these officials indeed made fun of him. He was more infuriated than insulted. It was already well known in the neighboring small town, as in the district, that "old Morstin was half crazy." The story circulated that at home he wore the uniform of a Rittmeister of Dragoons, with all his old orders and decorations. One day a neighboring landowner, a certain Count, asked him straight out if this were true.

"Not as yet," replied Morstin, "but you've given me a good idea. I shall put on my uniform and wear it not only at home but out and about."

And so it happened.

From that time on Count Morstin was to be seen in the uniform of an Austrian Rittmeister of Dragoons, and the inhabitants of Lopatyny never gave the matter a second thought. Whenever the Rittmeister left his house he saluted his Supreme Commander, the bust of the dead Emperor Franz Joseph. He would then take his usual route between two little pinewoods along the sandy road which led to the neighboring small town. The peasants who met him would take off their hats and say: "Jesus Christ be praised!," adding "Herr Graf!" as if they believed the Count to be some sort of close relative of the Redeemer, and that two titles were better than one. Alas, for a long time past he had been powerless to help them as he had in the old days. Admittedly the peasants were unable to help themselves. But he, the Count, was no longer a power in the land! And like all those who have been powerful once, he now counted even less than those who had always been powerless: in the eyes of officialdom he almost belonged among the ridiculous. But the people of Lopatyny and its surroundings still believed in him, just as they believed in the Emperor Franz Joseph whose bust it was their custom to salute. Count Morstin seemed in no way laughable to the peasants and Jews of Lopatyny; venerable, rather. They revered his lean, thin figure, his gray hair, his ashen, sunken countenance, and his eyes which seemed to stare into the boundless distance; small wonder, for they were staring into the buried past.

It happened one day that the regional commissioner for Lwow, which used to be called Lemberg, undertook a tour of inspection and for some reason had to stop in Lopatyny. Count Morstin's house was pointed out to him and he at once made for it. To his astonishment he caught sight of the bust of the Emperor Franz Joseph in front of the house, in the midst of a little shrubbery. He looked at it for a long while and finally decided to enter the house and ask the Count himself about the significance of this memorial. But he was even more astonished, not to say startled, at the sight of Count Morstin coming towards him in the uniform of a Rittmeister of Dragoons. The regional commissioner was himself a "Little Pole" which means he came from what was formerly Galicia. He had himself served in the Austrian Army. Count Morstin appeared to him like a ghost from a chapter of history long forgotten by the regional commissioner.

He restrained himself and at first asked no questions. As they sat down to table, however, he began cautiously to inquire about the Emperor's memorial.

"Ah, yes," said the Count, as if no new world had been born, "His late Majesty of blessed memory spent eight days in this house. A very gifted peasant lad made the bust. It has always stood here and will do so as long as I live."

The commissioner stifled the decision which he had just taken and said with a smile, as it were quite casually, "You still wear the old uniform?"

"Yes," said Morstin, "I am too old to have a new one made. In civilian clothes, you know, I don't feel altogether at ease since circumstances became so altered. I'm afraid I might be confused with a lot of other people. Your good health," continued the Count, raising his glass and toasting his guest.

The regional commissioner sat on for a while, and then left the

Count and the village of Lopatyny to continue his tour of inspection. When he returned to his Residence he issued orders that the bust should be removed from before Count Morstin's house.

These orders finally reached the mayor (termed "Wojt") of the village of Lopatyny and therefore, inevitably, were brought to the attention of Count Morstin.

For the first time, therefore, the Count now found himself in open conflict with the new power, of whose existence he had previously hardly taken cognizance. He realized that he was too weak to oppose it. He recalled the scene at night in the American bar in Zurich. Alas, there was no point any more in shutting one's eyes to these new bankers and wearers of crowns, to the new ladies and gentlemen who ruled the world. One must bury the old world, but one must give it a decent burial.

So Count Morstin summoned ten of the oldest inhabitants of the village of Lopatyny to his house – among them the clever and yet innocent Jew, Solomon Piniowsky. There also attended the Greek Catholic priest, the Roman Catholic priest, and the Rabbi.

When they were all assembled Count Morstin began the following speech,

"My dear fellow citizens, you have all known the old Monarchy, your old fatherland. It has been dead for years, and I have come to realize that there is no point in not seeing that it is dead. Perhaps it will rise again, but old people like us will hardly live to see it. We have received orders to remove, as soon as possible, the bust of the dead Emperor, of blessed memory, Franz Joseph the First.

"We have no intention of removing it, my friends!

"If the old days are to be dead we will deal with them as one does deal with the dead: we will bury them.

"Consequently I ask you, my dear friends, to help me bury the dead Emperor, that is to say his bust, with all the ceremony and respect that are due to an Emperor, in three days' time, in the cemetery."

VI

The Ukrainian joiner, Nikita Koldin, made a magnificent sarcophagus of oak. Three dead Emperors could have found accommodation in it.

The Polish blacksmith, Jarowslaw Wojciechowski, forged a mighty double eagle in brass which was firmly nailed to the coffin's lid.

The Jewish Torah scribe, Nuchin Kapturak, inscribed with a goose quill upon a small roll of parchment the blessing which believing Jews must pronounce at the sight of a crowned head, cased it in hammered tin and laid it in the coffin.

Early in the morning – it was a hot summer day, countless invisible larks were trilling away in the heavens and countless invisible crickets were replying from the meadows – the inhabitants of Lopatyny gathered at the memorial to Franz Joseph the First. Count Morstin and the mayor laid the bust to rest in its magnificent great sarcophagus. At this moment the bells of the church on the hill began to toll. All three pastors placed themselves at the head of the procession. Four strong old peasants bore the coffin on their shoulders. Behind them, his drawn saber in his hand, his dragoon helmet draped in field gray, went Count Franz Xaver Morstin, the closest person in the village to the dead Emperor, quite lonely and alone, as becomes a mourner. Behind him, wearing a little round black cap upon his silver hair, came the Jew, Solomon Piniowsky, carrying in his left hand his round velvet hat and raised in his right the black and yellow flag with the double eagle. And behind him the whole village, men and women.

The church bells tolled, the larks trilled and the crickets sang unceasingly.

The grave was prepared. The coffin was lowered with the flag draped over it, and for the last time Franz Xaver Morstin raised his saber in salute to his Emperor.

The crowd began to sob as though the Emperor Franz Joseph and with him the old Monarchy and their own old home had only then been buried. The three pastors prayed.

So the old Emperor was laid to rest a second time, in the village of Lopatyny, in what had once been Galicia.

A few weeks later the news of this episode reached the papers. They published a few witticisms about it, under the heading, "Notes from all over."

VII

Count Morstin, however, left the country. He now lives on the Riviera, an old man and worn out, spending his evenings playing chess and skat with ancient Russian generals. He spends an hour or two every day writing his memoirs. They will probably possess no significant literary value, for Count Morstin has no experience as a literary man, and no ambition as a writer. Since, however, he is a man of singular grace and style he delivers himself of a few memorable phrases, such as the following for example, which I reproduce with his permission: "It has been my experience that the clever are capable of stupidity, that the wise can be foolish, that true prophets can lie, and that those who love truth can deny it. No human virtue can endure in this world, save only one: true piety. Belief can cause us no disappointment since it promises us nothing in this world. The true believer does not fail us, for he seeks no recompense on earth. If one uses the same yardstick for peoples, it implies that they seek in vain for national virtues, so-called, and that these are even more questionable than human virtues. For this reason I hate nationalism and nation-states. My old home, the Monarchy, alone, was a great mansion with many doors and many chambers for every condition of men. This mansion has been divided, split up, splintered. I have nothing more to seek for, there. I am used to living in a home, not in cabins."

So, proudly and sadly, writes the old Count. Peaceful, self-possessed, he waits on death. Probably he longs for it. For he has laid down in his will that he is to be buried in the village of Lopatyny; not, indeed, in the family vault, but alongside the grave of the Emperor Franz Joseph, beside the bust of the Emperor.

Translated by John Hoare

ROBERT MUSIL

The Blackbird   1936

The two men I must mention in order to tell three short stories
– in the course of which it will become clear who the narrator is –
had been friends from childhood; let's call them Aone and Atwo.
Long term friendships such as theirs grow more and more peculiar
the older one gets. In the course of years one changes from head to
toe, from the smallest hair on your skin to your very heart, but the
relationship itself remains remarkably the same. It alters as little as
do the relations which every individual has with the various
persona that he successively calls "I." It doesn't matter whether
you feel like the thickheaded boy with blond hair who once was
photographed; no, basically you cannot even say that you like this
foolish little egoistic monster. Similarly, you are neither in accord,
nor contented, with your friends; indeed, many friends can't stand
each other. In a certain sense these are the deepest and best
friendships. They contain the incomprehensible element with no
adulteration.

The upbringing shared by the two friends Aone and Atwo had
been nothing short of a religious one. They had, of course, both
been educated at a boarding school that commended itself on
having given appropriate emphasis to religious principles. The
ambition of the pupils, however, lay in never observing them. For
example: the institution's church was a large and beautiful one
with a stone steeple, and was reserved for the sole use of the
school; no outsider ever entered, and while a few students in the
front pews alternately knelt and stood as required by the holy rites,
other groups could always play cards in the rear by the
confessional boxes, smoke cigarettes on the stairs leading to the
organ, or vanish up into the steeple, under whose gabled roof a
balcony was held aloft like a plate with candles, and there, on this
parapet, at a dizzying height, acrobatic stunts were performed that
could have cost the necks of even less sin-laden boys.

One of these provocations of God consisted in doing a
handstand on this parapet. You slowly raised yourself up and then
remained there, eyes downward, standing on your hands and
swaying back and forth. Anyone who has performed this feat on

solid ground will know how much self-confidence, boldness, and luck are needed to repeat it on a foot-wide ledge atop a church steeple. Many daring and agile lads would not attempt it, even though on flat land they could stroll about on their hands at will. For example, Aone didn't. Conversely, and this may well serve to introduce him as narrator, Atwo in his boyhood was the inventor of this test of aplomb. You rarely saw a body like his. He didn't have the physique which comes from sports, as do many, but rather seemed to be effortlessly woven from muscles by nature. Atop this body was a narrow, smallish head, with eyes like lightning coiled in velvet, and teeth which sooner made one think of the sleekness of a beast of prey than expect the meekness of a mystic.

In their college years both friends championed a materialistic theory of existence that regarded man as a physiological and economic machine, without soul or god. This he may very well be, though it didn't matter to them in the least; the lure of such a philosophy doesn't lie in its truth but in its demonic, pessimistic, terribly intellectual character. By this time their relationship to one another was already the comradeship of young men. Atwo was studying forestry and spoke of going far away as a forestry engineer, to Russia or to Asia, as soon as his studies were ended. Instead of such boyish dreams his friend had already hit upon a more grown-up fantasy and busied himself with the upward struggling working-class movement. When they met once again, shortly before the Great War, Atwo had his Russian exploits behind him, was employed in the office of a large corporation and seemed to have suffered considerable disappointments, even though he was doing tolerably well. In the meantime, his old school friend had gone from fighting in the class struggle to editing a newspaper which printed a great deal about social harmony and was owned by a big investor. From that time on they were inseparably bound by their mutual disdain for one another.

Once more, however, they lost touch and finally, when they were thrown together again for a short time, Atwo related the following, in the way that one dumps out a sackful of memories before a friend in order to continue on with the empty bag. Under these circumstances it matters little what Aone replied, and their conversation can be related almost as if it were a monologue. It would be more significant if one could describe exactly how Atwo looked, for his appearance had a decisive bearing on the meaning of his words. But that's difficult. At best one might say that he called to mind a sharp, slender sinewy riding crop that, resting on its supple tip, leaned against a wall. In this half-erect, half-sunken

Narrative vs. Reality

posture he seemed quite at ease.

* * *

"Among the oddest places in the world are those Berlin courtyards," said Atwo, "where the backs of two, three, or four buildings point their behinds at each other. Cooks sit in rectangular openings in the middle of the walls and sing. You can tell by looking at the red-hued copper utensils on shelves how loudly they clatter. Far below, a man's voice bawls out abuse to one of the girls up above, or heavy wooden shoes clomp back and forth on the hard brick pavement. Slow. Hard. Restless. Meaningless. Endless. Is it so or not?

"The kitchens and bedrooms face the courtyards; they lie close to one another like love and digestion in the human body. Floor by floor the nuptial beds are stacked up above each other, for every bedroom in the building has the same location. The wall with the window, the wall between the bedroom and the bathroom, and the wall with the closet all fix the location of the bed to within half a meter. Likewise, floor by floor the dining rooms, the white-tiled bathrooms, and the balconies with their red lamp shades pile up, one on top of the other. Love, sleep, birth, digestion, unexpected reunions, careworn and sociable nights lie close above one another in these buildings like columns of stacked-up breadrolls in an automat. In middle-class apartment houses such as these your personal destiny has already been settled when you move in. You will admit that human freedom lies principally in when and where you do something, for what people do is almost always the same. It's a hell of a thing if in addition you make the layout of everything the same. Once I climbed on top of a wardrobe merely to exploit the vertical dimension, and I can say that the disagreeable conversation in which I was involved looked quite different from up there."

Atwo laughed at his recollection. Aone felt almost as if they were sitting on a balcony with a red lamp shade, which belonged to his own apartment, but he remained silent, for he knew all too well what he might have replied.

"Moreover I'll admit even today that there's something monstrous in this regularity," Atwo himself allowed. "At that time I thought that I saw something like a desert or an ocean in this specter of anthill living and desolation. Even though the thought of it turns my stomach, a Chicago slaughterhouse is, after all, something quite different than a flowerpot! But the remarkable thing was that while I had this apartment I used to think about my parents with unusual frequency. You'll recall that I had as good as lost all contact with them, but all of a sudden this sentence began running through my head: They have given you life. And this comical thought returned time and time again, like a persistent fly that can't be chased away. There's nothing particularly curious about this sanctimonious phrase, which gets drummed into everyone's head in childhood. But when I considered my apartment I said all the same, 'Look. Now you have bought your independence, for so and so many marks yearly rent!' Perhaps I even sometimes said, 'Now you have fashioned a life of your own.' And that's where things stood – in the middle between department store, death insurance, and pride. Yet it seemed to me exceptionally noteworthy, indeed even a mystery, that here something had been given to me whether I wanted it or not, and what's more, something which formed the basic legend of everything else. I believe this proposition concealed a treasure trove of irregularity and unfathomability that I had buried. And then came the story with the nightingale.

"It began on an evening like many others. I had stayed at home, and after my wife went to bed I sat down in the study; perhaps the only difference from similar evenings was that I didn't pick up a book or anything else, but even that had occurred before. After one a.m. the street begins to grow quieter. Conversations become fewer and fewer. It's lovely to follow with one's ear the advance of the night. By two, noise and laughter downstairs clearly indicate drunkenness and lateness. I became aware that I was waiting for something, though I had no inkling of what it might be. Toward three the sky began to get lighter – it was May. I felt my way through the dark apartment to the bedroom and noiselessly lay down. I no longer expected anything but sleep and, in the morning, a day like the one that had just ended. Soon I no longer knew if I was awake or asleep. A dark green light seeped through the drapes and between the blinds; thin white streaks of the dawn wound their way into the room. It could have been my last waking impression or a tranquil dream vision. Then I was awakened by something approaching. Sounds came nearer. Once, twice I drowsily perceived them. Then they sat on top of the adjacent building, and from there leaped into the air like dolphins. Or I might have said like star flares, for the impression of spheres of light lingered. When they fell back down they burst softly against the windowpanes and sank slowly into the depths like great silver stars. I sensed the presence of magic. I lay awake on my bed, but differently than in the daytime; I felt like the figure on its coffin lid. It's very hard to describe, but when I reflect on it it was as if I had been turned inside out. I was no longer a solid, space-filling form, but something like a depression in space. The room was not hollow but was permeated by a substance that doesn't exist in the daytime, darkly transparent and darkly transpalpable – I too was made of it. Time ran in fever-small, rapid pulse beats. Why shouldn't what has never happened before happen now? 'It's a nightingale that's singing out there,' I said to myself, half aloud.

"Well, perhaps there are indeed more nightingales in Berlin than I thought," continued Atwo. "I believed then there weren't any in these stone mountains, and that this one had flown to me from afar. 'To me!' I thought, and sat up with a smile. 'A heavenly bird! So they really exist!' In such a moment, you see, one is ready to believe in the supernatural in the most natural way, as though one had spent one's entire childhood in a magical world. Immediately I thought: 'I will follow the nightingale. Goodbye, my love. Goodbye, indeed, love, house, city . . . !' But before I had gotten up, before I had clearly decided whether I would climb up to the roofs or would follow it along the streets, the bird had become silent and had obviously flown farther off.

"Now it was singing on another roof for another sleeper," Atwo reflected. "You will suppose that this ends the story? It's only just the beginning, and I don't know what the ending will be!

"I was abandoned, and oppressed by a profound despondency. 'It wasn't a nightingale at all. It was a blackbird,' I said to myself, exactly as you would like to say. It's well known that they mimic other birds. I was fully awake now, and the stillness was irksome to me. I lit a candle and studied the woman who lay next to me. Her body looked a pale, brick-red color. The white border of the blanket lay across her skin like a strip of snow. Wide shadow-lines, whose origin couldn't quite be made out, although of course it had to be connected with the candle and the position of my arm, wound about her body. 'What does it matter,' I thought meanwhile, 'if it really was only a blackbird?' Oh, on the contrary, precisely the fact that it had been merely an ordinary blackbird that could so derange me – that is much more significant! You know that one only cries over a single disillusionment; after a second, a smile is already on the way. And the whole time I continued looking at my wife. All this was interconnected, though I don't know how. 'For years I have loved you, like nothing else in the world,' I thought, 'and now you lie there like a burnt-out husk of love. You have become totally strange to me, and now I have emerged at the other end of love.' Was that satiety? I don't remember having experienced satiety. I'll describe it to you like this: it's as if an emotion could tunnel through your heart as if through a mountain, on whose far side lay another world with the same valley, the same houses, and the same little bridges. But I simply didn't know what it was – I still don't know today. Perhaps I'm wrong to tell you this story in connection with two others that followed it. I can only tell you what I took it for when I experienced it: a signal had come to me from somewhere. That was my impression of it.

"I lay my head next to her unsuspecting, sleeping body. Her breast seemed to rise and fall excessively, and the walls of the room rose and fell about her like the high seas about a ship that is far from land. I probably would never have left, but if I were now to steal away, it seemed to me, I would remain the little boat abandoned in solitude and that a great and seaworthy ship had negligently sailed over me. I kissed the sleeper; she didn't feel it. I whispered something in her ear, and perhaps I did it so circumspectly that she didn't hear. Then I laughed at myself, and scoffed at the nightingale, but stealthily dressed. I believe I sobbed, but I really did leave. It was staggeringly easy, although I tried to tell myself that no respectable person would behave like this. As I recall, I was like a drunkard, who curses the street he's walking on to assure himself of his sobriety.

"Naturally, I've often thought of going back. At times I longed to return from across half the world, but I never did. She had become untouchable for me. I don't know whether or not you understand me, but one who is deeply aware of an injustice will no longer rectify it. And by the way, I don't want your absolution. I want to tell you my stories in order to find out whether or not they're true. For years I've been unable to speak my mind to anyone, and frankly, if I were to catch myself talking aloud about this I'd be uneasy.

"So make no mistake; my rationality concedes nothing to your enlightenment.

"Two years later I found myself in a tight spot. It was in South Tyrol, in a blind section of a battle-line that curved from the bloody trenches of Cima di Vezzena to Lake Caldonazzo. There the line ran deep in the valley like a sunny ripple, over two hills with lovely names, and climbed up again on the other side to lose itself in quiet mountains. It was in October. The sparsely-manned trenches were overhung with foliage. The lake burned soundlessly in blue. The hills lay there like great withered wreaths, 'like grave-wreaths,' I often thought, without fearing them. Hesitantly and divided, the valley flowed around them, but beyond the line we held it fled from such pleasant diversions and led like a trumpet-blast, brown, wide and heroic, into the hostile distance.

"In the middle of the night we occupied an advanced position. We were so exposed in the valley that the enemy could have hit us by throwing stones, but they were content with simple artillery fire. On mornings after such nights everyone wore a strange expression, which didn't disappear for several hours. Everyone's eyes were enlarged, and upon the army of shoulders the irregularly held heads looked like a trampled lawn. Nevertheless, on all those nights I often raised my head above the rim of the trench and cautiously, like a lover, looked back over my shoulder; then I'd see the Brenta Mountains, bright heavenly blue like stiffly pleated glass, standing in the night. On these nights the stars were especially large, and looked like they had been stamped out of gold paper, and shimmered greasily as if baked from dough, and the sky was blue even at night, and the moon's thin, maidenly crescent, all silver or all gold, floated enraptured in its midst. You must try to imagine how beautiful it was; in a secure existence nothing is that beautiful. Sometimes I couldn't bear it and, filled with joy and yearning, crept out into the night as far as the green-gold black trees. I raised myself up among them like a small, brown-green feather in the plumage of the quietly sitting, sharp-beaked bird Death, which is more bewitchingly black and iridescent than anything you've ever seen.

"By contrast, in the main sector during the daytime you could actually ride about. In such positions, where you have time for reflection, for terror, you first learn to know the danger. Each day it gathers its victims: a set weekly average, such and such percent. Even the division's general staff officers were reckoning as impersonally as an insurance company. Actually everyone does. One instinctively knows one's chances and feels secure, if not exactly in favorable circumstances. This is the remarkable peace one experiences when one is continually at the front lines. I have to say this beforehand so that you don't falsely imagine my situation. To be sure, it happens that you feel yourself suddenly compelled to search for a particular well-known face you have seen several days before – but it's no longer there. Such a face can be more shocking than is reasonable, and can hang in the air like the shimmer of a candle flame. So one has less fear of death than usual but is susceptible to all sorts of excitations. It's as if the fear of one's end, which weighs constantly upon one like a stone, had been rolled away, and now, in the indeterminate proximity of death, a strange inner freedom blossoms.

"Once during this time an enemy aircraft flew over our peaceful position. This didn't occur often because the mountain range, with its deep ravines opening narrowly between fortified peaks, had to be flown over at a high altitude. We were standing on one of the 'grave-wreaths,' and in a split second the sky was dotted with bursts of shrapnel from the batteries as if by a nimble powder-puff. It looked amusing, almost delightful. The sun shone through the airplane's tri-colored wings above our heads as if through church windows or colorful tissue paper, and the only thing the moment lacked was some music by Mozart. To be sure, the thought ran through my head that we were clustered together like a racetrack crowd and made an easy target. Someone even said, 'Better take cover!' But clearly there'd be no pleasure in scuttling down a hole in the ground like a field mouse. Transfixed, I heard a faint ringing sound approaching my upturned face. Of course, it could have been the other way round, so that I first heard the ringing sound and only then realized the approach of danger; but at the same moment I already knew: it is an aerial dart! These were pointed iron rods, no thicker than a carpenter's pencil, which airplanes used to drop at that time from high altitudes, and if one struck you in the head it would pierce your entire body and come out again through the soles of your feet; but they rarely hit anyone and were soon given up. So, then, this was my first one. Bombs and machine-gun fire sound quite different, and I knew at once what I was dealing with. I tensed, and the next second I had the strange sensation, at odds with all probability: 'It's going to hit me!'

"And do you know what it was like? Not like a terrifying presentiment but rather like a never expected piece of luck! At first I was puzzled that I should be the only one to hear the ringing. Then I thought the sound would disappear again. But it didn't. It was still far off, and as it drew nearer became perspectively louder. I carefully observed the other faces, but no one else had perceived it. And in that instant, when I realized that I alone heard this tenuous singing, something rose forth out of me toward it – a ray of life; every bit as endless as that of death which was coming from above. I'm not inventing this; I'm trying to describe it as simply as possible. I'm convinced that I have expressed myself with absolute sobriety. Of course, I know that to a certain degree it's like a dream where one imagines that one is speaking quite clearly while the words themselves are externally incoherent.

"This lasted for a long time during which I alone heard the

approaching event. The sound was a thin, singing, simple high sound, like that which is produced when the rim of a glass is made to vibrate, but there was something unreal about it. 'You've never heard that before,' I said to myself. And this sound was directed at me. I was linked to this sound, and didn't doubt in the least that something decisive was about to happen to me. I didn't have a single thought of the kind one is supposed to have in the instant prior to death; everything I felt was directed toward the future. I must simply state that I was certain that in the next moment I would feel the presence of God in the presence of my body. That's no little thing for a person who hasn't believed in God since he was eight years old.

"Meanwhile the sound from above became more substantial; it swelled and grew menacing. I asked myself several times if I shouldn't give warning, but I didn't want to do that, even though I or one of the others might be struck. Perhaps this fancy – that high above the battlefield a voice was singing to me – was nothing but a damnable conceit. Perhaps God is nothing more than this: that we poor beggars, in the narrow confines of our existence, can vainly boast of having a rich relative in heaven. I don't know. But without a doubt the air had now begun to ring for the others as well. I noticed shadows of uneasiness flitting across their faces, but not a single one of them said a word either! I looked at these faces once again. Fellows to whom nothing could be further from their thoughts stood without knowing it like a group of disciples awaiting a message. And suddenly the singing had become an earthly sound, ten feet, a hundred feet above us, and then died away. He, it, was there. In the midst of us, but closest to me, something shattered into an unreal noiselessness, something was swallowed and silenced by the earth. My heartbeats were calm and regular. I couldn't have been frightened for even a fraction of a second. I wasn't unconscious for even the tiniest sliver of time, but the first thing I noticed was that everyone was looking at me. I was standing on the same spot as before, but my body had been wrenched savagely sideways and had executed a deep, semi-circular bow. I felt that I was coming to from a delirium and didn't know how long I'd been out. No one spoke to me. Finally someone said, 'Aerial dart,' and everyone wanted to look for it, but it was lodged a meter deep in the ground. At that moment I was inundated with a passionate feeling of gratitude and I believe my entire body blushed. If someone had said that God had entered my body I wouldn't have laughed, but neither would I have believed it. I wouldn't even have believed that I bore off a splinter from Him.

Nevertheless, every time that I remember this I'd like to experience something of the sort once again, only more clearly.

* * *

"Actually, I did experience it again, but it was no more intelligible," Atwo began his last story. He seemed to have become uncertain, but precisely because of this one could perceive that he was ardently eager to hear himself tell it.

It concerned his mother, who had never possessed a large share of Atwo's love, though he maintained that hadn't been so. "Superficially we didn't get along," he said, "and, after all, that's only natural when an old woman lives in the same small town for decades and her son, according to her standards, had achieved nothing in the world. She made me as uneasy as the imperceptibly broadened reflection of myself in a mirror might, and I hurt her by not coming home for years at a time. Every month she would write me an anxious letter filled with questions; even though I usually didn't respond, there was some odd connection, and I remained close to her nevertheless, as was ultimately shown.

"Perhaps decades ago she had passionately impressed upon her mind the ineradicable image of a small boy, in which God only knows what hopes she may have placed, and since I was that long-since vanished boy her love clung to me as if every sun which till then had set still hovered somewhere between light and darkness. There you'd have this secret vanity again except it isn't vanity. For I can truly say I don't care for my own company, and the way so many people act – the way they complacently look at photographs of their younger selves, or enjoy remembering what they did at this or that time in their lives – this ego-savings-account system is totally incomprehensible to me. I'm neither particularly capricious, nor do I live just for the moment, but when something is over I'm over too; if I realize, in walking down a street, that I've often come this way before, or if I see the house I used to live in, I feel a sudden and intense dislike of myself, as though I had recalled a disgraceful deed. What has been flows away as one changes, and it seems to me that no matter how one changes one wouldn't do so at all if the person one relinquished were altogether irreproachable. But precisely because I usually feel this way it was amazing when I realized that all my life a person had clung to an image of me, in all probability one which never corresponded to me, but which was in a certain sense my charter, the mandate of my creation. Do you understand me when I say that in a figurative sense my mother was a lioness confined in the real existence of a very limited woman? She wasn't clever by our standards; she had neither self-restraint nor broad horizons; when I think back over my childhood one couldn't call her kind, either. She was irascible and at the mercy of her nerves, and you can imagine the sort of occurrences resulting from this combination of passion and narrow vision. But I maintain that there exists a stature or character which, when personified in our everyday experience, is as incomprehensible as when in fabled times gods assumed the shapes of serpents and fish.

"Soon after the aerial dart incident I was captured during combat in Russia. Later I took part in the great transformation there and wasn't in any particular hurry to return, for the new life long pleased me. I still admire it now, but I realized one day that I could no longer mouth several essential dogmas without yawning. This entailed danger to my life, so I fled to Germany, where individualism was in full, inflationary bloom. I engaged in all sorts of dubious enterprises, in part out of necessity and in part for the joy of once again being in an old country where one can do wrong without having to feel ashamed of oneself. Things didn't go very well for me; sometimes I was in an exceedingly bad way. Things weren't going too well for my parents either. Several times my mother wrote to me, 'We cannot help you, but if it would help to get the little you will one day inherit, it would be my wish to die.' She wrote that, even though I hadn't visited her in years, nor shown her any sign of affection whatever. I must confess that I thought it was a somewhat exaggerated manner of speaking to which I attributed no significance, although I never doubted the authenticity of the feeling, however sentimentally it might be expressed. But then something very odd occurred: my mother actually did fall ill, and it's possible she dragged my father along with her, as he was very devoted to her."

Atwo reflected. "She died of a disease that she must have had without anyone suspecting it. One could point to a variety of natural explanations for the coincidence, and I fear that you'll hold it against me if I don't do this, but once again the incidental circumstances were the most noteworthy. She had absolutely no wish to die. I know that she fought, and bitterly complained about, an early death. Her will to live, her resolutions and wishes were all opposed to the event. Nor can one say that a resolve at the root of her character opposed her superficial intentions; if that were so she would already have thought of suicide or voluntary indigence, which she hadn't done in the least. She was wholly a victim. But haven't you ever noticed that your body has another will beside your own? I believe that everything we experience as having apparent mastery over us: will, emotion, sensation, and ideas, does so only under orders of limited authority, and that during difficult illnesses and convalescences, in uncertain battles and at every critical turning point in one's destiny there is a kind of primal decision of one's whole body in which the ultimate power and truth reside. But be that as it may, what was certain was that I immediately had the impression of something entirely voluntary in my mother's illness. You may call it imagination, but the fact remains that from the moment I received news of her illness, although there seemed no cause for alarm, I was markedly and completely changed. A hardness that had surrounded me melted instantly away. I can say no more than this: the condition I found myself in from then on had a strong resemblance to my awakening on the night I left home, and to my awaiting the singing dart from on high. I wanted to journey to my mother at once, but she kept me away on all sorts of pretexts. First it was that she would be delighted to see me, but I should wait for her slight illness to pass so she could welcome me in full health; later she told me that my visit might prove too agitating for her at the moment. Finally, when I pressed, she said the decisive turn for the better was at hand, and I should be patient for just a while longer. It appears as if she were afraid that a reunion would raise doubts in her mind. Then everything resolved itself so hastily that I only just managed to arrive in time for the burial.

"I found that my father was also ill and, as I told you, soon I could do nothing but help him die. He had previously been a decent man, but during these weeks he was peculiarly obstinate and moody, as if he held a grudge against me and felt annoyed by my presence. After his burial I had to dispose of the household effects, and this lasted several weeks. I was in no hurry. The people of the small town visited me now and again, out of old habit, and told me where in the living room my father used to sit, and my mother, and they themselves. They scrutinized everything very carefully and offered to buy this or that piece. They're so basic, these provincial people, and once one said to me, after he had thoroughly investigated everything, that it was really terrible – an entire family stamped out within a few weeks! No one counted me. When I was alone I sat quietly and read children's books – I'd found a whole chest full of them in the attic. They were covered with dust and soot, partly dried out and partly moldy, and if you struck them they gave off clouds of soft blackness. The marbled endpapers had worn away, leaving groups of jagged islands behind. But when I forced my way into the pages I conquered their contents like a seafarer navigating between these dangers. Once I made a strange discovery: I noticed that the darkened spots at the top where you turn the pages and below in the margin were slightly different from those caused by moldering, then I found all kinds of unidentifiable marks, and finally wild, faded pencil-tracks on the title pages. All at once I was overcome by the realization that these signs of enthusiastic wear-and-tear, these hasty marks and pencil scratches were the traces of a child's fingers, my own fingers, preserved for thirty and more years in a chest under the roof, preserved and forgotten by the whole world. Now, I'll tell you, it may not be anything special for other people when they reflect upon themselves, but for me it was as though my world were turned upside down. I also rediscovered a room, which, thirty years ago and more, had been my nursery. Later it served as a linen closet and the like, but basically it was left as it had been when I used to sit at the sprucewood table under the kerosene lamp, the lamp whose chain was held by three dolphins. Now I sat there again many hours a day and read like a child, like a child whose feet don't reach the floor. For you see, we're used to our heads towering up into nothingness without support because we have something solid beneath our feet, but in childhood we're not quite secure at either end. Instead of the grasping claws of later life we still have delicate, flannellike hands, and we sit in front of a book as if we were sailing through space over precipices on a small leaf. I tell you, under that table my feet really no longer reached the floor.

"I had fixed up a bed in this room and slept there. Then the blackbird came again. Once, after midnight, I was awakened by a wonderful, magnificent song. I didn't wake up immediately, but listened to it for a long time in my sleep. It was the song of a nightingale, but the bird wasn't sitting in the garden bushes but on the roof of a nearby building. I began to sleep with my eyes open. 'There aren't any nightingales here,' I thought. 'It's a blackbird.'

"You needn't think I've already told this story once today! When this thought occurred to me – there are no nightingales here, it's a blackbird – I awoke. It was four in the morning; the day entered my eyes. Sleep sank away as quickly as the traces of surf are absorbed in dry sand of the shore, and there in the open window, in light like a soft white woolen wrap, sat a blackbird. It was sitting there as surely as I am sitting here.

"'I am your blackbird,' it said. 'Don't you recognize me?' I didn't really remember right away, but I felt extraordinarily happy when the bird spoke to me.

"'I've already sat on this windowsill once before, don't you remember?' it continued, and now I replied:

"'Yes, one day you sat there where you're sitting now, and I quickly shut the window.'

"'I am your mother,' she said.

"Well, look, I may have dreamt that. But I didn't dream the bird. It sat there, then flew into the room, and I quickly shut the window. I went up into the attic and looked for a large wooden cage, which I remembered because the blackbird had already been there once before in my childhood, just as I mentioned. It had sat in the window and then flown into the room. I had used a cage, but it soon became tame and I didn't keep it locked up; it lived in my room unconfined and flew in and out. Then one day it didn't return, and now there it was again. I had no desire to try and determine whether or not it was the same blackbird. I found the cage, and along with it a new chest of books, and I can only say to you that I have never in my life been so good a person as I have since I've had the blackbird, though I probably can't describe to you what a good person is."

"Has she spoken often?" Aone asked slyly.

"No," responded Atwo, "she hasn't spoken. But I've had to provide her with birdseed and worms. It's a little awkward for me that she eats worms and I'm supposed to take her for my mother. But it's all right; it's just a question of getting used to it, and what don't you have to get used to in everyday life! Since then I've never let her go, and that's all I have to tell. That's the third story, and how it will end I don't know."

"But surely," Aone cautiously sought to confirm, "you implied that there's a single meaning in all of this?"

"Good heavens," countered Atwo. "Everything happened just as I said, and if I knew the meaning I wouldn't have had to relate all this to you. But it's like when you hear whispering or mere rustling, without being able to tell which it is!"

Translated by Thomas Frick and Wilhelm Wiegandt
and amended by Burton Pike

ÖDÖN VON HORVÁTH

Crossing the Border |97|

Mittenwald is a station on the German-Austrian border with a passport and customs checkpoint.

The border caused tremendous turmoil for some small-town Thuringian tourists. The administrative ceremony attending a border crossing struck them as peculiarly solemn. They shuddered. With timid admiration they looked at the bored policemen on the railroad platform.

A half hour before Mittenwald they were expectantly holding their passports in their hands. Many of them also had their baptism certificates, as well as a certificate of good conduct. All of their suitcases, backpacks, and boxes were lying wide open on the train seats, as if to say, "Please don't shoot us! We're good!"

They flinched when the customs official appeared in their car. "Anyone have anything to declare?" the customs official called unsuspectingly. "We do!" the small-town tourists screamed, precipitously holding their luggage right in front of his face. The customs official, however, ignored their loyalty and didn't even look. "Anyone have anything to declare?!" he outyelled them full of horror, and then raced out of the car for fear that someone actually would have something to declare for a change, meaning that he, for a change, would actually have to do something.

The passport inspection was more rigorous, since that was a more lucrative business. Usually there was at least one passenger on every train whose passport had just expired to whom you could then sell a border permit for a few marks or schillings, respectively. Such a person once told the passport official, "Excuse me, but I'm all for the *Anschluss*!" The passport official, however, vehemently forbade any insults while on duty.

In Mittenwald someone new entered Kobler's compartment. That is to say, he didn't exactly enter, but rather staggered in, since he was dead drunk. As it turned out, he was a partner in a shipping company, a driver from Innsbruck. "I've just been in a collision!" he greeted Kobler, belching like a prelate.

The collision consisted of his running over a motorcyclist near the border with his truck because he wanted to pass on the wrong side of the road, having forgotten about the border. The motorcyclist died instantly, whereas he survived terror-stricken, while his truck had to be towed away. But since his truck was well insured, he drank himself silly in light of his fortune amidst his misfortune. Now he was traveling back to Innsbruck. He hated the motorcyclist and conveyed to Kobler his sincere regret that there wasn't a second rider in the sidecar, for then, given his brisk pace, two would've been picked off and still nothing could've happened to him, since motorcyclists are always to blame. He's absolutely sure that in Bavaria you have to drive on the right, on the left in Tyrol, and in Voralberg on the right as well; he knows the rules of the road inside out because he himself used to be a traffic cop, you know, but unfortunately had allowed himself to be lured by the spirited charms of a malicious bitch into embezzling public funds. "I feel like I can tell you the whole story," he said frankly, and Kobler smiled uneasily.

The driver let go a thunderous fart and then grew maudlin. He was quite a moody person.

"There's no end of troubles in the world," he sighed.

"Will our train keep to the left now?" Kobler asked in order to change the subject because he feared the moody person might just turn around and slug him. The guy was truly disheartened. "We've only got one track, sir," he slurred.

He grew increasingly maudlin and expounded to Kobler about how even a motorcyclist is just a person, too, there's nothing you can do about that, and as far as cars are concerned national borders have always been complete nonsense, but, then, of course, you just have to have borders, otherwise you wouldn't be able to smuggle anything, even though in this particular case it's a matter of fraternal nations. "It's all so twisted!" he groaned, then added that now he's a partner in a well-established Innsbruck company. Then he cried.

Slowly the express train left the German Republic.

It traveled past two signs:

Kingdom of Bavaria	Federal State of Austria
Keep right!	Keep left!

Now they were passing through the northern limestone Alps, along the old Roman road between the Wetterstein and Karwendel mountains. The express train had to climb to an elevation of 1,160 meters in order to reach the Inn Valley, lying approximately 600 meters below. This was difficult terrain for express trains.

The Karwendel mountains are an imposing massif whose magnificent high valleys indisputably rank among the most remote Alpine areas. Grandiose gravel-covered slopes cut their way from jagged ridges to the valley floor, where they meet the debris from the other side. There is virtually no water and, therefore, hardly anything living. In 1928 it was declared a nature preserve in order to maintain the area's pristine state.

To the right, above the town of Seefeld, the top of Mount Hohe Munde shot out from a lyrical larch forest, and you could see the back of the Zugspitze now, too. And those familiar with the Öfelekopf could see it as well, that subordinate peak amidst the ring of Alpine majesty, as this eruption of the Earth's crust is tritely called.

Beyond Seefeld the trucker staggered off to the bathroom to vomit. He didn't return, having fallen asleep there.

Kobler was completely enthralled by God's magnificent mountains, for he had never beheld so many Alpine peaks at one time. Suddenly he thought, "What is a man next to a mountain?" The question moved him considerably. "Compared to a mountain, man is a big nothing. So I wouldn't want to live in the mountains all the time. I'd rather live in the plains. Or else the hills."

And then there was a big curve, and 600 meters below him Kobler saw the Inn Valley, from Ötz to Zirl, all of those big and bigger churches and cloisters, and between them small villages and secluded hamlets, and then more churches and cloisters along with a picturesque ruin as well as even more churches and cloisters. There it was before him: the Promised Land of Tyrol. And above it towered even mightier mountains; those were the Central Alps, Ötztal and Stubai. They were somber, black-green rulers with wild glaciers.

Thus the express train rolled along – past the terrifying abyss, above boldly constructed viaducts, and through many, many tunnels. The longest bore through Martin's Cliff. Once, while hunting, a medieval emperor lost his way there, an event commemorated by a plaque. No stone, however, tells the names of those who were killed during construction . . .

Then Kobler caught sight of a murky haze above the Inn Valley. Below the haze was Innsbruck, the capital of Tyrol.

All that Kobler knew about the city was that it had a famous golden roof, inexpensive Tyrolean wines, and that travelers coming from the West can see, on the left-hand side, several big brothels. Graf Blanquez told him about them once.

In Innsbruck he had to change to the express train to Bologna. That express train was coming from Kufstein and was delayed. "There's that famous Austrian tardiness for you!" he heard a lady say in a North German accent. But the Austrians who must have heard her comment on the platform simply smiled bashfully. "You poor, Prussian, regimental nincompoop," they thought. You could tell by the lady's intonation that her husband was in the army.

Her husband was a major with two ideals. His political ideal was a constitutional monarchy based on the British model. His erotic ideal, on the other hand, was decidedly more progressive – namely, companionate marriage. That's why his wife's voice sounded like that of a staff sergeant.

Austrians are such easygoing people.

Finally the express train arrived.

As far as Steinach am Brenner, that is, almost to the new Italian border, that is, for barely fifty minutes, an old Austrian Hofrat and a so-called man of the people, who played up to the Hofrat in search of his patronage, were sitting in Kobler's compartment. The man of the people was a foreman with no principles who joined the Heimwehr so that he could defraud his co-workers even more. His chief engineer, you see, was a Gauleiter in the Heimwehr.

The Hofrat had an old-fashioned gold pince-nez and a cunning gaze. His appearance was fastidious, especially his white head. All in all, he seemed to be a very vain individual, for he prattled incessantly just so he could hear the man's applause.

The express train veered away from Innsbruck and was already traveling through the Mount Isel tunnel.

"Now it's dark," said the Hofrat. "Very dark," said the man. "It's grown so dark because we're going through the tunnel," said the Hofrat. "Maybe it'll get even darker," said the man. "Damn, it's dark!" said the Hofrat. "Damn!" said the man.

Austrians are such easygoing people.

"I hope our Lord will allow me to see all the socialists hang," said the Hofrat. "You can count on the guy upstairs," said the man. "That's Mount Isel up there," said the Hofrat. "Andreas Hofer," said the man, adding: "The Jews are getting brazen."

The Hofrat's teeth were chattering.

"They ought to just lock that Halsmann up, throw him in the clink!," he crowed. "I don't give a damn if that Jewboy beat his Jew father or not. The prestige of Austria's judicial system is at stake here. You just can't let the Jews walk all over you!" "We beat up a Jew recently," said the man. "Oh, really," said the Hofrat delightedly. "The Jew was alone," said the man, "and there were ten of us. There was a hail of blows. Heimwehr blows!"

The Hofrat snickered.

"Yes, the Heimwehr!" he said. "Hail!" shouted the man. "Victory!" said the Hofrat. "And death!" shouted the man . . .

The Austrian Heimwehr is an organization of so-called self-defense for the Austrian bourgeoisie. This bourgeoisie, you see, feels very threatened because the Austrian working class balks at profits being made off the most basic human needs. In other words, rents are, relatively speaking, pretty low, so that owning a tenement hardly pays as much as it did in the good old days. Moreover, Vienna's red government has many new buildings full of light and airy apartments as a result of its conviction that all working people have the right to a roof over their heads.

The bourgeoisie, in contrast, is of the conviction that it's none of the city government's business if and how its residents live. "If they can't afford it, then they should live beneath God's firmament or else in a shelter. What good's an apartment if you can't pay for it!" the bourgeoisie argues.

Only time can and will tell which of the two classes is right.

In the meantime, the bourgeoisie is taking up arms against red Vienna, with the dream of quartering every Austro-Marxist. The army of these genial landlords is precisely that Heimwehr that cowardly and mendaciously dubs itself an organization of self-defense. Its soldiers are recruited from among perpetual subalterns, uneducated petit bourgeois, former noncommissioned officers, landlord's sons, roguish or terrorized or hopelessly stupid laborers, arrogant student riffraff, and the like, but especially from among poor, abused peasants, mobilized with the help of unscrupulous, calumnious clergymen. They were fetched from the deepest, darkest valleys, together with all those Tyrolean, Voralbergian, Salzburgian, and world-famous Styrian cretins. These cretins must surely constitute the most reliable and bravest division at the core of the Heimwehr, its vanguard, so to speak. Many of them have only nine toes but eleven fingers and don't even know their own names.

"In hoc signo vinces!" the archabbot recently proclaimed while blessing a Heimwehr flag. That's the crowd that wants to completely disenfranchise the hard-working and honest Austrian proletariat ad maiorem bourgeois means of production gloriam.

Once the express train had exited the Mount Isel tunnel Kobler stepped into the corridor. He couldn't stand being in his compartment any longer; the constant blather disturbed his thoughts.

He had to reflect. He felt a great need to do so, as though nature were urgently calling. Suddenly, you see, his real destination occurred to him, and he was very shocked to realize that he hadn't even thought about Egypt for a few hours.

He tried to collect himself. "There's nothing but glaciers out there, and in here there's nothing but beasts. Too many impressions get thrown at you," he said to himself. "Unforeseen," he added, a word that struck him as very genteel.

"I almost completely forgot about the pyramids," he continued, feeling uneasy. He felt like the man who on Thursday forgot what he had done on Wednesday.

He paced back and forth in the corridor.

Six ladies were sitting in one of the compartments. It was a ladies' compartment.

"If only they were six Egyptians!," Kobler fantasized. "And if only they weren't so old, and if only they weren't so wretched, and if only they had money . . ."

"If only!" he repeated. "If only I weren't Kobler, but the chairman of I.G. Farben. Then I could have twenty Egyptians, but it wouldn't do me any good, you know."

He grew terribly melancholic.

"One ought to be able to travel first class," he thought. "The wood hurts my behind. Bless my soul, I think I'm wounded!"

Translated by Craig Decker

INGEBORG BACHMANN

Youth in an Austrian Town 1961

On fine October days, as you come out of the Radetzkystrasse, you can see by the Municipal Theater a group of trees in the sunshine. The first tree, which stands in front of those dark red cherry trees that bear no fruit, is so ablaze with autumn, such an immense patch of gold, that it looks like a torch dropped by an angel. And now it is burning, and the autumn wind and frost cannot put it out.

Who, faced with this tree, is going to talk to me about falling leaves and the white death? Who will prevent me from holding it with my eyes and believing that it will always glow before me as it does at this moment and that it is not subject to the laws of the world?

In its light the town too is recognizable again, with pale convalescent houses under the dark hair of their tiles, and the canal that every now and then brings in a boat from the sea which ties up in its heart. The docks are undoubtedly dead now that freight is brought to the town quicker by train and truck; but flowers and fruit still fall from the high quay onto the pondlike water, the snow drops off the boughs, the melted snow comes rushing noisily down, then washes back and raises a wave and with the wave a ship whose bright colored sail was set on our arrival.

People rarely moved to this town from another town, because its attractions were too few; they came from the villages, because the farms had grown too small, and they looked for accommodation on the outskirts where it was cheapest. Here there were still fields and gravel pits, big market gardens and allotments on which year after year the owners grew turnips, cabbages and beans, the bread of the poorest settlers. These settlers dug their own cellars, standing in the seepage. They nailed up their own rafters during the brief evenings between spring and autumn, and heaven knows whether they ever in their lives saw the ceremony that takes place when the roof is put on.

This didn't worry their children, for they had already grown familiar with the ever-changing smells that came from far away, when the bonfires were burning and the gypsies speaking strange languages settled fleetingly in the no man's land between cemetery and airfield.

In the tenement in the Durchlasstrasse the children have to take off their shoes and play in stockinged feet, because they live above the landlord. They are only allowed to whisper and for the rest of their lives they will never lose the habit of whispering. At school the teachers say to them: "You should be beaten till you open your mouths. Beaten. . . ." Between the reproach for talking too loudly and the reproach for talking too softly, they settle down in silence.

The Durchlasstrasse, Tunnel Street, did not get its name from the game in which the robbers march through a tunnel, but for a long time the children thought it did. It wasn't until later, when their legs carried them farther, that they saw the tunnel, the little underpass, over which the train passed on its way to Vienna. Inquisitive people who wanted to go to the airfield had to walk through this tunnel, across the fields and right through all the embroideries of autumn. Someone had the idea of putting the airfield next to the cemetery, and the people in K always said it was convenient for burying the pilots who for a time made training flights here. The pilots never did anyone the favor of crashing. The children always yelled: "An airman! An airman!" They raised their arms towards them as though to catch them, and stared into the cloud zoo in which the airmen moved among animals' heads and masks.

The children take the silver paper off the bars of chocolate and whistle the *Maria Saaler Geläut* on it. At school the children's heads are examined for lice by a woman doctor. The children don't know what the time is, because the clock on the parish church has stopped. They always come home late from school. The children! They know their names when put to it, but they prick up their ears only when someone calls out "Children."

Homework: down strokes and up strokes in neat writing, exercises in profit and loss, the profit of new horizons against the loss of dreams, learning things by heart with the help of memory aids. Their task: to learn an alphabet and the multiplication tables, an orthography and the ten commandments, among the fumes of oiled floors, of a few hundred children's lives, dwarfs' overcoats, burnt India-rubbers, among tears and scoldings, standing in the corner, kneeling and unsilenceable chatter.

The children take off old words and put on new ones. They hear about Mount Sinai and they see the Ulrichsberg with its turnip fields, larches, and firs, mixed up with cedars and thorn bushes, and they eat sorrel and gnaw the corn cobs before they grow hard and ripe, or bring them home and roast them on the glowing embers. The stripped cobs disappear into the wooden box and are used as tinder, and cedar and olive wood is laid on top, smoulders, warms from far away and casts shadows on the wall.

The time of trophies, the time of Christmases, without looking forward, without looking back, the time of the pumpkin nights, of ghosts and terrors without end. In good, in evil – without hope.

The children have no future. They are afraid of the whole world. They don't picture the world; they picture only the geography of a hopscotch square, because its borders can be drawn in chalk. On one or two legs they hop the borders from one region to another.

One day the children move into the Henselstrasse. Into a house without a landlord, into an estate that has crawled out tame and hidebound from under mortgages. They live two streets away from the Beethovenstrasse, in which all the houses are spacious and centrally heated, and one street away from the Radetzkystrasse, through which the trams run, electric-red and with huge muzzles. They have become the possessors of a garden, in which roses are planted in the front and little apple trees and black currant bushes in the back. The trees are no taller than the children, and they grow up together. On the left they have neighbors with a boxer dog, and on the right children who eat bananas and spend the day swinging on a horizontal bar and rings which they have put up in the garden. They make friends with the dog Ali and compete with the children next door, who always know better and can do things better.

They prefer to be by themselves; they make themselves a den in the attic and often shout out loud in their hiding place, trying out their crippled voices. They utter little low cries of rebellion in front of spiders' webs.

The cellar is spoiled for them by mice and the smell of apples. They go down every day, pick out the rotten fruit, cut out the bad bits and eat what is left. Because the day never comes on which all the rotten apples have been eaten, because more apples are always turning rotten and nothing must be thrown away, they hunger after an alien, forbidden fruit. They don't like the apples, their relations or the Sundays on which they have to go for walks on the Kreuzberg above the house, naming the flowers, naming the birds.

In the summer the children blink through the green shutters into the sunshine; in winter they make a snowman and stick pieces of coal in its head for eyes. They learn French. *Madeleine est une petite fille. Elle regarde la rue.* They play the piano. "The Champagne Song." "The Last Rose of Summer." "The Rustle of Spring."

They no longer spell. They read newspapers, from which the sex murderer jumps out at them. He becomes the shadow thrown by the trees in the dusk as they come home from Bible lessons, and he causes the rustling of the swaying lilac along the front gardens; the snowball bushes and the phloxes part for a moment and reveal his figure. They feel the strangler's grip, the mystery contained in the word sex that is more to be feared than the murderer.

The children read their eyes sore. They wake up tired because they spent too long in the evening in wild Kurdistan or with the gold diggers in Alaska. They eavesdrop on a conversation between lovers and wish they had a dictionary in which to look up all the words they don't understand. They rack their brains about their bodies and a quarrel that takes place at night in their parents' bedroom. They laugh at every opportunity; they can scarcely contain themselves and fall off the bench for laughing, get up and go on laughing, till they get cramps.

But the sex murderer is soon found in a village, in the Rosental, in a barn, with tufts of hay and the gray photographic mist in his face that makes him forever unrecognizable, not only in the morning paper.

There is no money in the house. No more coins drop into the piggy bank. In front of children adults speak only in veiled hints. They cannot guess that the country is in the process of selling itself and the sky along with it, the sky at which everyone tugs until it tears and a black hole appears.

At table the children sit in silence, chewing for a long time on a mouthful, while a storm crackles on the radio and the announcer's voice flashes round the kitchen like ball-lightning and ends up where the saucepan lid rises in alarm above the potatoes in their burst jackets. The electric cables are cut. Columns of marching men pass through the streets. The flags strike together over their heads. "We shall march on and on till everything crashes in ruins," they sing outside. The time signal sounds, and the children start giving each other silent news with practiced fingers.

The children are in love but do not know with what. They talk in gibberish, muse themselves into an indefinable pallor, and when they are completely at a loss they invent a language that maddens them. My fish. My hook. My fox. My snare. My fire. You my water. You my current. My earth. You my if. And you my but. Either. Or. My everything . . . my everything. . . . They push one another, go for each other with their fists and scuffle over a counterword that doesn't exist.

It's nothing. Those children!

They develop temperatures, they vomit, get the shivers, sore throats, whooping cough, measles, scarlet fever; they reach the crisis, are given up, are suspended between life and death; and one day they lie there numb and shaky, with new thoughts about everything. They are told that war has broken out.

For a few more winters, until the bombs fling up its ice, there is skating on the pond under the Kreuzberg. The fine glassy surface in the center is reserved for the girls in flared skirts who perform inside edges, outside edges and figure eights; the circle round this belongs to the speed skaters. In the warming room the bigger boys pull on the bigger girls' skates and their earflaps touch the leather that is like swan's necks as it is stretched over thin legs. You have to have skates that screw on in order to count as a real skater, and those who, like the children, have only wooden skates attached with straps retire into remote corners of the pond or look on.

In the evening, when the skaters of both sexes have slipped off their boots, slung them over their shoulders, and stepped up onto the wooden stands to say goodbye, when all the faces, like fresh young moons, are shining in the dusk, the lights go on under the snow canopies. The loudspeakers are switched on, and the sixteen-year-old twins, who are known throughout the town, come down the wooden steps, he in blue trousers and a white sweater and she in a gauzy blue nothing over her flesh-pink tights. They wait nonchalantly for the music to strike up before leaping down onto the ice from the last step but one – she with a beating of wings, he plunging like a magnificent swimmer – and reach the center with a few deep, powerful thrusts. There she launches out into the first figure, and he holds out to her a hoop of light through which she springs, encircled by a haze, as the gramophone needle begins to scratch and the music grates to an end. The old gentlemen's eyes widen under their frosty brows, and the man with the snow shovel clearing the long-distance skating track round the outside of the pond, his feet wrapped in rags, rests his chin on the handle of his shovel and follows the girl's steps as though they led into eternity.

The children get one more surprise: the next lot of Christmas trees really do fall from heaven. On fire. And the unexpected present which the children receive is more free time.

During air raid alarms they are allowed to leave their exercise books lying on their desks and go down into the shelter. Later they are allowed to save up sweets for the wounded, to knit socks and weave raffia baskets for the men who are fighting on land, on sea and in the air. And to write a composition commemorating those under the earth and on the ground. And later still they are allowed to dig trenches between the cemetery and the airfield, which is already paying tribute to the cemetery. They are allowed to forget their Latin and learn to distinguish between the sounds of the engines in the sky. They don't have to wash so often any more; no one bothers about their fingernails now. The children mend their skipping ropes, because there are no longer any new ones, and they talk about time fuses and land mines. The children play "Let the robbers march through" among the ruins, but often they merely sit there staring into space, and they no longer hear when people call out "Children" to them. There are enough bits of rubble for hopscotch, but the children shiver because they are soaking wet and cold.

Children die, and the children learn the dates of the Seven Years' War and the Thirty Years' War, and they wouldn't care if they mixed up all the hostilities, the pretext and the cause, for the exact differentiation of which they could get good marks in history.

They bury the dog Ali and then his owners. The time of veiled hints is past. People speak in their presence of shooting in the back of the neck, of hanging, liquidating, blowing up, and what they don't hear and see they smell, as they smell the dead of St. Ruprecht, who cannot be dug out because they have been buried under the movie theater into which they slipped surreptitiously to see *Romance in a Minor Key*. Juveniles were not admitted, but then they were admitted to the great dying and murdering which took place a few days later and every day after that.

There is no more light in the house. No glass in the windows. No door on the hinges. Nobody stirs and nobody rises.

The Glan does not flow upstream and downstream. The little river stands still, and Zigulln Castle stands still and does not rise.

St. George stands in the New Square, stands with his club and does not strike the dragon. Next to him stands the Empress and she does not rise either.

O town. Town. Privet town with all its roots dangling. There is no light and no bread in the house. The children are told: "Keep quiet, keep quiet whatever you do."

Among these walls, between the ring roads, how many walls are still standing? Is the bird Wonderful still alive? He has been silent for seven years. Seven years are over. You my place, you no place, above clouds, beneath karst, under night, over day, my town and my river. I your current, you my earth.

Town with the Viktringer Ring and the St. Veiter Ring. . . . All the ring roads ought to be named by their names like the great starry ways that looked no larger to children, and all the alleys,

Citadel Alley and Corn Alley, yes, that's what they were called, Paradise Alley, not to forget the squares, Hay Square and Holy Ghost Square, so that everything here shall be named, once and for all, so that all the squares shall be named. Current and earth.

And one day nobody gives the children report cards any more, and they can go. They are called upon to step into life. Spring descends with clear, raging waters and gives birth to a blade of grass. There is no need to tell the children it is peace. They go away, with their hands in their ragged pockets and a whistle that is meant as a warning to themselves.

Because at that time, at that place, I was among children and we had created fresh space, I gave up the Henselstrasse, as well as the view of the Kreuzberg, and took as my witnesses all the fir trees, the jays, and the eloquent foliage. And because I have become aware that the innkeeper no longer gives a groschen for an empty soda siphon and no longer pours out lemonade for me, I leave to others the path through the Durchlassstrasse and pull the collar of my coat up higher when I cross it without a glance on my way to the graves outside, a passer-through whose origins are evident to no one. Where the town comes to an end, where the gravel pits are, where the sieves stand full of pebbles and the sand has stopped singing, you can sit down for a moment and take your head in your hands. Then you know that everything was as it was, that everything is as it is, and you abandon the attempt to find a reason for everything. For there is no wand that touches you, no transformation. The lime trees and the elder bush . . . ? Nothing touches your heart. No slopes from former times, no risen house. Nor the tower of Zigulln, the two captive bears, the ponds, the roses, the gardens full of laburnum. In the motionless recollection before departure, before all departures, what can be revealed to us? Very little is left to reveal things to us, and youth has no part in what is left, nor has the town in which it was passed.

Only when the tree outside the theater works the miracle, when the torch burns, do I manage to see everything mingled, like the waters in the sea: the early confinement in darkness while the airplanes flew above incandescent clouds; the New Square and its absurd monuments looking out upon Utopia; the sirens that wailed in those days with a sound like the lift in a skyscraper; the slices of dry bread and jam containing a stone on which I bit by the shores of the Atlantic.

Translated by Michael Bullock

INGEBORG BACHMANN

Among Murderers and Madmen   1961

Men are on the way to themselves when they get together in
the evening, drink and talk and express opinions. When they talk
without purpose they are on their own tracks, when they express
opinions and their opinions rise with the smoke from pipes,
cigarettes, and cigars and when the world turns to smoke and
madness in the village inns, in the private rooms, the back rooms
of the big restaurants, and in the wine cellars of the big cities.

We are in Vienna, more than ten years after the war. "After the
war" – this is how we reckon time. We are in Vienna in the
evening and swarming out into the cafés and restaurants. We come
straight from publishing houses and office blocks, from surgeries
and studios, and meet, get on the trail, hunt the best that we have
lost, like a deer, with embarrassment and to the accompaniment of
laughter. In the intervals, when nobody thinks of a joke or of a
story that must definitely be told, when nobody assails the silence
and everyone sinks into himself, someone now and then hears the
blue deer lament – once more, still.

In the evening I went with Mahler to our men's circle at the
Kronenkeller in the Inner Town. Everywhere, now that it was
evening in the world, the taverns were full, and the men talked and
expressed opinions and told stories like the wanderers and martyrs,
like the Titans and demigods of history and fable; they rode up into
the night land, settled down by the fire, the common open fire
which they poked, in the night and the desert in which they were.
They had forgotten their jobs and families. None of them wanted
to recall that at home their wives were now turning back the covers
and going to bed because they didn't know what to do with the
night. Barefoot or in slippers, with tied-up hair and tired faces, the
women wandered round at home, turned off the gas and looked
fearfully under the bed and in the cupboard, soothed the children
with absent-minded words or sat dejectedly by the radio and then
went to bed after all with thoughts of vengeance in the lonely
house. The women lay there feeling like victims, with wide-open
eyes in the darkness, full of despair and malice. They did accounts
with marriage, the years, and the housekeeping money, mani-

pulated, forged, and embezzled. Finally they shut their eyes, attached themselves to a waking dream, abandoned themselves to wild deluding thoughts, until they fell asleep in one last great reproach. And in the first dream they murdered their husbands, made them die in car crashes, of heart attacks and pneumonia; made them die quickly, or slowly and miserably, according to the magnitude of the reproach, and under their closed delicate eyelids tears welled up in sorrow for the death of their husbands. They were crying over their husbands who had gone out, ridden out, never come home, and finally they wept over themselves. They had come to their truest tears.

But we were far away, the club, the choral society, the school friends, the league members, groups, unions, the symposium, and the men's circle. We ordered our wine, put our tobacco pouches on the table in front of us and were out of range of their vengeance and their tears. We didn't die but grew livelier, rattled on and put forward our opinions. Not till much later, towards morning, would we stroke the women's wet faces in the dark and offend them again with our breath, the sour, strong fumes of wine and beer, or earnestly hope that they were already asleep and that we should not have to utter another word in the bedroom-tomb, our prison, to which we returned each time exhausted and peaceable, as though we had given our word of honor.

We were far away. We were together that evening as on every Friday: Haderer, Bertoni, Hutter, Ranitzky, Friedl, Mahler, and I. No, Herz was missing; he was in London that week preparing for his final return to Vienna. Steckel was also missing; he was ill again. Mahler said: "There are only three of us Jews here this evening" and he looked fixedly at Friedl and me.

Friedl stared at him uncomprehendingly with his little round watery eyes and pressed his hands together, no doubt because he thought that he wasn't a Jew at all, and nor was Mahler, his father perhaps, his grandfather – Friedl didn't know exactly. But Mahler put on his arrogant face. You'll see, said his face. And it said: I never make mistakes.

It was black Friday. Haderer was talking big. That is to say, the wanderer and martyr in him was silent and the Titan was having his say, so that he no longer had to belittle himself and boast of the blows he had received, but could boast of those he had given. On this Friday conversation took a different turn, perhaps because Herz and Steckel were missing and because Friedl, Mahler, and I didn't seem an obstacle to anyone; but perhaps it was only because the conversation had to become true some time or other, because smoke and madness allow everything to find utterance.

Now the night was a battlefield, a campaign, an alert, and they revelled in that night. Haderer and Hutter plunged into the memory of the war; they wallowed in reminiscences, in a lot of obscure talk; and neither of them would let up until they were transformed and wore uniforms again, until they were at the spot where they were both in command again, both officers, and had established contact with headquarters; where they had flown over with a "Ju 52" to Voronezh, but then suddenly they couldn't agree on what they should have thought of General Manstein in the winter of 1942, and they simply couldn't agree on whether the 6th Army could have been relieved or not, whether the plan of deployment itself was to blame or not; then they landed retrospectively on Crete, but in Paris a little French girl had told Hutter she preferred the Austrians to the Germans, and when day broke in Norway and when the partisans had encircled them in Serbia they had come to the point . . . they ordered the second liter of wine, and we also ordered another one, because Mahler had started telling us about some intrigues in the Medical Association.

We drank Burgenland wine and Gumpoldskirchen wine. We drank in Vienna and the night was not yet over for us by a long way.

On this evening, when the partisans had already won Haderer's esteem and had only incidentally been harshly condemned by him (because it never became quite clear what Haderer really thought about this and other things, and Mahler's face said to me once again: I never make mistakes!), when the dead Slovenian nuns were lying naked in the wood outside Veldes and Haderer, put off his stroke by Mahler's silence, had to drop the nuns and stopped in the middle of his story, an old man whom we had long known came up to our table. He was a wandering, dirty, dwarfish fellow with a drawing-pad who bothered the customers with offers to draw them for a few schillings. We didn't want to be disturbed and certainly not drawn, but because of the embarrassed silence Haderer unexpectedly and magnanimously invited the old man to draw us, to show us what he could do. We each took a few schillings out of our wallets, put them in a pile, and pushed the money across to him. But he took no notice of the money. He stood there happily supporting the pad on his bent left forearm with his head thrown back. His thick pencil darted about the pad at such a speed that we burst out laughing. His movements looked as though they came from a silent film, grotesque, shot too fast. As I was sitting nearest to him he handed the first sheet to me with a bow.

He had drawn Haderer:

With duelling scars in his small face. With the skin stretched too tight over his skull. Grimacing, continually acting the expression on his face. His hair meticulously parted. A gaze that tried to be piercing, compelling, and wasn't quite.

Haderer was a head of department on the radio and wrote over-long dramas which all the major theaters regularly produced at a loss and which gained the unqualified approval of all the critics. We all had them at home, volume by volume, with a handwritten dedication. "To my esteemed friend...." We were all his esteemed friends – apart from Friedl and me, because we were too young and hence could only be "dear friends" or "dear, young, gifted friends." He never accepted a manuscript from Friedl or me for broadcasting, but he gave us recommendations to other editors and publishers, felt himself to be our patron and the patron of some twenty other young people without there being any visible sign of what this patronage consisted in or what results it produced. Naturally it wasn't his fault that he had to console us and at the same time spur us on with compliments; it was the fault of "that gang of daylight robbers," as he called them, of the senile authorities in the ministries, the education offices, and the radio; he drew the highest possible salary among such authorities and at measured intervals received all the honors, prizes and even medals that country and city had to bestow; he delivered speeches on great occasions, was regarded as a man suitable for making public appearances and yet at the same time as one of the most outspoken and independent spirits. He swore at everyone, that is to say he always swore at the other side, so that at one time one side was pleased and at another time the other, because now the one was the other. To be more exact, he simply called things by their names, but fortunately he rarely did the same with people, so that no one in particular felt attacked.

Sketched like this by the beggar-artist he looked like a malicious death's head or like one of those masks that actors still sometimes fashion for themselves in playing the parts of Mephistopheles or Iago.

I hesitantly handed the sheet of paper on. When it reached Haderer I watched him closely and had to admit to myself that I was surprised. Not for a moment did he appear hurt or offended, he showed his superiority, he clapped, perhaps three times too often – but he always clapped and praised too often – and cried "Bravo" several times. With this "Bravo" he also expressed the fact that he alone here was the great man entitled to bestow praise, and the old man reverently bowed his head, but he hardly looked up because he was in a hurry to complete Bertoni's head.

Bertoni was drawn like this:

With his handsome athlete's face which one could guess to be sun-tanned. With his sanctimonious eyes that wiped out the impression of radiant health. With his cupped hand over his mouth, as though he were afraid of saying something too loud, as though he might let slip a thoughtless word.

Bertoni worked on the *Tagblatt*. For years he had been ashamed of the continual lowering of the standard of his *feuilleton*, and now he merely smiled sorrowfully when someone drew his attention to a slip, inaccuracies, the lack of good contributions or correct information. What do you expect – in these days! his smile seemed to say. He couldn't halt the decline on his own, although he knew what a good newspaper ought to look like, oh yes, he knew that, had known it early in his career, that was why he liked to talk about the old newspapers, about the great days of the Vienna press and how he had worked under its legendary kings in the old days and learned from them. He knew all the stories, all the scandals of twenty years ago; he was at home only in that time and he could bring this time to life, could talk about it without a break. He also liked to talk about the dismissal era that followed, how he and a few other journalists had got by during the first years after 1938, what they had secretly thought and said and hinted, in what danger they had been before they too put on uniform, and now he still sat there wearing his cap of invisibility, smiled, could still not get over a great many things. He formed his sentences carefully. No one knew what he thought, hinting had become second nature, he behaved as though the Gestapo were always listening. The Gestapo had given birth to an everlasting police force before which Bertoni had to cringe. Even Steckel couldn't give him back a feeling of security. He had known Steckel intimately before he had to emigrate, had become Steckel's best friend again, not only because soon after 1945 Steckel had vouched for him and got him back onto the *Tagblatt*, but because in many respects they could reach better understanding with each other than with the rest of us, particularly when "those days" were under discussion. At such times they spoke a language which Bertoni must have imitated at some early period, and now he no longer had any other and was glad to be able to talk it with someone again – a light, evanescent, witty language that didn't really go with his appearance and behavior, a language of innuendoes that had a double appeal to him now. He didn't hint at things, like Steckel, in order to make a matter clear, but hinted past them into a despairing vagueness.

The draftsman had put the sheet down in front of me again. Mahler leaned over, glanced at it and laughed arrogantly. I passed it on with a smile. Bertoni didn't say "Bravo" because Haderer had got in first and deprived him of the chance of expressing himself. He merely looked at the drawing of himself sorrowfully and thoughtfully. After Haderer had quieted down, Mahler said across the table to Bertoni: "You're a handsome man. Did you know that?"

And this was how the old man saw Ranitzky:

With a hasty face, the face of a man eager to please, who would nod before anyone expected agreement. Even his ears and his eyelids were nodding in the drawing.

Ranitzky, one could be sure of that, had always agreed. Everyone fell silent when Ranitzky, with a word, touched on the past, for there was no point in being frank with Ranitzky. It was better to forget that and to forget him; when he sat at the table he was tolerated in silence. Sometimes he nodded to himself, forgotten by everyone. He had been two years without a job after 1945 and perhaps even under arrest, but now he was a professor at the university again. He had rewritten all the pages in his *History of Austria* dealing with recent history and republished it. When I once tried to question Mahler about Ranitzky, Mahler said to me briefly: "Everyone knows that he did it out of opportunism and is incorrigible; he knows it himself. That's why nobody tells him. But one ought to tell him all the same." Mahler, in any case, told him by his expression every time they met or when he answered him or merely said: "Listen . . ." and made Ranitzky's eyelids start fluttering. Yes, he set him trembling every time he greeted him with a shallow, fleeting handshake. Then Mahler was at his cruelest, when he said nothing or merely straightened his tie, looked at somebody and indicated at the same time that he remembered everything. He had the memory of a merciless angel, he remembered all the time; he simply had a memory, no hatred, but just this inhuman ability to store everything up and to let one know that he knew.

Hutter, finally, was drawn like this:

Like Barabbas, if it had appeared natural to Barabbas that he should be set free. With childish confidence and triumph in his round, sly face.

Hutter was a man who had been set free and felt no shame, no scruples. Everyone liked him, even I, perhaps even Mahler. We had gone so far with the times that we kept saying, Let this man go free! Hutter succeeded in everything, he even succeeded in not having his success held against him. He was a provider of capital and financed everything possible, a film company, newspapers, magazines, and recently a committee for which Haderer had gained his support and which was called "Culture and Freedom." He sat every evening with other people at a table in town, with the theater directors and the actors, with businessmen and high-grade civil servants. He published books but he never read a book, as he never saw any of the films that he financed; nor did he ever go to the theater, but he came to the theater tables afterwards. For he honestly loved the world in which all this was discussed and in which things were prepared. He loved the world of preparations, of opinions about everything, of calculations, intrigues, risks, shuffling the cards. He liked to watch the others when they shuffled and joined in when their cards got worse, intervened or watched as the trumps were played and intervened again. He enjoyed everything, and he enjoyed his friends, the old and the new, the weak and the strong. He laughed where Ranitzky smiled (Ranitzky smiled his way through and generally smiled only when somebody was being murdered by the circle, an absent person whom he would have to meet next day, but he smiled so subtly and ambivalently that he could tell himself he didn't join in, he only smiled, said nothing and thought his own thoughts). Hutter laughed loudly when somebody was being murdered and he was even capable, without thinking anything of it, of repeating what was said. Or he would get furious and defend the absent person, refuse to let him be murdered, drive the others off, save the man who was in danger and then immediately roll up his sleeves and take part in the next, if he felt like it. He was spontaneous, really able to get excited, and all reflection, consideration, was alien to him.

Haderer's enthusiasm over the draftsman now abated, he wanted to get back into the conversation, and when Mahler forbade the old man to draw him he was grateful and waved the man away, whereupon he pocketed his money and bowed once more to the great man, whom he must have recognized.

I had confidently hoped that the conversation would come round to the next elections or to the vacant post of theater director, which had provided us with a topic for three Fridays already. But this Friday everything was different, the others wouldn't stop talking about the war they had been drawn into, none of them escaped the suction, they gurgled in the morass, grew noisier and noisier and made it impossible for us to start a different conversation at our end of the table. We were forced to listen and to stare into space, to crumble the bread on the table, and every now and then I exchanged a glance with Mahler who slowly expelled the smoke of his cigarette from his mouth, blew rings, and seemed to be entirely given over to this smoke game. He held his head slightly tilted back and loosened his tie.

"Through the war, through this experience, we have come closer to the enemy," I now heard Haderer say.

"Who?" Friedl made a stuttering attempt to enter the conversation. "The Bolivians?" Haderer hesitated, he didn't know what Friedl meant, and I tried to remember whether they had also been at war with Bolivia at the time. Mahler laughed soundlessly, it looked as though he were trying to draw the smoke rings back into his mouth.

Bertoni explained quickly: "The British, Americans, French."

Haderer had recovered his self-possession and interrupted him vehemently: "But I never looked upon them as enemies! I'm simply talking about the experiences. I wasn't referring to anything else. We can speak and write differently because we have them. Just think of the neutrals, who lack these bitter experiences and who have lacked them for a long time." He put his hand over his eyes. "I'm glad not to have missed anything, not to have missed those years, those experiences."

Friedl said like an obstinate schoolboy, but much too quietly: "I'd have been glad to miss them."

Haderer looked at him non-committally; he didn't show that he was angry but tried to hand out a sermon that would please everybody. But at this moment Hutter put his elbows on the table and asked so loudly that he completely disconcerted Haderer: "Yes, what about that? Couldn't one say that culture is only possible through war, struggle, tension . . . experiences – I mean culture, what about that?"

Haderer made a brief pause, first warned Hutter, then reproved Friedl, and then, surprisingly, spoke of the First World War in order to evade the second. They talked about the Battle of the Isonzo; Haderer and Ranitzky exchanged regimental reminiscences and thundered against the Italians – first against the Italians as enemies and then against the Italians as allies in the last war; they talked about "being stabbed in the back," about "unreliable leaders," but preferred to return to the Isonzo and finally lay in the barrage on the Kleiner Pal. Bertoni took advantage of the moment when Haderer thirstily put his glass to his mouth and began implacably to tell an incredible and involved story from the Second World War. It concerned the order given to himself and a German

philologist in France to organize a brothel; there was no end to the
misadventures that beset them, and Bertoni became involved in the
most comical debaucheries. Even Friedl suddenly shook with
laughter. I was surprised, and still more surprised when he
suddenly tried to appear familiar with the operations, ranks, dates.
For Friedl was the same age as myself and at most, like me, had
entered the army during the last year of the war, straight from
school. But then I saw that Friedl was drunk and I knew that he
became difficult when he was drunk, that he was joining in the
conversation only to make fun of it and out of desperation, and
now I could hear the mockery in his words. But for a moment I had
distrusted him too, because he had gone back to the others, had
entered into this world of tomfoolery, tests of courage, heroism,
obedience and disobedience, that man's world in which everything
that normally held good was remote, everything that held good for
us during the day, a world in which no one knew any more what he
could boast of and what he felt ashamed of and whether anything
in this world in which we were citizens still corresponded to this
boast and this shame. And I thought of Bertoni's story about
stealing pigs in Russia, but I knew that Bertoni was incapable of so
much as pocketing a pencil in the newspaper office, he was so
correct. Or Haderer, for example, who had received the highest
decorations during the first war and people still say was entrusted
by Hötzendorf with a mission calling for great boldness. But
Haderer, when one looked at him here, was a man who was not
capable of any boldness whatever and never could have been, at
least not in this world. Perhaps he had been capable of it in the
other world, under another law. And Mahler, who is cold-blooded
and the most fearless man I know, told me that back there in 1914
or 1915, as a young man with the medical corps, he had fainted and
taken morphia in order to be able to stand the work in the military
hospital. Then he had made two suicide attempts and been in a
mental hospital till the end of the war. So all of them operated in
two worlds and were different in the two worlds, divided and never
united egos which were never allowed to meet. They were all
drunk now and swaggering and had to pass through the purgatory
in which their unredeemed egos were screaming, wishing soon to
be replaced by their civilian egos, the loving social egos that had
wives and jobs, rivalries and needs of all kinds. And they hunted
the blue deer which early on had emerged from their one ego and
never come back, and so long as it did not come back the world
remained a madness. Friedl jogged me, he was trying to stand up,
and I was startled when I saw his gleaming, swollen face. I went

out with him. We twice looked for the washroom in the wrong direction. In the passage we pushed our way through a group of men who were crowding into the large hall in the cellar. I had never seen such a crush in the Kronenkeller nor had I ever seen these faces here. It was so striking that I asked a waiter what was going on this evening. He didn't know any details, but he said it was an "Old Comrades reunion"; they didn't generally let the rooms for such gatherings, but Colonel von Winkler, I must have heard of him, the famous one, would be coming to celebrate with them; he thought it was a gathering in memory of Narvik.

In the washroom there was a deathly silence. Friedl leaned on the washbasin, reached for the roller towel and spun it round once.

"Can you understand," he asked, "why we sit together?"

I said nothing and shrugged my shoulders.

"You do understand what I mean?" Friedl said insistently.

"Yes, yes," I said.

But Friedl went on: "Do you understand why even Herz and Ranitzky sit together, why Herz doesn't hate him as he hates Langer, who is perhaps less guilty and is dead today? Ranitzky isn't dead. Why in God's name do we sit together! Herz especially I don't understand. They killed his wife, his mother . . ."

I thought about it hard and then I said: "Yes, I do understand it."

Friedl said: "Because he has forgotten? Or because, after a certain day, he wants it to be buried?"

"No," I said, "that isn't it. It has nothing to do with forgetting. Nor with forgiving. It has nothing to do with all that."

Freidl said: "But Herz helped Ranitzky to get on his feet again, and for at least three years now they've been sitting together, and he sits with Hutter and Haderer. He knows all about them."

I said: "We know too. And what do we do?"

Friedl said more vehemently, as if something had occurred to him: "Do you think Ranitzky hates Herz for having helped him? What do you think? He probably hates him for that too."

I said: "No, I don't think so. He thinks that's how it should be, and at most he fears that there is something behind it, that there is something more to come. He feels unsure of himself. Others, like Hutter, don't ask many questions and find it quite natural that times pass and times change.

"In those days, after '45, I too thought that the world was divided, and forever, into good and evil, but now the world is already dividing again, and again differently. It was almost impossible to take in, it all happened so imperceptibly, now we are mixed together again so that a fresh division can be made; once more we have the minds and the deeds that have sprung from other minds, other deeds. Do you understand? It has come to that, even if we don't want to see it. But even that isn't the whole reason for this wretched agreement."

Friedl cried out: "Well, what is it then? What's the reason for it? Go on, say something! Is it perhaps that we are all the same anyhow and that's why we're together?"

"No," I said, "we're not the same. Mahler was never like the others and I hope we shall never be like them either."

Friedl stared into space. "Yes, but Mahler and you and I are also very different from one another; each of us wants and thinks different things. Even the others aren't alike, Haderer and Ranitzky are very different, Ranitzky would certainly like to see his Reich return again, but definitely not Haderer, he has backed democracy and this time he will stick to it, I feel certain of this. Ranitzky is hateful, and so is Haderer, he remains hateful in my eyes in spite of everything, but they are not the same, and there is a difference if one sits at a table with one of the two or with both of them. And Bertoni . . ."

As Friedl yelled his name, Bertoni came in and turned red under his tan. He vanished behind a door and we remained silent for a while. I washed my hands and face.

Friedl whispered: "Then everyone is in league with everyone, and I am too, but I don't want to be! And you are also in league!"

I said: "We're not in league, there is no league. It's much worse. I think we all have to live together and can't live together. In every brain there is a world and a demand that excludes every other world, every other demand. But we all need one another, if anything is ever to become good and whole."

Friedl laughed maliciously. "Need. Of course, that's it; perhaps I even need Haderer . . ."

I said: "That isn't how I meant it."

Friedl said: "But why not? I shall need him; it's easy for you to talk in general terms, you haven't got a wife and three children. And if you don't need Haderer you may one day need somebody who is no better."

I didn't answer.

"I've got three children," he yelled and then he showed me, by moving his hand to and fro eighteen inches above the floor, how small his children were.

"Stop it," I said. "That's no argument. We can't talk like that."

Friedl grew angry. "Yes, it is an argument, you have no idea what a powerful argument it is, for almost everything. I married at twenty-two. What can I do about it? You have no idea what it means, no idea at all!"

He screwed up his face and supported himself with all his strength on the washbasin. I thought he was going to sink to the ground. Bertoni came out again, didn't even wash his hands and quickly left the room, as if afraid of hearing his name again, and more than his name.

Friedl swayed and said: "You don't like Herz? Am I right?"

I replied reluctantly: "What makes you think that? . . . All right then, I don't like him. Because I reproach him with sitting down with those people. Because I keep reproaching him with it. Because he helps to prevent us from being able to sit with him and a few others at a different table. He sees to it that we all sit at one table."

Friedl: "You're crazy, even crazier than I am. First you say we need one another and now you reproach Herz for that. I don't reproach him for it. He has the right to be friendly with Ranitzky."

I said excitedly: "No, he hasn't. No one has the right. Neither he nor anyone else."

"Yes," said Friedl, "after the war we thought the world was divided forever into good and evil. But I'll tell you what the world looks like when it is divided cleanly.

"It was when I came to London and met Herz's brother. It took my breath away. He knew nothing about me but he wasn't even satisfied by the fact that I was so young, he asked me straight away: Where were you in those days and what did you do? I told him I was at school and that my elder brother had been shot as a deserter; I also told him that in the end I had to take part, like all the pupils in my form. After that he asked no more questions, but he began to inquire about various people he had known, including Haderer and Bertoni, about a lot of people. I tried to tell him what I knew, and it came out that some of them were sorry about what had happened, that some felt embarrassed – yes, it was impossible to say more with the best will in the world – and others were dead, and most of them denied and covered up; I said that too. Haderer will always deny, always falsify his past, won't he? But then I noticed that this man was no longer listening to me at all, he was completely absorbed by one thought. And when I began to talk about the differences again and said for the sake of justice that perhaps Bertoni had never done anything bad in those days and at most had been a coward, he interrupted me and said: 'No, don't make any distinctions. For me there is no difference and never will be. I shall never set foot in that country again. I shall never walk among murderers.'"

"I can understand that, in fact I understand him better than Herz. Although – " I said slowly, "that's no solution either, only for a while, only so long as the worst remained at its worst. One is not a victim for a lifetime. That's no solution."

"It seems to me that there is no solution whatever in this world. We grapple with life and aren't even capable of clarifying this dismal little situation for ourselves, and before us others have grappled with it, have been unable to clarify anything and have run to their doom. They were victims or executioners, and the deeper one descends into time the more impassable it becomes, I often feel completely lost in history, don't know where I can hang my heart, on which parties, groups, forces, for everything seems to obey an infamous law. And all one can do is to be on the side of the victims, but that leads nowhere, they don't show us any way."

"That's the terrible thing about it," yelled Friedl. "The victims, the many, many victims don't show us any way at all. And for the murderers times change. The victims are the victims. That's all. My father was a victim of the Dollfuss period, my grandfather a victim of the Monarchy, my brothers victims of Hitler, but that is no help to me, do you understand what I mean? They simply fell down, were run over, were shot, stood against the wall, ordinary people who didn't think much or have many opinions. Well yes, two or three of them thought a bit, my grandfather thought of the coming Republic, but tell me, what was the use? Couldn't it have come without that death? And my father thought of social democracy, but tell me who can claim his death? – not our Workers' Party that wants to win the elections. It doesn't need a death for that. Not for that. Jews were murdered because they were Jews, they were nothing but victims, so many victims – but surely not so that today we should at last tell our children that they are human beings? It's a bit late, don't you think? No, that is something no one understands, that the victims serve no purpose. That is just what nobody understands and that is also why no one feels it an insult that these victims should also have to suffer so that we shall come to realize certain things. These realizations aren't needed at all. Who here doesn't know that one should not kill? That's been known for two thousand years. Is it worth wasting another word over that? Oh, but there is plenty of talk about it in Haderer's last speech, there it has just been discovered, he twists and twines humanity round in his mouth, he quotes the classics, quotes the Fathers of the Church and the latest metaphysical platitudes. But that's crazy. How can anyone make a speech about that? It's completely insane or malicious. Who are we that people should have to say such things to us?"

And he began again: "Let someone tell me why we sit here together. Let someone tell me that and I'll listen. Because it is unparalleled, and what comes out of it will also be unparalleled."

I don't understand this world any more – we often used to say that to one another during the nights in which we drank and talked and stated our beliefs. But everyone had moments when it seemed that it could be understood. I told Friedl I understood everything and he was wrong not to understand anything. But then all at once I didn't understand anything any more either, and now I thought to myself that I couldn't even live with him, and of course still less with the others. One couldn't possibly live in one world with a man like Friedl, with whom one was in agreement over many things but for whom a family was an argument, or with Steckel for whom art was an argument. There were times when I couldn't even live in one world with Mahler, whom I liked best of all. Did I know whether, at my next decision, he would come to the same one? "Looking back" we were in agreement, but what about the future? Perhaps I should soon be separated from him and Friedl – we could only hope not to be separated after all.

Friedl whimpered, straightened up and reeled to the nearest lavatory door. I heard him vomiting, gargling and rattling in the throat, and in between he said: "If all that would just come out, if one could spew it all out, all of it, all of it!"

When he came out he beamed at me with a contorted face and said: "Soon I shall drink brotherhood with that lot in there, perhaps even with Ranitzky. I shall say . . ."

I held his face under the tap, dried it, then I seized his arm. "You won't say anything." We had already been away too long and had to get back to the table. As we passed the big hall the men of the "Old Comrades reunion" were making such a din that I didn't catch a word of what Friedl was saying. He was looking better again. I believe we were laughing about something, about ourselves probably, as we pushed open the door of the private room.

The air in the room was even thicker and we could barely see across to the table. When we came closer and passed through the smoke and discarded our madness, I saw a man sitting next to Mahler whom I didn't know. These two were silent and the others were talking. As Friedl and I sat down again and Bertoni gave us a hazy look, the stranger stood up and shook hands with us, murmuring a name. There was not the least friendliness in him, absolutely nothing approachable, his eyes were cold and dead, and I looked questioningly at Mahler, who must have known him. He was a very tall man in his early thirties, although he looked older at first glance. He wasn't badly dressed, but it looked as though someone had given him a suit that was a little bigger than even his size demanded. It was some time before I was able to catch snatches of the conversation, in which neither Mahler nor the stranger took any part.

Haderer to Hutter: "But then you must also know General Zwirl."

Hutter delightedly to Haderer: "But of course. From Graz."

Haderer: "A highly educated man. One of the finest Greek scholars. A very dear old friend of mine."

Now there was reason to fear that Haderer would reproach Friedl and me with our insufficient knowledge of Greek and Latin, ignoring the fact that it was people like him who had prevented us from acquiring this knowledge at the proper time. But I was not in the mood to discuss one of Haderer's favorite subjects or even to challenge him, instead I leaned over to Mahler as though I hadn't heard anything. Mahler was saying something in a low voice to the stranger and the latter was answering loudly, staring straight in front of him. He answered each question with one single sentence. I guessed that he must be a patient of Mahler's or at least a friend who was treated by him. Mahler always knew all kinds of people and enjoyed friendships which we knew nothing about. In one hand the man held a packet of cigarettes, with the other he smoked as I had never seen anyone smoke before. He smoked mechanically, drawing on the cigarette at absolutely regular intervals, as though smoking were the only thing he could do. From the stub of the cigarette, a very short stub on which he burned himself without wincing, he lit the next one and smoked on for all he was worth.

Suddenly he stopped smoking, held the cigarette trembling in his huge, ugly red hands and nodded his head. Now I heard it too. Although the doors were shut a bellowed song echoed across to us from the hall on the other side of the passage. It sounded like "Back home, back home, we'll meet again. . . ."

He drew hastily on his cigarette and said loudly to us, in the same voice in which he had answered Mahler's questions:

"They're always coming back home. I suppose they haven't quite got there yet."

Haderer laughed and said: "I don't know what you mean exactly, but that really is an incredible disturbance and my esteemed friend Colonel von Winkler could have kept his men a bit quieter. . . . If things go on like that we shall have to look round for other accommodation."

Bertoni interjected that he had already spoken to the landlord, who had said that this "Old Comrades reunion" was an exceptional occasion, some big anniversary. He didn't know exactly. . . .

Haderer said he didn't know exactly either, but his esteemed friend and former comrade. . . .

I had missed what the stranger, who had continued speaking while Haderer and Bertoni drowned his voice, had said to us – Friedl must have been the only one who listened to him – so it wasn't clear to me why he suddenly said that he was a murderer.

". . . I was under twenty when I knew it for a fact," he said, like somebody who isn't telling his story for the first time, but can talk about nothing else wherever he goes and doesn't need any particular listener but is quite content with any he can find. "I knew that I was predestined to become a murderer as some people are predestined to become heroes or saints or average men. I lacked nothing to that end, no characteristic, if you like to put it that way, and everything drove me to one goal: to murder. All I lacked was a victim. At that time I used to run through the street, here" – he pointed in front of him through the smoke, and Friedl quickly leaned back to avoid being touched by the hand – "here I ran through the alleyways, the chestnut blossoms gave off their scent, the air was always full of chestnut blossoms in the Ring Streets and in the narrow alleyways, and my heart was dislocated, my lungs were pumping wildly, and my breath came out of me like the breath of a hunting wolf. Only I didn't know yet how to kill and whom to kill. I had only my hands, but would they suffice to strangle a throat? I was much weaker in those days and undernourished. I knew nobody I could have hated, I was alone in the city, and so I didn't find the victim and went almost insane over it in the night. It was always at night that I had to get up and go downstairs and out, and stand at the windy, deserted, dark street corners and wait. The streets were so quiet in those days, no one passed, no one spoke to me, and I waited till I began to shiver and whimper with weakness and my madness faded away. That only lasted a short time. Then I was put in the army. When I was given a gun I knew that I was lost. One day I should shoot. I handed over responsibility for myself to this gun barrel, I loaded it with bullets, which I had invented just as I had invented gunpowder, that was certain. At rifle practice I always missed the target, not because I couldn't aim straight but because I knew that the bull's eye wasn't a real eye, that it was only a substitute, a practice target that produced no death. It irritated me, it was only a deceptive bait, not reality. I shot, if you like to put it that way, accurately off-target. I used to sweat terribly during these rifle practices; afterwards I often went blue in the face, vomited and had to lie down. I was either insane or a murderer, I knew that for sure, and with a last residue of resistance to this fate I talked about it to the others, so that they might protect me, so that they might be protected from me and know whom they were dealing with. But the peasant boys, artisans, and clerks who were in my room thought nothing of it. They pitied me or ridiculed me, but they didn't take me for a murderer. Or did they? I don't know. One of them used to call me "Jack the Ripper," a post office clerk who went to the cinema a lot and read books, a clever fellow; but I don't think he really believed it either."

The stranger stubbed out his cigarette, looked quickly down and then up, I felt his cold, prolonged gaze on me and I didn't know why I wanted to sustain this gaze. I did sustain it, but it lasted longer than the gaze exchanged by lovers and enemies, it lasted till I could no longer think and was so empty that I jumped when I heard the loud, regular voice again.

"We came to Italy, to Monte Cassino. That was the greatest slaughterhouse you can imagine. There flesh was so mangled you might think it was a delight to be a murderer. But it wasn't, although by then I was quite certain that I was one and for six months had been going round in public with a gun. By the time I came into the position on Monte Cassino I hadn't a vestige of soul left in me. I breathed the smell of corpses, the smell of burning and dugouts like the freshest mountain air. I didn't feel the others' fear. I could have had a big day with my first murder. For what was simply a battlefield to the others was to me a murder-field. But I'll tell you what happened. I never fired my rifle. I leveled it for the first time when we had a group of Poles in front of us; there were troops from every country in action at Monte Cassino. Then I said to myself: No, not Poles. I didn't like the names the others gave people in their slang talk – Polacks, Yanks, Niggers. So no Americans, no Poles. I was just a simple murderer, I had no excuse, and my language was clear, not flowery like the others." "Wipe out," "rub out," "smoke out," such expressions were unthinkable to me, they revolted me, I couldn't utter them. My language was clear, I said to myself: You must and you want to murder a human being. Yes, that was what I wanted and I had wanted it for a long time, for exactly a year I had feverishly desired it. A human being! I couldn't fire, you must see that. I don't know if I can explain it to you fully. It was easy for the others, they did as they were told, they generally didn't know if they had hit anybody or how many, nor did they want to know. Those men weren't murderers, were they? They wanted to survive or win medals, they thought of their families or of victory and the fatherland, though scarcely at that moment, not any more, they were trapped. But I thought unceasingly of murder. I didn't fire. A week later, when the battle held its breath, when we saw no more of the Allied troops, when only the planes tried to finish us off and by no means all had died who were to die there, I was sent back to Rome and court-martialed. I told them all about myself, but they wouldn't understand me and I was put in jail. I was condemned for cowardice in the face of the enemy and for undermining morale, there were a few other points too which I don't remember exactly any more. Then I was suddenly taken out of jail and sent north for treatment in a psychiatric clinic. I believe I was cured, and six months later I was put in another unit because there was nothing left of the old one, and we moved east into the battles of the retreat."

Hutter, who couldn't bear such long speeches and would have liked to persuade someone else to tell stories or jokes, said, breaking a pretzel: "Well, and how did the shooting go then?"

The man didn't look at him, and instead of drinking again like all the others at that moment, he pushed his glass away into the middle of the table. He looked at me, then at Mahler and then at me again, and this time I turned my eyes away.

"No," he said finally, "I was cured. So it didn't work. You will understand that, gentlemen. A month later I was arrested and spent the rest of the war in a camp. You will understand, I couldn't shoot. If I could no longer shoot at a human being, how much less at an abstraction, at the 'Russians.' The word meant nothing to me. It conjured up no sort of picture, and you have to have some kind of picture in mind."

"A queer bird," Bertoni said to Hutter in a low voice; nevertheless I heard it, and I was afraid the man had heard it too.

Haderer beckoned to the waiter and asked for the bill.

We could now hear a swelling chorus of men's voices from the big hall; it sounded like the chorus in an opera when it has been banished behind the scenes. They were singing: "Homeland, your stars. . . ."

The stranger held his head bent, listening, then he said: "As though not a day had passed." And: "Good night." He stood up and walked, huge and quite upright, towards the door. Mahler also got up and, raising his voice, said: "Listen!" It was an expression he always used, but I knew that now he really did want to be listened to. And yet I saw that for the first time he was unsure of himself, he looked across at Friedl and me, as though in search of advice. We stared at him; there was no advice in our eyes.

We lost time over paying the bill, Mahler strode up and down, gloomy, meditating and impatient, suddenly turned to the door, tore it open, and we followed him because the singing had suddenly broken off, only a few isolated and collapsing voices were still to be heard. And at the same time there was a movement in the passage that betrayed an action or a disaster.

In the passage we ran into several men who were yelling confusedly; others stood in shocked silence. We didn't see the man anywhere. Someone was talking to Haderer, presumably the Colonel, white in the face and speaking in a treble voice. I heard scraps of sentences: ". . . incomprehensible provocation . . . I mean to say . . . ex-servicemen . . ." I shouted to Mahler to follow me, ran to the stairs, and in a few leaps was up the steps, which led dark, damp, and stony, like a shaft out of a mine, into the night and the open. He was lying not far from the entrance to the cellar. I bent over him. He was bleeding from several wounds. Mahler knelt down beside me, took my hands away from the man's chest and indicated to me that he was already dead.

The night echoed within me and I was in my madness.

When I came home in the morning and there was no more turmoil in me, when I merely stood in my room, stood and stood, unable to move and unable to find the way to my bed, I saw the blood on the palm of my hand. I didn't shudder. It was as if through the blood I had received protection, not to become invulnerable, but so that the effluvium of my despair, my desire for vengeance, my rage could not force its way out of me. Never again. Never more. And if they should consume me, these homicidal thoughts that had arisen in me, they would not strike anyone, as this murderer had not murdered anyone and was only a victim – sacrificed to nothing. But who knows that? Who dares say that?

Translated by Michael Bullock

THOMAS BERNHARD

The Italian   *1969*

After supper I walked with the Italian back and forth in front
of the summerhouse. He had been quite successful, he said;
postwar Florence and the death of his family had made him, in his
opinion, quite rich; earlier that morning he had enumerated
fourteen businesses that he owned, two farms, two mills, a cannery
– all in Tuscany – a house in Florence, a small estate "above
Silvaplana, a hut for my loneliness." At ever shorter intervals he
returned there, to what he called his "Fiesole." As he described his
general situation and views on business, the feared, and, under
circumstances, lethal air streamed out of the summerhouse in
which my father, as I now saw, had been laid out by my sisters
much too high on the bier; I was still occupied with thoughts about
Kliental and Zimmerwald, with the influence of Karl Liebknecht.
I thought incessantly about my work, above all about the
Heidelberg program. Out of politeness, so as not to offend the
Italian, I said that I had been planning a trip to southern Italy for a
long time. "I'd like to join a geologist who is going to Sicily in the
fall," I said. The Italian warned me about going to Sicily too early,
"not before the end of October." Our point of departure would be
Caltanisetta, I said; my friend's research is confined to the area
between Caltanisetta and Enna. The Italian recommended an
excursion to Agrigent ("That way, you'll spare yourself a trip to
Greece!"), Palermo, and Cefalù. He feared, I detected, that I might
suddenly ask him to go into the house to my father, or that I might
ask him whether – as is right and proper – he had already been to
my dead father, "the old gentleman": all of the guests had in the
meantime already paid their death visits, but not the Italian. I had
observed him the whole day; of all the people assembled, he
appeared to be the most interesting and also by far the most
intelligent. Not a talkative person, he had been alone the whole
time since his arrival. Once they had greeted him, my sisters hadn't
paid any more attention to him. But he also didn't desire any
contact.

I immediately took advantage of the situation to disappear into
the park with the Italian, to escape for a short while the tense

atmosphere in the house, the many people, my sisters' distress, the mourning-tumult; he wanted me to tell him something about the history of our house – outside, in fact – something which I did with a certain curiosity, but, of course, not without great mental strain. We were now walking back and forth, and, pursuing a totally extraneous idea, I showed the Italian – in order to keep him from seeing my father, a man whom he hardly knew but to whose funeral his family had sent him – the pile of theater costumes and instruments, coats, jackets, pants, trumpets, drums, and flutes which were in the shed at the side of the house. Before they could lay my father out on the bier, my sisters had cleaned out the house and, in their excitement, thrown the costumes and instruments, which had lain around the summerhouse for decades, onto a pile in the shed. I thought that these costumes and instruments, all very old and expensive items, might interest the Italian. I explained to him that each of these things had an especially deep significance for me, that they had an especially high value, "memories," I said, using the Italian's tone of voice. To me he appeared – judging from the remarks, through which he, in his way, set himself off from the others – to be very well educated and interested in art. I said that these things – for the most part sewed and decorated by my grandmother and sisters, and purchased by my great-grandfather and his brothers – were the most beautiful that I had ever seen or heard of, and that I knew the props of many great theaters throughout Europe. The shed was illuminated by the light of the two wake-candles which came from the summerhouse through a crack in the boards. I said that the Italian should be careful not to get dirty, because the shed was filthy, full of spider webs, full of dust. First I showed him the costumes of the rich. Then the costumes of the poor. Then the costumes of the exalted. Then the costumes of the comical. One after another I pulled them out before his eyes and held them up to the light. The Italian wanted to know who had written the play which my sister's children would have performed this very evening "between eight-thirty and ten-thirty, *in and in front of the summerhouse*," had our father not died during the last rehearsal, had he not shot himself – which I had already described in detail – in his room, as is well known, in a most gruesome way. "An accident," the Italian had said earlier. And he absolutely wanted to know whether the play was a comedy or a tragedy, or whether it was both tragic and humorous. I responded, telling him that the author of the play was my younger sister's oldest son, and that I had not read it, "not a single line"; it was supposed to be a surprise except for those playing in it – "I don't even know its title." I said it would be a good idea to get someone to give me the play as soon as we returned to the house, so that I could still read it tonight, for "now it will never be performed," and it could even distract me – even from my literary aspirations, which, at that point in time, were tormenting me – since sleep would be out of the question. I said that I would most certainly like the play, since I knew the nature of the person who wrote it, "a very delicate being"; it would, in a pleasant way, give me something to think about. For more than a hundred years, I said, a play had been written by one of our children – usually by one of our sons – for the last evening in August; it was really amazing, I remarked, how good these plays always were; how well-written and performed they had been; there are in my older sister's desk drawer nearly three dozen plays; the oldest in existence were by my grandparents; one of them, I can still recall from reading it, had the title "The Sparrowhawk." All of these plays – which, after being thoroughly rehearsed, were performed only once – are a treasure trove for students and theater critics, for every actor who can be taken seriously. I should even like, I said, to make them sometime the focus of an essay, perhaps under the title: "Our Summer Plays." All of these plays, the comedies as well as the tragedies and musicals, were all written in one single night; even I had written one when I was eleven, "in the darkness of the summerhouse," I said. The Italian in us had inspired us for the theater, I said, and was happy upon saying this to find a friendly, attentive, and even talkative partner in the Italian, who, up until that moment, had stood opposite me in a sometimes painfully reserved way. He now said that his family in Florence had also once a year performed theater, "always behind masks," he said, "and always in winter," and never original pieces, but rather, and oddly in the land of comedy, only plays of English or French origin, "Shakespeare, Molière. . . ." The adults, he added, had also taken part in these plays. Had the summerhouse been built for this purpose, he inquired. "For theater and festivities," I said. He didn't understand the word "festivities," so I attempted to explain it to him, which I did, I think, with success. I must say, however, he always spoke such good German that I was irritated at the beginning of our acquaintance. The air now coming into the shed had a certain sharpness to it due to the nearness of the incessantly loud creek at the edge of the woods which was still roaring after the recent downpours. I had not yet shown the Italian all of the costumes when it occurred to me that he was perhaps bored with me. What were these things to him? They meant nothing to him, the Italian from Florence, who had only been sent for two days to my father's funeral – what were these costumes, these instruments to him? I suggested that we go into the house, it would be – though loud – warm inside and perhaps he would like "a hot cider," I said, having noticed how the Italian had drunk one with such great pleasure in the early afternoon. The Italian, nonetheless, wanted to see *all* of the costumes. I told him from memory each of the corresponding roles as well as who had played or could have played each one. That consumed almost an hour's time. The costumes for the latest play, I told him, were not among these; they were left unfinished in my younger sister's room lying on the floor. The musical instruments also appeared to please him. He and his mother had once fled, he said, a burning opera house in Padua, where he had been studying; his mother had died four weeks later in a Florentine hospital as a result of the shock. Since then he had not set foot in another theater building. He had, however, gone inside our summerhouse. For a while we were silent and then he said: "We never write to each other." It immediately struck me how introspectively he had said that, and I regretted not being able to speak a single word of Italian; my father's claim was certainly correct that one can never speak too many languages. I felt so wretched. And the Italian spoke such good German! I asked him whether this time in the shed or my theatrics concerning the costumes and instruments had irritated or bored him – the whole thing, I said apologetically, had been a welcome distraction from the horrors of the present situation, "indeed from my own self," I said. "I also have," I said, "a pretext for not being in the house, where they're most certainly looking for me; they would never suspect that I'd be in the park. They're wondering where we are." "But I can't refuse," I said, "a guest's request to take a walk."

The moment we entered the woods the Italian asked whether I was familiar with Italian literature. I was baffled by such a question coming from a businessman – actually I have time and time again noticed that it is precisely businessmen who ask such questions. I responded with no, but added that I had read Michelangelo's sonnets and Petrarch's poetry when I was thirteen. I was not familiar with more contemporary literature, I indicated, except for Pavese, Ungaretti, Lampedusa, and certain political writings which from time to time I was compelled to draw upon in my own studies. I uttered the name Serrati, but the Italian had never heard of him. With Campanella I also had no luck, whereas the liberal Mazzini and the opportunist Modigliani only elicited a head-shake from the Italian. He then asked me whether I liked traveling or traveled much. I said yes. He wanted to know how old I was and whether I was "still a student." I said no. The difficulty it would have created kept me from telling the Italian anything about myself, even the most straightforward of personal data. He told me as he stopped to pull a spruce branch out of his face – and I turned around, as I realized for no good reason – that it was difficult for him to carry on a conversation with the people in the house, the mourning-guests, "with the occupants," as he said impeccably, whose names for the most part he did not know ("All of them strangers!"), he said, even though he was related and had been introduced to them as soon as he had arrived. He felt a certain affinity to me, he said; in the company of strangers one always gravitates to the first person who utters a friendly word. I was that person, "mysteriously young," he said. And since the whole time I had felt it inappropriate to ask him how old he was, he then rather suddenly said, as he walked in front of me, that he was forty-eight years old. He liked the fact that I, as opposed to the others, was able to move about so "freely" in the face of this "unfortunate accident." This, he said, had also affected him.

From the house we both heard my sisters' excited discussion; single words, indeed whole sentences were, due to the favorable direction of the wind, completely intelligible even in the woods. Their debate came out of the kitchen where they had probably retreated in order to discuss undisturbed one of their urgent but pointless matters. The Italian was also amused by our interception of the argument. Probably believing that no one would be in the park or in the woods at this time in such cold weather, my sisters had moved closer to the open window; growing louder and louder, their conversation revolved around, as we could hear and understand, the repeated use of the words "in front of" and "in back of." I pointed out to the Italian that this had to do with the funeral procession and who would be in front and who would take up the rear. After one of them aggressively tossed out the word "bishop," everything became still. From the clearing one could see the summerhouse. It occurred to me that the children would have performed their play precisely at this time. There would have been an equally large group of people – though from the immediate area – assembled in the house, the park, and in front of the summerhouse; fewer relatives and more neighbors – in different dress and mood. I pondered the difference between "visitors of the Summer Play" and "visitors of the dead," as I stood on the mass grave. The Italian was completely unaware of it. I was uncertain whether I should tell him that he and I were standing on two dozen buried bodies. "Here in this clearing," I said, getting control of myself at the last second, "we played tag as children," and explained to him how we played the game. He responded saying that Florentine children play the same game of tag. Even in the darkness I could make out the contours of the mass grave, the "light spot" in the weeds. I don't believe I have been to the clearing in more than ten years, and now I was there for the fourth time in three days, and with the Italian, as well. Suppressing that which was more dreadful, I said with alacrity: "My father wanted to lie in state in the summerhouse, as his father had also wanted." And then: "He often called it the '*slaughter*house.'" For the fourth time in three days, I thought. And then, so that I could inform the Italian about the mass grave – what seemed for many reasons to be an important thing to do – I saw to it that we moved on, and under my direction we made a detour to the bridge. The Italian was astonished when, standing on the bridge, I said: "There is a mass grave here, in fact, right there in the clearing we just left. Two dozen Poles lie there under the ground, buried," I said. In short phrases I told him, as I had told those before him, the story which my father had passed along, that in the clearing two dozen Poles are buried, "common soldiers," I said, "two officers." Though I was only twelve years old at the end of the war, I could still remember the Poles, "they had been quartered in the summerhouse, they had been waiting out the end of the war, they had taken refuge in the summerhouse." From my father I knew that they had been shot one night, two weeks before the end of the war, by Germans who suddenly appeared from the woods. Their corpses are said to have remained in the house for two weeks and caused "a horrible stench" – the occupants of the house had been forbidden to enter it. The Germans had threatened to shoot my father and all others who had wanted to carry them out of the house in order to bury them. "Adolescents," I said, "fifteen-year-olds, sixteen-year-olds." I had now told this story for the third time since my arrival. "Actually only my father saw the executed men." The Italian looked at the summerhouse and said: "The '*slaughter*house.'" I said that on the day of the murders, I had heard from my room the Poles screaming in the summerhouse. For years, whenever I was near the summerhouse, or anywhere in the world at night, I had heard that screaming. For decades, right up to this present day, I have struggled with that screaming which automatically gets louder each time I approach the summerhouse. "My whole life I have believed," I said, "that I will never be able to escape the Poles' screaming as they were lined up against the wall." The Italian turned around. "Supposedly, there was one by the name of Potoki among the murdered Poles," I said. The Italian listened silently to my story, my statement. For a long time, I continued, only my father knew about the mass grave, nobody else. The appropriate authorities had been notified a long time ago, I indicated, but nothing right up to today had ever been done about the mass grave, the "Poles'-grave," as my sisters had named it. "We never go to the clearing," I said, "strange that I went to the clearing with you. Also with Freistädter. The Hungarian." "An atrocity," said the Italian and asked me whether this expression was correct. I affirmed its correctness. "It was like a trap," I said, "when the Poles entered the summerhouse." "Shot to death," the Italian said, in reference to my father again as he looked at the summerhouse. "An accident?" Again I thought: Did the man lying in the summerhouse with a bullet through his skull commit suicide? "Such a gruesomely destroyed face," said the Italian. I asked again – in order to change the subject – about the political situation in Italy. "I'm only interested in politics insofar as it is of use to my business; my honesty is perhaps a bit shocking," he said, so as to dispense with, as I could see, an unpleasant discussion. "The wrong people are sitting in Rome," he said oversimplifying things, "the wrong people are sitting in every capital, in every nation, in parliament and government, always the wrong people." I immediately thought about the Chartist movement in England, and then about Zimmerwald, things which almost continuously occupied my thoughts – even when I often forcefully repressed them. And now it was the Spartacus League and the Soviet system, Rosa Luxemburg and Klara Zetkin. For two hours I had forgotten my work, everything that for months had been causing my brain tremendous distress. And only one other time was I able to get out of my thoughts when, after a short while, the Italian had invited me to visit him in Florence; after we were over the bridge, he said: "The darkness which prevails here . . . ," and then trailed off into silence. There is, he said, "no means of escaping oneself." What he meant by that, and precisely at that moment, I don't know; we were standing right in front of the open window, right in front of the dead man.

Translated by Eric Williams

THOMAS BERNHARD   1967

Crimes of an Innsbruck Merchant's Son

Shortly after making the acquaintance of his person I had a most illuminating insight into his development – into his childhood, in particular. Over and over again he would describe the sounds and smells of his long-since distant home, the eeriness of that gloomy merchant's house: his mother, the silence of the goods, and the birds trapped in the darkness of the high vault; the appearance of his father who, in the merchant's house in the Anichstrasse, relentlessly issued the commands of a ruthless ruler of property and people. Georg always spoke of his sisters' lies and defamations. Siblings often resort to such devilish tactics against one another; sisters have a criminal mania for exterminating their brothers, brothers their sisters, brothers their brothers, and sisters their sisters. His home had never been a house for children, as is the case with most other houses, homes – particularly those in better neighborhoods, with better air quality – but a dreadful, dank, and enormous house for adults into which were born not children, but ghastly reckoners, blustering infants with a nose for business and for suffocating charity.

Georg was an exception. He was the center but, on account of the uselessness, the disgrace that he represented for his entire family – a family that was constantly shocked and embittered by him and forever striving to obliterate things – a detestably warped and crippled center which they wanted out of the house at all costs. Nature had deformed him so opprobriously and to such an extent that they always had to hide him. After they had been disappointed to the depths of their fecal and victual loathsomeness by medical arts and science, they begged, in perfidious solidarity, that Georg contract a terminal illness that would take him from this world as quickly as possible. They were prepared to do anything and everything so that he would die, yet he did not die. And even though together they all did everything so that he would become fatally ill, not once (neither in Innsbruck, where he grew up a few hundred yards from me, separated from me – neither one was aware of the other – by the Inn River, nor subsequently during our studies in Vienna in our fourth-floor room in a house in the

Zirkusgasse) did he become *deathly* ill. Within the family he only grew bigger and uglier and frailer, ever more useless and needier. But his organs, which functioned better than their own, remained unimpaired . . . This development embittered them, particularly since, at the moment in which he was thrown by his bellowing mother into a corner of the laundry-room floor, they had already resolved to avenge themselves – in their way – for the abominable surprise of the birth of an initially enormous, clammy, and fat, and subsequently, although increasingly bigger, nevertheless increasingly delicate but healthy, unsightly "cripple of a son" (as his father called him) – to compensate themselves for this outrageous injustice. Like a conspiracy, they decided to rid themselves of Georg – in such a way as not to come in conflict with the law – before he, as they brooded, could inflict potentially lethal damage upon them by virtue of his mere existence. For years they thought the time, since they would have endured it, was near, but they had deceived themselves, let themselves be deceived. Georg's health, his lack of infirmity as far as his lungs, his heart, all of his other important organs were concerned, was stronger than their will and their wisdom.

Terrified on the one hand, and megalomaniacal on the other, they determined, as he rapidly grew bigger and healthier and more delicate and more intelligent and uglier, that he, they maintained as a matter of fact, had not issued forth from their centuries-old merchant stock to be left among them. After multiple stillbirths they would have deserved one of their own, an upright one, not a bent beam of merchant blood which, from the outset, they were all supposed to support and subsequently carry, lift even higher, all together, parents and sisters, lift *up* even higher than they already were; and they received – whence was uncanny to them, since, in the end, it did come from the father out of the mother – a creature which, in their eyes, was a useless, ever more deeply thinking animal that even laid claim to clothing and pleasure and that, instead of supporting you, had to be supported, instead of nourishing you, had to be nourished, and that should have been cosseted, yet was not cosseted. On the contrary, to them Georg was and remained a clump of flesh that, given his complete uselessness, was always in the way and couldn't be stomached, and, as if that weren't enough, even wrote poetry. Everything about him was different. They considered him to be the greatest disgrace to their family, which otherwise consisted of only hard-boiled realists completely lacking in imagination. He oftentimes spoke in our room in Vienna's Zirkusgasse, which we rented after having met and teamed up in a restaurant in the Second District, of his "childhood prison in Innsbruck," and whenever he thought he would have to say "cowhide whipping," a term that became increasingly difficult for him, he would wince before his listener, before me, who, for years, was his solitary listener. Cellar vaults and hallway vaults and story vaults, all of which were much too big, much too enormous for him, stone steps too high for him, trap doors too heavy, coats and pants and shirts too big (his father's worn coats and pants and shirts), his father's too shrill whistling, his mother's screaming, his sisters' tittering, rats jumping, dogs yelping, frigidity and hunger, narrow-minded seclusion, much too heavy school bags, loaves of bread, sacks of corn, sacks of flour, sacks of sugar, sacks of potatoes, shoveling and steel bicycle racks, incomprehensible orders, assignments, threats and commands, punishments and castigations, blows and beatings formed his childhood. Even after he had been away from home for years, he was still tormented by his having to drag down into the cellar and then back up out of the cellar (a dragging that caused him considerable pain) halves of smoked pigs. Years afterwards and from a distance of over four hundred miles, in Vienna, he would, when it was dark, still anxiously traverse, with his head bowed down, the parental merchant courtyard in Innsbruck; he would, shaken by fever, descend into the parental merchant cellar in Innsbruck. Whenever he, slapped into their merchant calculations on a daily basis, miscalculated, then he (not quite six years old the first time) would be confined by his father or his mother or one of his sisters to the cellar vault and, for a while, solely be referred to as a "criminal." At first, only his father called him a criminal. But subsequently, as he recalled, his sisters, and even his mother, joined in calling him a "criminal." Completely "ineducable," she, whom he now, years later, separated by many mountains from her, believed, during his studies in Vienna, to see in a more reasonable light, always, as far as Georg was concerned, totally submitted to the more dominant part of the family, that is, to the father and the sisters. With frightful regularity father and mother would whip him several times a week with the cowhide.

    In the houses of Innsbruck merchants, sons would howl during his childhood like pigs in the houses of Innsbruck butchers. Surely things were most dreadful in his house. His birth, they assured him at every opportunity, gave rise to their ruin. He was constantly called "unconstitutional" by his father. His father would use the word "unconstitutional" to gash him incessantly. His sisters exploited him for their intrigues and, given their sagacity, to an ever increasing level of perfection. He was everyone's victim. If I peer into his childhood and into his Innsbruck, I peer into my childhood and into my Innsbruck – with such coincident alarm into mine, which was not ruled by the same dreadfulness but by a much greater opprobrium, for my parents did not, as did his, act out of brute force, but out of a radically philosophical one, a force that originates in the head and only in the heads.

Early in the morning every day, a saddening bitterness, deeper than nature otherwise allows, would thrust our agonizingly inept heads into a singular and utterly torpid suppositional state. Everything in us and about us and around us indicated that we were lost – I as much as he – whatever we had to look at and think through, whatever we had to walk and stand and dream, no matter what it was about. For days, Georg was frequently in his most remote, as he called it, higher phantasies, and he would, as I ceaselessly had to observe, coincidentally always pace back and forth in his despair, which also cast gloom over me, laws, their drafters, and those who, on a daily basis, would rudely cast all laws asunder. From a certain point in time onwards we two would jointly proceed as if forever jointly through the entire, vast, diseased scheme of colors in which nature was compelled to express itself as the most painful of all human pains in each and every one of us. For years, we lived, although on the surface of the capital, within a system – created by us for us and visible only to us – of protective canals. In these canals, however, we unceasingly inhaled lethal air. We walked and crawled towards each other almost always only in those canals of our youthful despair and youthful philosophy and youthful scholarship . . . Those canals led us out of our room in the Zirkusgasse – where, usually affected by powers of judgment and the prodigious abundance of history, we would sit, affected by ourselves, on our chairs at the table, over our books, frightful botchings, idolizations, mockeries of our, indeed, of the entire, geological genealogy – into the old, age-old body of the city and then back into our room . . . We spent, had to spend, eight atrocious semesters together, Georg and I, in a way that I have only intimated, in our room in the Zirkusgasse. We were permitted no break whatsoever. For those entire eight semesters, during which jurisprudence was spoiled for me and pharmacology no less for Georg, we were incapable, given our stooping, our common crippling (I, too, was already crippled) – because, as previously indicated, for all and sundry we were always having to move in our canals and, therefore, hunch over – of rising, out of necessity, to an even oh so slightly higher position. During those entire eight semesters we did not once have the strength to stand up and leave . . . We did not even have the strength – because we did not have the desire – to open the window in our room in the Zirkusgasse and let some fresh air in . . . not to mention the fact that we had only one of those *invisible strengths* . . . Our hearts, as well as our minds, were so firmly withdrawn that once, as far as is humanly possible, we were very close to suffocating each other, had not something, which could not come from us nor from one of us, occasioned such an external or internal metaphysical intervention in us, an alteration of our state from two equal states, Georg's and mine . . . Through an enormously complicated procedure against us, our souls, in what, for us, was still the rather atonic atmosphere of the capital, shrank together. Like so many of our age, we wholeheartedly were deeply buried in the implicit idea that nowhere, neither internally nor externally, did the possibility of fresh air and all that it can give rise to, *unleash* or *obliterate*, exist. And there was, in fact, no fresh air for us back then in our room in the Zirkusgasse, no fresh air for eight semesters.

Each of us had a name that originated many, as far as we were concerned, countless generations ago in the mountains, a name that, on the left bank of the Inn as well as on the right, grew increasingly greater, but now, however, as the subverter of ourselves, had been, following all of those parental execrations and arithmetic sleights of hand, displaced into this, as we were compelled to see, obscenely, plaintively atrophied capital. Each of us was enveloped by our meaningful name and could not get out. Neither knew the other's prison, the guilt, the crimes of the other, but each assumed that the other's prison, the guilt and crimes of the other were his own. Our mistrust of and towards each other had, in the course of time, intensified to the extent that we increasingly belonged together, no longer wanted to abandon each other. Thus, we despised each other and were the most contrary creatures you could imagine. Everything of the one seemed to be of the other, that is, *from the other*. In no way, however, did we resemble each other – not in our affairs, not in one single sentiment, not at all. And yet each of us could have been the other, everything of the one could have come from the other . . . I often said to myself that I *could* be Georg, what Georg was, but that was not to say that nothing of Georg was *from* me . . . How other students, having been sent to the capital, vivaciously found pleasure and rejuvenation among the city's possible distractions remained a mystery to us. Nothing enthused the two of us. We took pleasure in nothing. The city's spirit was a dead one, its entertainment apparatus too primitive for us.

From the outset, we, he and I, proceeded perspicaciously, submitting everything to what, in virtually every instance, was our deadly criticism. Our attempted escapes ultimately failed. Everything oppressed us. We sickened; we constructed our canal system. Already in the first few weeks we withdrew from Vienna's silent delusions of grandeur, from the city in which no history, no art, no science exists any more, in which there was nothing. But even prior to my arrival in Vienna, while still on the train, I (like he) was, we both, independent of each other, were assaulted by a fever, an illness, that progressively saddened us, I by a *distraction to lethal irritability*, logically drawing from all externals into my subconscious as well as my complete consciousness and, sitting in one of the many dark compartments of the express trains which are pulled through our country at high speeds, perceiving myself and perceiving that which forever is connected to me, surprised by my first suicidal thought – the first signs of suicidal thoughts in quite some time. What a gray and extraordinarily severe melancholia I suddenly had to contend with amidst the hills of Melk! During this trip, which I had been forced to take against my will, I frequently, and especially when coming upon dangerous curves, such as those close to the Danube near Ybbs, wished to be dead – a quick, sudden, and painless death that leaves only an image of repose behind. The journey of young people from the provinces to the capital to commence a dreaded course of study, one which most of them do not want, almost always proceeds under atrocious circumstances in the minds and emotions of those affected and deceived and thus tormented. Suicidal thoughts by someone fearfully approaching, by train in the twilight, college or university in the capital, someone who, by all means, is far less courageous than anticipated, is the most natural thing. How many, and not at all few, among those I have known, those I grew up with and those mentioned to me, have, shortly after taking leave of their parents at their home-town train stations, thrown themselves from the train . . . As for Georg and me, we never revealed our perspectives on suicide to each other. We only knew from each other that we felt at home in them. We were as confined to our room and our canal system, as in a higher game, one comparable to higher mathematics, in our suicidal thoughts. In our higher suicide game, we often left each other completely alone for weeks. We studied and contemplated suicide. We read and contemplated suicide. We holed ourselves up and slept and dreamed and contemplated suicide. While contemplating suicide we felt alone, undisturbed, no one paid attention to us. We were always free to kill ourselves, yet we did not kill ourselves. As strange as we were to each other, there were never any of those hundreds of thousands of inodorous human secrets between us, just the secret of nature *in and of itself* which we knew about. Days and nights for us were like the verses of a steady, unending, dark song.

On the one hand, his family members knew from the outset that he was unsuitable for the paternal vocation of merchant and thus for assuming control of the business in the Anichstrasse, a business that demanded one of their kind. On the other hand, however, they clung for a long time to the hope that Georg, the cripple, could perhaps overnight, from one cowhide whipping to the next, still become what they had wanted him to be from the outset: the successor to the grocer who was now already in his sixties! In the end, however, as though by arrangement, they decided behind his, Georg's, back, all of a sudden and forever, upon his older sister, and from that moment on they crammed everything they possibly could, all of their mercantile energies and all of their mercantile knowledge, into that person whose fat legs caused her to walk about the merchant house like a weighty pig – into that fat, bloodshot, rustic Irma. Wearing puffed sleeves in summer as in winter, she, who had just turned twenty and was engaged to a butcher's assistant from Natters, developed into a pillar of merchant enterprise whose calves were constantly oozing pus. At the exact same moment in which they appointed his sister (no doubt with a view toward her fiancé!) to be her father's successor, they permitted him to study. They were afraid of losing face. They did not, however, as he would have wished, allow him to study pharmacology in Innsbruck – where, in addition to a commercial apprenticeship he had attended and successfully completed high school – or in nearby Munich, but only in Vienna, a city that he as well as they had always detested, one lying far to the East. They wanted to have him, to *know* that he was, as far away from them as possible, and the capital really did lie at the ends of the earth. Every young person today knows what it means to be banished there! His attempts to make them understand that Vienna, the capital, had, for decades now, been the most backward of all European university cities were of no avail. There was nothing one could have recommended studying in Vienna. He was forced to go to Vienna and, if he wasn't willing to forego the most meager of monthly pittances I have ever known parents to provide their children, he was forced to remain in Vienna, that most dreadful of all old European cities. Vienna is *as* an old and lifeless city, *as* a vast cemetery which all of Europe and all the world has forgotten and passed by, we thought, such a huge cemetery of crumbling and decaying curiosities!

During our recent time together, and particularly intensely towards the end of the year, I always felt as if he had been me, whenever, before falling asleep, he would insinuate all of the things we knew nothing about . . . His inability to make himself understood just once in his life was also mine . . . His childhood, which struck him as endless and not, like that of the author of *Moby Dick*, to last a thousand years: an incessantly futile attempt to gain the confidence of his parents and the other people in his surroundings, at least his most immediate surroundings. He had never had a true friend – but who knows what that is – just people who ridiculed, clandestinely feared him. He was always one who, in his way, by virtue of his deformity, disturbed the harmony of others, of many others. He was eternally disturbing . . . Wherever he went, wherever he chose to be, he was a hideous stain on a beautiful, comforting background . . . People (for him) were only there to entrap him, no matter who or what they were, what they represented, what they dared to represent. Everything set a trap for him. There was nothing that didn't set a trap for him – not even religion. In the end, he was suddenly obscured by his own feelings . . . His waking up was no doubt also an awakening to the madness of hopelessness . . . All of a sudden he flung open the door to my (I who had felt safe) childhood with the brutality of a sick, oppressed, desperate person . . . Every morning he would awake in the permanently sealed cell of a new immemorial day.

Whereas characters recognizable as quite merry, even boisterous, repeatedly moved before the somber scenery of my childhood, that never happened to my friend. Only terrifying incidents were visible to him. Whenever he looked into the past and what had been played there and was still being played, it was even more terrifying. Accordingly, he, he repeatedly said, wanted to look as seldom as possible, indeed, not at all, into the past, which is like the present and the future, *is* the present and future. But that didn't work. His childhood was an immense glacial stage, his youth, his entire life, existing merely to frighten him, and the leading roles on that stage were solely and perpetually played by his parents and his sisters. They continually devised something new to distress him. He would sometimes cry, and when I asked him why he would respond: because he cannot draw the curtain on the stage; he is too feeble to do so. With increasingly less frequency is he able to draw the curtain on the stage. He is afraid that one day he may not be able to draw it at all. Wherever he may go, wherever he may be, in whatever condition, he is forced to watch his play. The most dreadful scenes played over and over again in his Innsbruck home, in the merchant's house – his father and mother as the driving forces behind his lethal scenery. He would continually see and hear them. In his sleep he would often say the words "father" and "mother," along with the words "cowhide" and "cellar" or, hounded to death by one of his pursuers, "No! Stop!," which was linked to his many punishments. In the morning, his body, although crippled (his skin was that of a terminally ill girl), refined by a degree of chasteness otherwise prohibited by nature, would be soaking wet. A fever, one unable to be measured, had weakened him even before he had risen. We usually did not eat breakfast, since eating and drinking nauseated us. The world for us was a perversely brute and perversely philosophical plague, a disgusting operetta. Last February, Georg was constantly sad and, in his sadness, always alone. In the evening, under conditions well-known to both of us, he, younger by a year, had to be supported by hand movements, movements of the head, frightened by the names of all of those deceased or still living creatures and objects that he so feared. The few letters addressed to him, like those to me, only contained admonitions to recover and were completely lacking in kindheartedness. He once uttered the word "indelicate." He thought the world was, at the very least, indelicate. We both would have needed to be very different in order to turn our backs on the cemetery that was the capital, that *is* the capital. We were too weak to do so. Everyone in the capital is too weak to leave it. The last thing he said was, "This city is a cemetery that's becoming extinct!" Following this remark, which, like all of his other recent ones, had entirely the same value, didn't start me wondering, I proceeded, it was the fourteenth, in the evening, ten-thirty, to go to bed. When I awoke, shortly before two on account of a noise – Georg had kept completely still, most likely because under no circumstances did he want to wake me (and now I know how agonizing that must have been for him) – I had the dreadful realization that Georg's parents now refer to their son as a crime against himself and a crime against his family. At ten the next morning, Georg's father had already arrived in Vienna from Innsbruck and demanded clarification of the occurrence. Upon my return from the clinic where Georg had been admitted, Georg's father was already in our room, and I knew, even though it was still dark on account of the bad weather, that things would never change on this day, that the man, who was packing up Georg's belongings, was his father. Although he, too, was from Innsbruck, I had never before seen him. As my eyes grew accustomed to the darkness, understanding even how to exploit that darkness – I shall never forget the sharpness of my eyes – I saw that that person, who was wearing a black overcoat with sheepskin lining, that that person, who gave the impression of being in a hurry and threw everything of Georg's into a pile in order to remove it, that that person, and that everything connected to him, bore responsibility for Georg's misery, for this catastrophe.

Translated by Craig Decker

BARBARA FRISCHMUTH

1983

Oh, My Dear Augustine

What sort of Vienna, what sort of Augustine-Vienna am I trying to describe here? Starting in the Landstrasse district where you had, have a room or an apartment, from the windowsill (where you also eat breakfast) of which you can see the horse-drawn carriages heading off in the morning to their stands downtown? Or is it better for me to begin in the afternoon when, after a full day in the service of tourism, they're slowly trotting home, past the detergent factory, into the heart of the Erdberg area? Do I really see you before me – you whom I'm trying to create based on that erstwhile character – as, filled to the gills with coffee, that Turkish broth that is supposed to make you think straight, you trudge down the unevenly worn, constantly twisting staircase, feeling the impact of your footsteps in your head (yet another hangover for you)?

You're barely onto the street when all of the district's bad air assails you, the excreta from exhaust systems mixed with the stench of dug-up sewer pipes and people unexpectedly in a rush. And, just as you always do when you're sick and tired of something, you flee – this time into the tobacco shop, I can be sure of that. In spite of any and all fluctuations in the market, you've remained loyal to the same brand of cigarettes, which you request, and without having to ask for it the tobacconist also gets you a copy of the *Kronen-Zeitung*, that fashionable daily tabloid which, along with your other spiritual nourishment, you cannot do without. You're especially interested in the horoscopes. *Frau Helga*'s daily predictions about the fortunes of your sign constitute an essential contribution to the continuity of your day-to-day existence. The international news gets on your nerves. Actually, you wanted to travel to Turkey soon. Leather jackets are so cheap there, and the exchange rate is relatively good. You scan the domestic news because, as you say, you don't give a damn about it anyway. Murders start you thinking. There's something titillating about a mafia feud, complete with shooting, in a beltway cafe. Of course it's a sad affair, a man exterminates himself together with his family, but a friend of yours would be interested in the vacant apartment.

Culture? You sigh. For that they have money. But it would never occur to anyone to make a state-supported wine garden available to you. You would show them what a provider is. At most, you'd only need one or two of the many, many millions the national theaters devour every year. You would be a total work of art, so to speak, corporally and spiritually one.

You no longer get upset about the comments the same people have been making for years. What do they want, you'd say, he's basically right, from his point of view. As long as he's not railing against me . . .

Among the classifieds you're interested to see whether someone is selling a classic car at a favorable price, like an early BMW. Not because you're crazy about it, but to show the boys how it was, back then, in the fifties . . . (I have no idea where I'm going, but I'll get there faster.) And, of course, the sports section. You're a fan of Team Austria, aren't you, or is it the Vienna team? I don't know much about soccer. I can't keep up with you there.

This city, I hear you say in my thoughts, is an old woman with a double chin and warts, who's put on her finest evening wear for an appearance at some senior citizens' club. And if I continue in my thoughts, I come upon the saint in the Rochus Church, Bonatus is his name, a martyr. His relics are clothed in gold brocade with embroidered pearls, custom-tailored, all along the arch of his ribs, only his viscerocranium, his ulna, and the bones of his extremities lie exposed to the observer's eye, similar to the baroquely decorated bones in St. Peter's Church. You have a sense of the macabre, that's why you often use them as a place to meet one of your little girlfriends, to whom you then present yourself in the proper light – namely, a transitory one.

There's nothing horrible about death for me, you say to one of them, would you want to pass away with me? And there's nothing for her to do, of course, but to giggle excitedly, and you stand there with your half-promise. You ask yourself what would happen if she doesn't pass away with you. And the more you talk about it, the more you're able to think of death as that brittle, harmless skeleton to which it's almost possible to establish something like a friendly relationship.

The world is gray, you say, even when everything is in color. The glow has to come from within, and if nothing wants to burn there, then you have to stoke the fires a bit. The question is where and whether it should be a shot of schnapps, a glass of wine or a bottle of beer. Not before five, you say upon further consideration, and give the world no chance to put on its first touch of rouge for you. And you surreptitiously stretch out your hand to see whether and how much it shakes when you catch yourself somehow maintaining equilibrium.

Actually you have a lot to attend to. It would be a slight exaggeration to call it an occupation. But if you think about it carefully, you're supposed to be in three places at once right now, so you forgo the triple-booking and spontaneously decide to do something worthwhile. This new idea elates you so much that you start to bounce along the sidewalk.

If I construct things correctly, then you used to do a lot of temping. You were a gofer for a music publisher; a driver for various art galleries; attended to singers on tour; and even proved successful at organizing alternative programs. You associated with nothing but interesting people, fully conscious of being the most interesting one. You appear lovable to most, inscrutable to those with a sense for the unique, and the ones who really like you find you *terribly difficult*, a combination of *very sensitive* and *an ass*, as a progressive film editor once put it.

Now you're a company without personnel. Your offices are located in various downtown cafés that have not yet been renovated. You're mobile and shun excessive production costs. What you sell is worth the money that many invest in your overwhelming ideas. You've watched so many so carefully for so many years that you commit none of the errors fatal to your line of work.

Your ancestors came as far as Landstrasse. Some of them, from a long way off in the East, stopped along this one of the great access roads, at a suitable distance from the Ringstrasse, and earned their living as tailors, barbers or shoemakers, services that were in much demand back then. At three in the morning even you sometimes discover your Slavic soul, throwing glasses against the wall and giving the Gypsy violinist your last hundred schillings. You call it depression, while your friends say that today Augie is feeling nostalgic.

Of course you know where to go to eat. Without working meals your business doesn't advance either, and your criticism is so biting that the innkeeper sags at the knees if he catches one of your reprimanding glances. But in reality you prefer to nourish yourself with liquids most of all, with that thrilling feeling, with each new bottle, of how much longer? Experience teaches you that you always manage to slip away. And the lesson to be learned from that is that experience doesn't have sufficient foresight.

You've cut the cord at home. That is, the apartment has been divided and you have your own entrance. Mama's old, and sometimes you go over to her place for a cup of coffee, but her whining gets on your nerves. Besides, she has two girlfriends as well as a cocker spaniel, which you take for a walk if she has to lie down.

Sometimes one of your girls sticks around for a few days. But you have a sensitive nose and send them away if they don't wash or change their underwear often enough. Besides, it bothers you to see them lying around in your bed during the day without their make-up. They should find some sort of work; you can't stand around staring into space all day, either. You're uncommonly generous with gifts, but don't want to have to be responsible for supporting anyone. A married man, you say, is like a mouse with a tin mug on its tail, unable to creep into a hole any more. (A Tatarian proverb.)

You somehow owe it to yourself to have fathered a child here and there. Contact is limited to paying child support and birthday and Christmas visits with gifts. A child belongs with its mother, you say. Once they get to be as old as I am, they'll understand.

I maintain you're a night owl. And you never tire of being annoyed at how early bars have to close in this city. That's why you're especially fond of those few pubs that don't even open until two or four in the morning. You don't even begin to hit your stride until after midnight, and between one and three you're in top form. Then you can take anything from anybody, and everybody can take everything from you, for when Augie is big, then he's strong. Very strong, as the boys say, when you disparage all forms of authority and even spoil their enjoyment of that singer/songwriter from the Stadthalle. Ha ha, they laugh in unison, when you set that type of tone. And the fact that you accept so little of what is nowadays lends you an aura of incorruptibility, which otherwise wouldn't exactly suit your character. Your wit is cruel because it works deep under the skin, and when you're in top form you don't even spare yourself, so that you're able to keep a crowd laughing in suspense until, underneath all of your vulgar expressions, they realize on the following day the wretchedness of their own existence. You sweep them away into the most iridescent recess of your obscurest paradise and take them for a walk through an expansive pasture of superelevated platitudes, a sharp-toothed shepherd who renders the wolves downright taciturn. And since, in this case, you're in command of the prevailing mood, you can also see to its change, and God help you if, among this crowd, there's someone whose nose doesn't suit you. You fill it with such a stench that he's no longer able to see and hear. No one will come to his rescue, because you have all the magic. And who would want to appear ridiculous in the presence of a magician who might pull that runaway rabbit out of his pants pocket? Or, even worse, the wallet of the person sitting across from him. One has to be prepared for everything when you're under the influence of your own self.

You're simply ingenious according to your special friends, the ones who, for reasons of pure entertainment, are permitted to invite you to go out drinking now and then. You know more about the world than anybody else, but your position consists primarily of backing down. People like you don't fight, they survive. When you can, and when you can't. Your aversion to life, at any rate, would counterbalance your lust for it. If necessary, you would show yourself the same contempt you hold for others.

You portend the evil you don't intend to stave off. At most, you helpfully intervene among your close acquaintances, precisely to the point at which an intoxicating sense of power frequently comes over you. From a purely personal standpoint, you then say, I can't stand him. I'll put that swindler in his place. Whatever else he does doesn't matter to me at all.

Your dodge is that peacock's fan, which you strike whenever things appear to be heading towards mating season. And your brilliant eyes really aren't bad at all, a palette of the richest colors masterfully mixed by you. The way you're dressed is part of the picture as well, a bit shabby but noble, with emphasis on the coat, since you often go walking at night.

It becomes increasingly clear to me that you enjoy eating in the better Balkan restaurants. You like the food and the people, you say, and think that life should be more than just work. Except for the time when you're supposed to accomplish something yourself, something rougher, as you call it, with co-workers. Then you suddenly have a very definite notion of workplace discipline and morale, and demand perfect results.

Strictly speaking, you only invest in yourself. Neither in an act nor an object. Even your capabilities you only employ as a casual display package in the shop window that dominates your appearance. You don't write anything down, and you don't make any images. As far as music is concerned, you rhythmically vibrate according to your mood. You are, so to speak, the work of art, and no one can reproduce you very quickly. After all, you know what you owe yourself, and you refine your unrepeatability.

You're an urban creature, a downtown kind of guy, to be precise, who only moves beyond the beltway to go to a wine garden, and then, for some years running now, only by taxi. You never drive yourself any more, even though you were tremendously lucky back then, but even you won't go that far in provoking your own downfall. It was, when you think back to it, one of your most inspiring intoxications, and today you still have the feeling that you had spontaneously lifted off when, after the curve, you proceeded over the embankment and down into the Danube Canal. The few seconds you were floating were so great that you did precisely what you were always talking about back then: *bailed out*. Just in time. The impact was violent, the sobering effect rather incomplete. You practically don't remember how you climbed onto the barge hanging from the bank by a short chain. Waking up was more spectacular. An incredible sunrise on the edge of the Prater, and you, air-dried, in somewhat stiff clothes (fortunately it was warm that night), slowly swinging into that summery morning. You even had your papers with you, soggy as they were, in your inner jacket pocket. Nobody wanted to believe your crazy story until somebody borrowed your car. Even then a few people thought you had pushed it in yourself on account of the insurance. (And even I had difficulties conceiving of something that could compete with the plague, but I think the thing with the car just about does.) Ever since that incident you consider yourself invulnerable, on the one hand, and take stock in statistics, on the other. Risks simply increase from time to time. And whenever you dream at night about *getting out* the hair on the nape of your neck stands on end. You sink into the dirty soup of the Danube Canal and awake wheezing wildly. You love sunrises as a result. Especially when the weather's nice you try to make good use of the night for your professional life (many clubs consider it an honor if you interact with the disc jockey) so that you can then enjoy the sunrise on your way home and climb calmly into bed as if nothing more could happen thereafter.

People know that your opinion counts for something in this line of work, and a tip from you is worth more to a young musician than some moderate success at cheap honky-tonks in the provinces. Not that you haven't thought about your own record company . . . but you don't want to get involved that concretely, the whole expense, and besides, other people should be the ones scuffling about. The main thing is that you know what's good. And that those who matter know it as well. The fact that they ask you confers an indisputable significance upon you.

You still enjoy taking a girl to the Prater. You buy corn on the cob and cotton candy, and in the fun house you surreptitiously undo her bra, causing her to *disappear* immediately and you to imagine how she's fiddling around in the ladies' room until the thing is on properly again. And when the roller coaster makes her sick you laugh and eat a couple of hot dogs with great pleasure. You regret that the Prussian Freak Show has turned into a sex shop, and collect old postcards showing the woman with three breasts and the people with bird heads. You never force your tenderness upon anyone, so your kisses are usually ardently awaited, and everyone thinks they're out of harm's way with you.

When it comes to love affairs, you're a connoisseur, and in your almost senile wisdom you take only the cream of the crop, leaving the fleshy rest for others. The occasional feeling of loneliness you pay for that optimum quality has subsumed your features, which were not exactly ascetic to begin with, into a subdued-looking face. Which only sometimes gets distorted if you come up against demands that leave you without desires. You calmly take note of the suicide attempts made by your little girlfriends. Of course, it would be really stupid if something actually happened. Nevertheless, travelers should not be detained, as you always say. It certainly enhances your reputation if little girls are unhappy on your account. You rarely get involved with women. Then your magic lags and looks like some harmless deception.

You would never let your friends down, the question is just who are your friends when. For the sake of camaraderie you're capable of just about anything, and you'd risk your own life for a true friend, providing, of course, that he also stands by you and that he's never ever made fun of you. And that he's someone who's worth it, whose company you really value, someone with whom you've already been through a lot. You'd even spend a few weeks in jail for a friend like that and, if I'm not mistaken, your response would be: at least now I have a chance to think. It's true, you know, that day-to-day events constantly eclipse your philosophical side. In that sense you're a victim of the present as well, taken in by the hectic nature of things, even if in a somewhat unconventional way. You hate having to change pubs several times a night just so that you can have a better sense of the range of your interests.

You have an odd conception of time. So often you say *back then*, and I can't shake my suspicion that you're always referring to the postwar period, even when you're talking about the Biedermeier. To cook simply, you say, for example, but lovingly, without the thousands of spices with which they adulterate things nowadays. And an apple was still an apple; nowadays even a worm won't bite into one. People had a sense of how to live *back then*, now you can just forget about that. The way you let your hand glide over a finely crafted piece of furniture says a lot about your attitude towards the present. And you unabashedly falsify your own memories by simply perceiving, from your present standpoint, experiences differently. It was a good thing, you say, that we didn't have everything then, and we were tough, with our freezing cold john and washbasin down the hall. And back then we still had a sense of the world and what should become of it, but nowadays nobody has any idea of how long things will just keep going.

You no longer go to the country, because in your opinion everything's been ruined ever since everybody started building a *cabin of their own*. But you're very interested in technical developments in the field of electronics, and your dream would be a quadraphonic juke box, with a design from the fifties and the sound of the future. You're even interested in fashion, providing it's made of flawless materials and sets those people who dare to wear it apart from the rest. Clothes say something about the respect one has for one's own body, and you place great emphasis on a well-tailored suit, even though you wear it pretty casually. You expect your girlfriends to have a superior sense of the tailor's trade, and only when you think you can take a few things for granted do you offer this or that hot tip. But you're also able to appreciate when someone's come up with something decisive for their façade. I have eyes in the back of my head, you would respond if asked, and I want to see something that excites me, instead of constantly having to look at the boring bulges of forever frustrated souls, who haven't been struck by anything since the blackness of existentialism. That's the point at which your sense of people intersects with your emphasis on your own being. You know exactly what kind of impression you want to make upon others, and it's very important for you not to confuse cause and effect in this regard. You think highly of yourself and want to convey this feeling accordingly. It simply does make a difference which sunglasses people wear.

You realize with a certain distress that even you are, naturally, getting older. Can't do anything about that, you secretly try to console yourself; the main thing is to stay cool. Never ingratiate yourself to anyone, otherwise some day no one will want you at all. Better they ask ten times for you and you play hard to get, that's your secret. This stake doesn't apply to the game, and you can only win if you distance yourself to such an extent that no one notices your triumph. You've so internalized this philosophy that even when you're completely intoxicated you don't reveal any more of yourself than you usually do when playing cards with your friends.

Who knows, you say to yourself, if I'll even make it to old age. Your doctor frequently talks about a few years at most if you don't radically change your drinking habits. You respond to his advice by ordering only the very best brands now. You've even considered buying your own vineyard in order to control production. But ever since reading that it would take at least ten years for all of the chemicals to disappear from the soil, you have no patience for that, and so prophylactically stick to the most expensive ones.

Recently, at particularly sentimental times, you even think of your children. Especially since the night when one of the boys whose vague sense of happiness allowed them to be maneuvered by you was your son, and you didn't even recognize him. It wasn't until he helped you (you were definitely drunk) into the taxi in the morning that it dawned on you what was up, and you said, now you're finally old enough to do things with. And the boy simply asked, but what? That's when you realized that he was incompatible with your lifestyle.

Maybe you should have a dog. A dog with personality, of course, whether or not it's a purebred is beside the point. It would have to be suited to you and have character. Not just any kind of creature who would constantly lick your fingers. Maybe even one from the animal shelter, one without a master, who, on account of bad experiences, knowingly decides on you. In short, a small, highly intelligent bastard, one who'll fetch the waiter for you when you want to pay, and not some fat, bleary-eyed thing like your mother's spaniel. "Augie and his dog," they'd say, and downtown would have one more legend to tell. Thus, while still alive you tinker with your obituary, for you, too, would like a bit of all that possible immortality. After all, you've certainly contributed to that of others. Poldi W. and Karl F. have a lot to thank you for in that regard. Not to mention Mali Nagl, the Ella Fitzgerald of the wine garden.

You are and always will be a musician at heart. I don't think I'm wrong in supposing that. The fact that you didn't become a professional musician may be due to the hardships of your childhood, to the lack of opportunities, and to a professional ethos that interferes with all of your other desires. That is probably the only thing you would do differently if you had your life to live over again. In this life, however, you limit yourself to making judgments. Unhampered by your own bagpipe-style, you can develop your opinions most enigmatically, and the industry hangs on your every word. You have a good nose, and people pay close attention to your participation, which isn't exactly high (you'll never get rich that way) but sufficient to push your way of life through. You most certainly set stock in yourself as a work of art, and there are enough believers to whom you convey a convincing course.

You belong to this city, just like the river that doesn't flow through it, whose color occurs primarily in song. You're as pleasant as backbiting among the living and as recalcitrant as the adulation following death by starvation. Your life is the dream people want to wake up from every day, and your death will be as inconspicuous as getting tanked at night in some plush bar. People will remember you and once again talk of your times as the *good old* ones, even though a few days ago you put your glass back on the table with a resounding crash.

My God, your last girlfriend will sob to the waiter, Augie's died. And it happened so quickly. Since a hospital, as you repeatedly declared, would be out of the question for you. The kind of man you are simply gets struck down.

Translated by Craig Decker

BARBARA FRISCHMUTH   1983

A Neighbor of Mine and Musil's

I would like to live in Salmgasse. Salmgasse is an enchanting
lane, shaped like a J and located in Vienna's Third District.
Especially in its lower third, in the curve of the J, there are a few
Habsburg-yellow buildings, massive structures with very simple
façades. But behind them . . .
Recently one of the gates stood open – the masons restoring
the plaster were coming and going – and I entered the inner
courtyard. Sun rooms, trees, a garden, wrought-iron balconies: in
short, almost everything you don't expect in the middle of the city.
Ever since I've been living in the spirit of Salmgasse, and
whenever I can manage it, I detour through that J on my way to the
nearest streetcar stop. Musil, by the way, lived for many years
around the corner, in Rasumofskygasse, and the garden where
Agathe and Ulrich . . . but I don't want to know all the details.
So I'm living in this house in Salmgasse – the entrance is on
Siegelgasse – on the very top floor, if possible, behind one of those
sun rooms, looking down into the garden. It snowed, a serious
snowstorm, much too early this year, and the snow is clinging to
the trees, which still have their leaves. A plastic tricycle sits
between the rose bushes and only glistens laterally now, a
complementary Austrian flag, white, red, and white.
Then I see our neighbor, just as he disappears in the stairway.
He's wearing a heavy frock coat lined with mole fur. The mole, he
said, is the lowest common denominator to which custom tailoring
and fancy can be reduced. He's supposed to have a dog, too. What
kind of dog would you like as a neighbor?, I ask my son – an
unnecessary question since I know he'll say a St. Bernard. A St.
Bernard, my son says. And how do you think that would be with all
of those stairs to climb? A building like this doesn't have an
elevator. But the apartment is big, my son says. But I have no use
for such an enormous dog in my story, so away with him! To the
country, to the mountains, to St. Gotthard as far as I'm concerned.
Perhaps he has a famous pedigree and must go to some out-of-the-
way kennel in order to reproduce his particular bloodline.
I keep running into him, our neighbor. He was the only tenant

in the building who knocked on our door when we moved in and invited me to his apartment for coffee. Great, I said, but why don't you stay here, I still have some coffee left.

He's old, pretty old, but very dignified. I suspect he sleeps with a mustache-trainer.

Have you been living in this building for a long time? I ask intentionally, since at some point I would like to get to Musil. He nods. With a certain eight-year interruption . . . I understand, I reply. And where were you during your exile? I, he says, flexing his hands – thank God you can't see it any more – spent three weeks shoveling the Panama Canal. Then I had my first café. In Panama? And then one in New York. He laughs, and reminds me so much of that former professional dance partner and subsequent owner of a café in the Prater with whom I often used to play backgammon and whom, on account of his humor, I'll never forget.

I hope I don't disturb you, he says, when I come home at night. Sometimes I come home very late. Ah ha, I say, you really carry on, and he turns his signet ring with a satisfied smile. Of course, I'm curious to see his apartment. So, I say, next time I'll come to your place. Tuesdays are best, he says. Tuesday is my day off.

For the time being I'm not going to tell my son anything about our neighbor. He would surely want some sort of young person who might play soccer with him.

Salmgasse, of course, would put me even closer to Café Zartl. Sometimes I eat breakfast there and glance at the *Weltwoche*, the *Frankfurter Allgemeine Zeitung*, the Styrian dailies. They just don't subscribe to the *Spiegel*. And whom do I see walk in? Our neighbor (that has to be, on account of the story). Just a moment, he says, and, covering his mouth, begins to tell me things. Things, I tell you . . .

He had recently been in the National Library again – a remarkable structure, impressive and surely expensive to maintain – and took a look at the small green booklet, the 1979 debt report of the Austrian Postal Savings Bank, available there. Shocking! The foreign debt alone! Shocking! Not to mention the budget deficit! This country is bankrupt, my neighbor whispers in my ear, and therefore, well, you know, the tank shipments were able to be stopped just in time, but all those thousands and thousands of arms to the Middle East . . . And then I suddenly had to think of the taxi driver with whom I drove through the slush yesterday at the speed of walking, who asked me if anyone had protested.

Snowflakes, slowing turning into rain drops, are hanging from the ends of his mustache. Before I leave you to the world's news, what do you say to that? And my neighbor points with his thumb behind him in the direction of the snowstorm. Europe will slowly freeze over, but who cares. We're the prime target for all of those medium-range missiles. The super powers don't give a damn about the little countries.

By all means I wanted to see his apartment – symmetrical to mine, just inverted, perhaps a little less sun, but cooler in summer as a result. As if I had known about all of those books!

Be careful, my neighbor says, that nothing falls on your feet. And with a masterful reach he pulls from one of the towering piles of books just the one he wants, like some oriental scholar. Do you think I'd ever let a carpenter into my refuge again? my neighbor says. There's plenty of room, you just have to know your way around. And he leads me through the archingly ordered pathways which, from the perspective of the ceiling lamp, must look like a French garden.

Come, my neighbor says, clearing off a leather wing chair. Then he serves me coffee with cognac and winks. That's what the old ladies drink in those Budapest cafés. You know the ones, those seat-warmers, who spend half a day sipping a glass of wine. But cognac, they really do drink that.

My hobby is toponymy, my neighbor says, as he spreads various maps – ones he drew himself, of course – over his knees. Toponymy is an essential source of history. It's easy for me; I grew up multilingually. When you consider how much people mess about on account of deficient language skills. It all starts with the Bible and continues from there, without end . . . And now he bears a striking resemblance to that deceased Trotskyite doctor, that old acquaintance from my early youth, who spent a long time in Palestine – well before Israel – and who at an advanced age authored a wild pamphlet against the gospels as an historical source.

But, my neighbor says, without its related disciplines toponymy is as isolated as a village in the woods. And just about anything can be considered a related discipline, even literature. That was my cue. Whether he could remember that man with the bushy eyebrows and green eyes? What do you mean, green eyes? I just assumed. Oh, he says, you mean the chain smoker? Well, you know, a talented man, but completely unsuccessful. I mumble something about his hundredth birthday. What?, my neighbor exclaims. That can't be! Was he older than I?

Cigarette?, my neighbor asks. He himself is smoking a cigar. Sometimes this place smells like a smokehouse, he says chuckling, but as a bachelor I can set the rules as I please, and if I care to, I can leave the full ashtrays lying around. You were never married? Let's not talk about that, my neighbor says. Two failed attempts. One was an Armenian, the other a Tatar. So I voluptuously manage to exist as a dual divorcé-widower. We raise our glasses to that, and for a short time we're one heart and mind, as I only would have wanted to hear the story of one of the two women anyway.

Gradually I will have to inform my son about our neighbor. And vice versa. Oh, my neighbor says, the small boy with the big bookbag. Does he know how to play chess? I hesitate. If you would be so kind . . . Is he gifted? I shrug my shoulders. If he's gifted, I can teach him. Otherwise, we can play dominoes.

Gifted, I say, what does being gifted have to do with it? The important thing is how one is taught. Not at all, our neighbor snorts, and I see him grow angry. I'll be the one to decide whether or not he's gifted. Then I see my old teacher before me, the one who taught Chinese ethnology the whole year long, who was always so accommodating and helpful until he flew into a rage, at which point you had to worry that he would have a stroke right then and there.

But then our neighbor calms down. I never believe anything mothers say, he tells me, and straightens his fringed scarf.

Adieu, he says, as I return the book I had been leafing through to its place. And then he kisses my hand and asks whether people still dance the tango. And as I listen to the melody in astonishment, he's already taking huge steps with me through the long hallway, and a vague memory tells me that many, many years ago I danced the tango like this with an old gentleman in a café in Wroclaw.

Can't you make me something to eat now?, asks my son, the small one with the big bookbag. And afterwards I'd like someone to go ice-skating with me.

You can go ice-skating all winter long, I tell him, but today I'm finally going to show you Salmgasse.

Translated by Craig Decker

PETER HENISCH

1980

Baronkarl

Locale
Favoriten: Vienna's Tenth District
The Laaerberg: An elevation therein

1

When he appeared on the Laaerberg he still looked halfway
normal. Sure, he had a beard and long hair, but that, after all, was
fashionable at the time. He sat in the beer garden of the Nettles
Bar, musing over his mug of beer and occasionally making notes
in a marbled composition book. Anyone can sit there, of course.
But, as is the case when someone no one knows sits somewhere
day after day and somehow doesn't belong there, people begin to
get curious. At first they just looked askance and whispered to one
another. Sometimes they laughed, because one of them would
crack a joke about him which, apparently, annoyed him. Then he
would glance up from his notebook and over to them, but soon was
back scribbling, all the more fervently. Until one day when Sigi
Fassel, whom they all call Jango, stood up and, with his typical
cowboy gait, swaggered over to him.

Hey, J.C., he asked, what are you looking for here?

I'm looking for stories. Can you tell me some?

Tell you some? Well, I can't tell you anything. But I'd gladly
punch you in the face.

That would have quickly settled the matter, for hardly anyone
stands a chance against Sigi Fassel, and least of all a shrimp like
him. But just then the old sot of a Latin teacher – who doesn't
exactly fit in himself with the crowd at the Nettles Bar, but with
time they got used to him – intervened. Excuse me, he said, but
who would be so coarse? What kind of stories are you looking for,
young man?

So the guy started talking about his fascination with this
milieu. And about the periphery as the site of contradictions –
whatever that means. So the Latin teacher took his glass of wine
and walked over to him, swaying but dignified. And Sigi Fassel
stood by, hanging his arms and jawbone, not knowing what a Jango

is supposed to do in a situation like this.

For his part, J.C., whom he gladly would have punched in the face, was no longer impressed. Instead, he continued talking to the Latin teacher who, in turn, responded, and it was impossible to understand a single word. So Sigi Fassel took off – not back to his posse, even though they whistled to him, but to his moped. Hopped onto the saddle, stepped so hard on the gas that the metal impressively reared up like a mustang, and was gone.

J.C. and the Latin teacher, however, didn't pay any attention to his tremendously forceful exit. They, as they say, were deep in conversation. The Latin teacher ordered another mug of beer for J.C., J.C. another glass of wine for the Latin teacher. And they sat and drank and chatted incessantly. It was probably the old sot of a Latin teacher who put the bug into his ear about Baronkarl.

Perhaps like this: Have you ever heard of Baronkarl, young man?

And in case he hadn't or was only vaguely aware of him: You should write about that guy. Now there's a topic for you.

From that point on, at any rate, he was no longer looking for just *any* stories but rather *specific* ones: namely, about Baronkarl. With each passing day he dared to ask more, and with each passing day the people on the Laaerberg responded more obligingly. Most of them gladly talked about Baronkarl; as they told their stories, quite a few had a moist twinkle in their eyes. Baronkarl had an incredible reputation. Baronkarl was something like the patron saint of the district.

2

Once, when she was still young, an old woman recounts, she went shopping and a terrible storm came up. So she set her shopping bag down and tried to open her umbrella, since it was raining. But the wind was so strong that it kept turning her umbrella inside out. Once the bad weather had passed the only thing to do with the umbrella was throw it away.

No sooner said than done. She looks for a public trash receptacle and deposits her umbrella there, pointed end first. Suddenly there is such abusive swearing coming from the receptacle that she recoils in shock. That can't be a cat or a dog, she thinks, and very nearly runs over the janitress.

Jesus, Mary, and Joseph, she says, what happened? You look like you just saw a ghost! But for a long time the woman is unable to speak. She just points mutely at the ominous receptacle.

The janitress is not particularly quick on the uptake. But all at once she starts to laugh.

Don't you know, she says, what's over there? That's the headquarters of Karl Báron.

I see, the woman says. And who is that?

You don't know him?

No.

Then you certainly haven't been living in this district for very long.

Listen, Karl Báron of Vienna's Favoriten district, he's . . . Baronkarl . . . but see for yourself! At that moment the lid comes off the receptacle and someone wearing a black suit climbs out. He's not wearing any shirt underneath, however, just some kind of military underwear. But, all the same, a bowler hat on his head. And a wilted flower in his buttonhole. Or maybe it was just an onionskin. But then it was an especially beautiful one.

Just imagine, the man was covered with deep red onionskins that someone had thrown out in the trash. That was a sight, the old woman smiles. I'll never forget that as long as I live.

Then Baronkarl sat down on the curb and pulled a dusting brush out of his breast pocket. He brushed himself off extremely meticulously. And whistled a popular tune while doing so.

3

Nobody knows, the teacher says, exactly where he came from. The only thing that's for certain is that at some point following World War I he was there. And living in trash receptacles. Which, of course, was prohibited, even back then. Officially it's called a transgression of registration laws or vagabondage. Although it's highly questionable whether you can designate someone who more or less has settled down, prefers a specific trash receptacle as his residence, and otherwise limits all of his activities to a narrowly defined area – Vienna's Tenth District – as a vagabond.

All of his activities . . . what did he do?

Well, Baronkarl was a "Biertippler." That's someone who lives on "Bierhansel." And "Bierhansel" is what's left in the kegs they leave out behind the pubs. "Biertippler" would tip the kegs so that the dregs ran out into their canteens, which they usually wore on their belts and from which they would drink the "Bierhansel."

There were a lot of those "Biertippler." Why exactly did Baronkarl become so popular?

I'll tell you why, the teacher says. Baronkarl was simply

different from all the rest.

4

Baronkarl, an old cabby recounts, was a joiner in his youth. He was quite a skillful craftsman, but he always had a love of music in him. He learned to play the violin from Bandleader Prystichal, who was the brother of the famous military bandmaster. Baronkarl didn't need a teacher for the fluegelhorn and as a small child he was already squeezing an accordion. The longer he was a joiner, the more he talked about being free and how he finally wanted to be his own boss.

But on May 5, 1905 – I know the date from my father who was a coachman in Favoriten at the time – an event occurred that completely changed his life. As Baronkarl was bending down to pick up a nail that had fallen, a co-worker inadvertently hammered him hard on the head. Karl fell down on the spot and had to be carried home. For two weeks he schlepped around with a huge bump, and his head was humming and buzzing. He walked around restlessly, mumbling what were usually incomprehensible things to himself, and then all of a sudden, laughing loudly, he declared: That's the end of work for me!

His father, of course, immediately sent him to Steinhof, Vienna's psychiatric hospital. But after a few months there they discharged the guy as harmless but incurable. The blow to his head, the doctors determined, obviously deranged him. Others, however, maintain that Karl just used the accident in order to be labeled a fool and committed to Steinhof. For only as a fool, he supposedly said later, can one live halfway sensibly in a world like ours.

From that point on, in any case, any kind of regular employment reminded Baronkarl of his accident. When I see people toiling from dawn till dusk and the sun disappears on them, he supposedly said, I always think about that hammer on my head. And you really do have to be crazy to work so hard for somebody else who then gets more even though he does less. Maybe they nailed me a little too firmly, for instead of putting me to sleep they woke me up just in time.

About Baronkarl (Theory Number One)

Baronkarl was a disheveled aristocrat.
His family owned lots of property and was rolling in money.
Disheveled, by the way, isn't really the right word.
He just didn't put much stock in living like a dandy.

For it didn't suit him
To wear a white shirt and tie, they say.
And he could do without
A bank account and a big inheritance, the story goes.

He would rather be a "Biertippler" with a canteen,
Wearing patched pants and an apron
And sleeping in trash receptacles,
Until the city workers woke him in the morning.

About Baronkarl (Theory Number Two)

Baronkarl was once an arithmetic teacher.
Baron was just his surname.
He must have had a run-in with the school authorities.
Or maybe being a teacher didn't please him anymore.

For it didn't suit him
To wear a white shirt and tie, they say.
And he could do without
A steady income and a pension, the story goes.

He would rather sit in beer gardens
And trade lottery tips with his drinking buddies.
He certainly didn't get rich doing that.
But that wasn't important to him at all.

About Baronkarl (Theory Number Three)

Baronkarl ran out on his old lady.
She, supposedly, was fabulously wealthy and also a real bitch.
One day he just got fed up.
And threw his house key into the canal.

For it didn't suit him
To wear a white shirt and tie, they say.
And he could do without
Having a woman in bed and children, the story goes.

From that point on Frau Baron dined alone.
While her Karl cadged from people at the market.
Many of them bought him coffee with whipped cream.
Not even when he was hungry, would he ever steal.

5

Baronkarl, an unemployed blacksmith recounts, frequently watched my father and me work as we knelt down by the horses. He would wait until the barkeep around the corner opened up; that was always his first stop. Baronkarl would tip his hat and respectfully greet my father. God bless the honorable craftsman, he would say.

Often he would hang around a while and tell us stories. Like the one about the sunken village lying at the bottom of a sea of bricks. Or the one about the labyrinthine series of small garden plots whence, once you entered, you could never escape. Oh come on, Baronkarl, my father would say, those are all just fairy tales.

Well then, Baronkarl replied one day, I'll tell you a true story. Not all that long ago Egypt was up there on the Laaerberg. The Jews, led by Moses, walked across the sea and their feet stayed dry. The Egyptians, however, got stuck in the mud.

I was an Egyptian. Well, of course. That only makes sense. And I caught sight of a woman who was a beautiful Jewess. My God, was that broad a looker! But cruel, very cruel . . . Yes, Herr Meister, my heart's been bleeding ever since.

I was still a young boy at the time and didn't understand a word. But once the bar was open and Baronkarl was gone, my father explained the meaning of it all to me. A few years ago, he said, they shot a film here in the district. Many of the unemployed, including Baronkarl, availed themselves of the opportunity to earn a few schillings as extras.

Back then, however, Baronkarl was not yet living in his receptacle. He was a young man like all the others, if perhaps a bit unrealistic. But the woman he met during the filming drove him mad. And because he couldn't get her he decided to become something of a recluse. And that's his secret.

About Baronkarl (Theory Number Four)

Baronkarl was a runaway monk.
He just couldn't bear the monastery.
Poverty or chastity wouldn't have bothered him in the least.
But he absolutely detested obedience.

So one day he went over the wall
And hung his frock on a tree
And cast off the scent of holy water,
Or rather, turned it into wine.

But a bit of the friar stayed with him,
For he was never immoderate,
And as for the ladies, the fair sex,
He never touched them his whole life long.

6

Others respond to the question why Baronkarl became Baronkarl as follows: Baronkarl was a soldier in the Great War. On the Eastern front he risked life and limb for Kaiser and Fatherland. But when he and his surviving comrades returned from the war, people suddenly didn't believe in those words any more.

Some of them continued droning their "God Save the Kaiser," but others proclaimed: We don't need a Kaiser! Long live the Republic! That was downtown. They raised the red flag in front of Parliament. Baronkarl, however, wanders into the outskirts. Steps in front of his trash receptacle and circumspectly, almost appreciatively, begins to shed his clothes. He drops his uniform to the ground. As soon as he's undressed himself down to his skivvies he opens the lid on the receptacle and climbs in.

Many, however, maintain that he had returned earlier because, by himself and for himself, he no longer believed in what the others were fighting for. He no longer – and, to be sure, just in the nick of time – thought it worthwhile to risk life and limb. Who knows whether, at some later point, he would have even returned at all, since many of those who were with him on the battlefield remained there. They then called that "remaining on the field of honor." But Baronkarl renounced that particular honor. He fought his way through, not as a soldier who returns home from the war, but as a deserter. Hence, he didn't move into the receptacle on a whim, but in order to disappear. For disappearing and subsequently reappearing (alive, that is) a municipal trash receptacle is just fine.

7

Some people connect Baronkarl to the Brick Bohemians. The Brick Bohemians led an inhumane existence down in the Wienerberger brickyard. Having arrived in the imperial city from what is now Czechoslovakia, they were forced to submit to working conditions that were far worse than most. Entire families lived in dugouts or slept in brick ovens. They weren't paid their wages in cash but rather in coupons that could be redeemed only in the brickyard's own stores. They were thus bound to the brickyard.

Baronkarl, according to this version, was the child of Brick Bohemians. That would also fit with the widespread assertion that he spoke with a Bohemian accent. Others, however, claim that he had an Hungarian accent. If Baron were his surname, then, contrary to customary practice, it would have had to be pronounced bar·ón.

Be that as it may, Baronkarl was gone from the brickyard and moved into his trash receptacle. That wouldn't have made much of a difference since, from childhood on, he was used to the living conditions among the Brick Bohemians. Only now he didn't work for beggar's wages; instead of working, he begged . . .

Many reject this version. But perhaps that's precisely why it's true.

8

In Paris they would call someone like that a "Clochard." In and around Vienna they call him a "Sandler."

In one photo he's sitting with his back against a clapboard wall, having fallen asleep, his chin resting on his chest. His head is bare, and the bags under his eyes shocking. He's wrapped in a tattered coat. Lying next to him is a bag that probably contains all his belongings. On top of that sits his hat. A picture of misery? — He autographed that picture.

His handwriting is straight and sure, with a few flourishes.

Karl, he writes, Baron of Favoriten.

But, the teacher says, that's understating things.

He was the uncrowned king of the district.

9

Baronkarl played many musical instruments and often delighted people with his music. That is, those who *wanted* to be delighted. The children in particular would run after him, just as they allegedly did with dear old Augustine who, however, never existed. But Baronkarl, he really did live. He was without a doubt flesh and blood. He set his hat down in front of him, but he would never use the money the passers-by threw in for himself.

Now, he would call out to the children, who among you hasn't had anything to eat today? And who among you hasn't had anything to drink today or nibbled on anything sweet? Then he would empty out his hat, put it on, and lead the way. To the bakery for bread, the pub for pop, and the confectionery for snacks.

He supposedly often peeled potatoes for the egg lady. Pounds of potatoes, which would earn him a big pot of soup. He didn't eat that by himself, however. He would drag it out into the yard, and they'd be waiting for him there, under the elm tree. Who would like some, he would ask, and then serve up the soup with a huge ladle. The poor and the unemployed would fill their canteens. For dessert Baronkarl would tell jokes. Of course, this kind of private soup kitchen was much more popular than the one in the monastery.

A kind soul once gave him a suit. Given the way Baronkarl looked, with his jacket and pants patched innumerable times, he took pity on him. Baronkarl tried on the suit. He looked decidedly proper in it.

He politely thanked him, took his old things under his arm, and went. But when the munificent donor ran into him two days later, Baronkarl looked the way he always did. Baronkarl, the fellow asked, what have you done with that beautiful suit? Well, Baronkarl replied, I met someone who was even poorer than I.

10

Back when I was a schoolboy, a pensioner recounts, I often met Baronkarl on the way to school. Every morning he would be tipping the kegs in front of the beer hall in the Buchengasse. In all honesty, at first he seemed a little weird to me, with his great big slouch hat, his greasy coat, and his bristly beard. But despite his odd, seedy appearance, I gradually realized that he was harmless, even good-natured.

The other children were yelling after him, and so I joined them. Karl, we would call, play something for us! And for a while he acted as though he hadn't heard anything. Then all of a sudden he would turn around on his heels, pull a comb or harmonica out of his bulging coat pocket, and make music like a faun. Or dance and drum on a pot.

But just as suddenly as he had begun to make music and a din, he stopped. Then he would sit down where he had just been standing, cross his legs, and prop his chin up with his hands. Now leave me alone, he would say softly, I have to think. And slowly we went on our way.

From the front he looked clever, like Till Eulenspiegel, but from the side always a bit philosophical, almost like Socrates. He surely had something of a Greek philosopher whose time had already passed or a Viennese Action Artist whose time had not yet come. Every once in a while he would stick cigarette butts in his ears and wiggle his lower jaw, which would make us laugh. But when Baronkarl was serious he was very serious and often made a truly dignified impression.

11

Karl's relationship to the police was not bad.

Most policemen knew and appreciated Karl as a real character. Nevertheless, sometimes a young, overzealous patrolman (or someone new to that line of work) would harass him. And, even though he caused quite a commotion, arrest him.

When he would show up at the station with a collared Karl, however, his colleagues would just laugh.

That's quite a catch you got there, you fool!

Don't you know who that is? That's Karl Báron, you know. You can't treat him like that. Now let him go immediately!

Occasionally, Karl would purposely set out to be arrested, and that went like this:

During very cold winters it was too cold even for him. Usually someone would invite him in. But every now and then he didn't have any luck.

What did he do then? He stood in front of the police station and started fiddling in the night. Not very melodiously, although he was certainly capable of that, but extremely wretchedly, a real caterwaul.

And what happened then? At first, nothing at all happened. But soon people started complaining from every window. Hence, the police had to do something and so, for their part, looked out their windows.

What's the matter, Baronkarl, they would ask. Is it too cold for you? Then come join us inside.

Baronkarl was a proud man, you know. He never would have admitted that it was too cold for him.

You think *I'm* cold?, he would reply. I was cuddling up with polar bears when *you* were still in diapers!

Answers like that annoy the police. The station window was shut again.

Karl Baron, however, continued fiddling. Dreadfully. Fierce cursing streamed from the windows. Little by little the whole quarter was awake.

Then a policeman would slip into his coat and go out into the snow to fetch Karl.

That's how Karl came to spend many a night at the police station for disturbing the peace.

Johnny (1)

Outside a seedy character shuffles by. Greasy hat, long, patched coat, a coal sack on his back. His left eye and mouth droop. He drools a bit, mutters and curses to himself.

Who's that?

Oh, him. That's hunchback Johnny. A "Sandler."

Like Baronkarl?

What do you mean? The teacher laughs.

Honestly, there's no comparison at all!

12

An innkeeper on the Laaerberg supposedly offered Baronkarl lodging. Baronkarl, he's supposed to have said, I have an empty storeroom. Would you like to move in? And Baronkarl consented to the proposal; it was a harsh winter. He came trudging through the snow with his things.

Of which there were not very many. People talk of two canteens, a stack of old newspapers, a penknife, and a piece of indelible lead. He used to hide all of that in his receptacle. Apart from the duds he used to wear.

Baronkarl would brush off the snow and enter the parlor. He would remove his shoes and air out his feet. And the innkeeper himself schlepped an iron stove into the storeroom. And the innkeeper's wife made a cozy fire for him.

At first, Baronkarl felt right at home in his new dwelling. Would sit there and mend his shoes, repair his coat. Would look out his transom window and follow the snowflakes. Or would read his newspapers and mark them with his indelible pencil.

In the guest room next to his he made himself at home. He won quite a few tricks playing cards. The innkeeper, good soul that he was, would often buy him a drink. And his wife spent a lot of time chatting with Karl.

The innkeeper's wife supposedly found Baronkarl quite appealing as a man. With his graying beard, Baronkarl was not at all unattractive, even if he was a bit short and stout. As soon as he was washed and had uttered a few fine words, something he supposedly was very adept at . . . But those are all rumors and, for the sake of discretion, we don't want to follow up on them.

Soon Karl grew restless in his storeroom. Pacing back and forth like a caged animal in the zoo. From the door to the transom window and back again. Constantly back and forth, despite the fact that the room was so small. He didn't show up in the guest room any more. The guests would ask whether he was sick. The innkeeper and his wife would shake their heads. Karl was simply a complicated eccentric.

Then one day he was gone. And didn't reappear in the area for a long time. The innkeeper and his wife would call for him, but soon stopped on account of the cold.

13

Another innkeeper wanted to hire Karl to sing in his wine garden. As has been said, Karl was not at all unmusical and he enjoyed singing. Besides, he is said to have known some very old songs, ones that otherwise would have been long forgotten.

So the innkeeper placed a harmonica around Baronkarl's neck and a couple bottles of beer in front of him. And Baronkarl closed his eyes and searched for a melody. People stopped their talking and moved closer. They sat around and waited. Then Baronkarl started to sing (or rather speak) in his very husky voice. And when he was singing (or rather speaking) even the schmaltziest songs lost all of their schmaltz. In between he would take big swigs from the rapidly emptying beer bottles. The people applauded, but Baronkarl didn't hear them at all.

His thoughts must have been elsewhere when, for instance, inverting the "correct" text, he would sing about how his father had *not* been a landlord and had *not* been a silk manufacturer. When he sang about his *two spirited horses* you could, they say, hardly take him for some fine chauffeur, but more likely a manure transporter. That, at any rate, was more authentic. And if someone said: Baronkarl, play this or that song for me, as if Baronkarl were just any old musician playing for money (he never did take a cent for singing or playing), he would pay no attention to him. Or else he would say: first I'll play what I want, then there will be a long break, and then *maybe* you'll hear what you want . . .

The fact that Karl stopped singing and playing for this particular innkeeper, rumor has it, is connected to a police action. You see, the guy increasingly sang and played songs he shouldn't have been singing or playing back then. It was around '34. And who knows what would happen if he were to do so today. Who will sweep our streets now? – was, for example, one of the questions that kept repeating in one of his refrains (supposedly dating from '18 or maybe even from '48 of the previous century). And the answer – Yes, the noble gentlemen with the gold stars, they'll be sweeping our streets now – yes, this answer supposedly resulted at least in his being reprimanded for failing to possess a music license and being ordered to shut up.

14

Many say Baronkarl was an artist in his youth. Painted pictures and perhaps even wrote poems as well. Once he submitted a poem to a newspaper, but received neither the poem nor a response in return. On another occasion he showed a fat gallery owner one of his paintings, but got nowhere.

From that point on Baronkarl did without the necessary public exposure. Lived his art in a different way or turned his life into art. Is he the same person as the Anker bread factory painter that so many speak about? His story, at any rate, goes like this:

During the period of high unemployment there was a painter on the Laaerberg. He, the one who's telling me about him tells me, would only paint the Anker bread factory. The Anker bread factory as seen from the Absberggasse, the Anker bread factory as seen from the Urselbrunnengasse. The Anker bread factory as seen from the lower-middle-class garden plots, the Anker bread factory as seen from the storage yards.

And, you know, the one who's telling me about the painter on the Laaerberg tells me, the Anker bread factory is as hideous as the work inside it. It stands there like the fortress of some robber baron, like some haunted castle from a bygone era. And it is, you know, like some sort of ghost, he thinks, the way it stands there like that, a relic. That's right, he says, a relic from the time when the fortresses of the robber barons weren't as well camouflaged as they are today.

If he, the Anker bread factory painter, had painted something beautiful, like a landscape, for instance, he could have earned a lot of money. Even or especially back then, with all that unemployment. For the poor, to be sure, were even poorer then, but the rich were perhaps even richer than usual. And one of them would have bought one of his paintings for a tidy sum. But the Anker bread factory painter would only paint the Anker bread factory. Sometimes a few people would stand around in a circle and watch him paint. Why, master, they would frequently ask him, do you only paint the Anker bread factory? But the Anker bread factory painter was not a loquacious person.

Instead of providing an answer, once or twice he would tell the story of the Fujiyama painter. For as long as he painted, the Fujiyama painter only painted Fujiyama. Rich people would come to him wanting to buy a Fujiyama from him. At your service, he would say, and pick up his brush. And then, as if by magic, he would produce Fujiyama on the canvas in a jiffy. With one single stroke, in less than one single minute. The rich people would look on in amazement and ask what it cost. The Fujiyama painter named his price. But Mr. Fujiyama painter, the rich people would reply, that's too much. Such a price for one single minute of painting Fujiyama! Then the Fujiyama painter would smile and open a door. And behind the door were countless Fujiyamas. I *needed* to paint all those Fujiyamas in order *to be able* to paint this one. That's what the Fujiyama painter would say. So the rich people had to be reasonable. And reached for their fat wallets and bought a Fujiyama from the Fujiyama painter. And he continued to paint Fujiyamas. And, if he hasn't died, is still painting today.

That's exactly the case, the Anker bread factory painter supposedly claimed, with the Anker bread factories I paint. But, in fact, that wasn't the case at all, since no one came to buy an Anker bread factory from him. Maybe, he who's telling me about the Anker bread factory painter philosophizes, maybe that's due to the difference between the Anker bread factory and Fujiyama. Fujiyama is a landscape, but the Anker bread factory is nothing but a pile of worthless junk.

No one knows why the Anker bread factory painter would only paint the Anker bread factory and nothing else. Many say that maybe he once worked in the Anker bread factory. Others think that he probably *wanted* to work in the Anker bread factory. It was, as has been said, a period of high unemployment, so all sorts of things were possible. In any case, one day he disappeared. Nobody knows why or where. Maybe he died. Or it simply no longer gave him any pleasure to paint the Anker bread factory. Or he realized how senseless it was.

Rumor has it, however, that they cured him of his painting. Not painting *per se*, but painting the Anker bread factory. Over time, his painting the Anker bread factory grew eerie for the people in the Anker bread factory. The movers and shakers there, but also those who shake what gets moved.

The latter certainly could have given the Anker bread factory painter a licking. And from what one hears, they did do so a couple of times. The others, however, the movers and shakers, had other possibilities. And in the end they also realized them.

Since then, he who's telling me this story tells me, nobody has ever painted the Anker bread factory again. Neither as seen from the Urselbrunnengasse nor as seen from the Absberggasse, neither as seen from the lower-middle-class garden plots nor as seen from the storage yards. And surely, he thinks, no one will ever paint it again. It is, you know, hideous, he concludes, like the work inside it.

15

One day a distinguished gentleman who had heard a lot about Baronkarl came to visit him. Where is this curious individual, he inquired, who lives in a garbage can? I would like to ask him something. So they led him to Baronkarl, who had just crawled out. It was early in the morning. And he was standing there in his long underwear and shaking out his garment.

The distinguished gentleman turned up his nose and looked intently at Baronkarl through his glasses. And cleared his throat so that Baronkarl would pay some attention to him. Baronkarl, the distinguished gentleman said from his clean suit, how do you manage? Living all the time in such filth, for so long, like some sort of vermin.

You see, Baronkarl replied, every morning I shake off my dirt. My dirt is external. It's all around me, but not inside me. And my relationship to fleas and bugs is clear: they suck the blood out of people like me. That's the difference between us.

For you, dear sir, in your clean linen, are you aware of all the dirt you're living in? And can you shake it off every morning? And are you sure you're not a bloodsucker?

16

Another gentleman, with a heavy watch fob hanging on his gut, supposedly visited Baronkarl one day. You know, Baronkarl, he said, I find you incredibly appealing. The way you cast all of us and our satiation in doubt. You know, Baronkarl, I think that's just great.

When he, the gentleman, came to that rather elevated word "satiation" he patted himself on the gut. And his watch fob rattled along with the money in his jacket. It's important to remember that at that particular time virtually no one was sated. Except, as usual, a few at the expense of the many.

Now, Baronkarl, he said, you listen to me. You see, Baronkarl, I'm going to make a proposition. You're an intelligent person, right? Therefore, I'm going to give you an opportunity to earn some money. He set a rather old bottle of wine at Baronkarl's feet. At this point Baronkarl was sitting on his receptacle, dangling his feet. The gentleman with the watch fob waited for Baronkarl to pick up the wine bottle. And waited for Baronkarl to say something.

Baronkarl, however, just dangled his feet and looked at the sun. In the Tenth District, you see, the sun sets a beautiful red. You, the gentleman with the watch fob said, will just do what you always do. Except that you'll write about it, for my journal.

As he said that, the gentleman with the watch fob was standing between Baronkarl and the beautiful red sun. Baronkarl, however, wanted to see the beautiful red sun as it was setting and not the gentleman with the watch fob. But in order to do that he would have had to be able to see through him – but his father wasn't a glazier. So Baronkarl did, in fact, look at him, and said to him: Please get out of my sun.

Baronkarl was Baronkarl, and that was that.
Being Baronkarl, however, sufficed for Karl.
People really liked Karl as Baronkarl.
As Baronkarl Karl was able to live.

And so Karl lived his life,
And people accepted that.
I'm honored, many would greet him,
And for many it was an honor to greet Karl.

17

What did Baronkarl do in '34?

Around Building 24B on Quellenstrasse people were shooting. The workers were entrenched behind trash cans, and everyone had run out of bread . . .

He certainly didn't join in the fighting. No, that wasn't his way. He probably just withdrew into his receptacle.

Many, however, claim to have seen and heard the music he was making right at that time. From the floodplain beyond the Danube you could hear the artillery. Then all of a sudden it grew very quiet. And over and over again he would play the Blue Danube Waltz on his violin, altering the text, however:

The Danube's so blue. The Danube's so red. The Danube's so black. And in just a little while: the Danube's so brown.

18

Even though it was a beautiful day Baronkarl once headed down Favoritenstrasse into town with an open umbrella. With great concentration he looked at the points of his worn and frequently mended shoes and counted his steps. A growing group of children and other curious people walked behind him. Karl, they asked him, what exactly are you doing? But instead of answering them, Karl just shook his head and put his finger to his mouth.

Hence, interest in his action increased. As he approached the Südtirolerplatz he was dragging along a crowd like the Pied Piper of Hamelin. So a policeman, who was probably fearing some sort of unemployment demonstration, stood in Karl's way. For God's sake, Karl, he called. What are you doing? Don't bring disaster upon the entire Tenth District!

Two thousand three hundred ninety-four, Baronkarl, gently pushing the policeman aside, calmly continues to count. Two thousand three hundred ninety-five, two thousand three hundred ninety-six . . . Can anyone among you tell me approximately how long one step is? One step, a few clever schoolchildren exclaim, one step measures approximately three-quarters of a meter. Thank you, Baronkarl replies, collapsing his umbrella. Now I can finally figure out how long Favoritenstrasse is.

Johnny (2)

Hunchback Johnny stands at the fence of the beer garden and watches. The barkeep at the Nettles puts a beer on the table. Over her shoulder she keeps an eye on Johnny. Get out of here, you creep, she says. Get lost!

But Johnny doesn't understand, doesn't want to understand. He's drooling out of the corner of his mouth. He's babbling. Toothless. The words remain unclear. But apparently they're not meant maliciously.

Take off, you unappealing thing, the barkeep rants.

Johnny listens, tilting his head. Maybe he's deaf.

The barkeep pours a bucket of filthy water on him.

Now scram, you idiot! Before you chase all my customers away.

What happened to Baronkarl under Hitler?
In response to that question many just shrug their shoulders.
Whatever became of him under the Nazis?
In response to that question most people just shake their heads.

Karl simply survived Hitler,
But we really don't know how.
Karl simply outlasted the Nazi period,
But no one knows exactly how he managed to do so.

We do know what happened to the gypsies on the Laaerberg back then.
And we do know what happened to the deserters from Rudolfshügel back then.
We do know what happened to the Jewish perfumer from the Reumannplatz back then.
And we do know what happened to the Mongoloid child from the Troststrasse back then.

But we never really thought about
What became of that rascal Baronkarl back then.
In all honesty, we never really cared about
What might have happened to old happy-go-lucky Baronkarl back then.

19

People tell the story of how, in March '38 (so many, they say, were suddenly wearing swastikas on their lapels and even in Favoriten they had smashed the windows of Jewish stores and forced the proprietors, along with their wives and children, to scrub the sidewalks), Baronkarl was walking around with a lantern in broad daylight. He shined his light directly into the faces of those who were merely observing the events (the light illuminated their foreheads, parts of their noses and mouths and, particularly intensively, their eyes) which, in turn, they say, so upset so many people that, without even asking him exactly what he meant with all this, they quickly took off. One of them, however, a courageous man, at least dared to pose the question, and Baronkarl, holding the lamp at his side, gave him a response. I'm searching for human beings, he supposedly said, and the answer struck the other man as somehow familiar, but he didn't know exactly why.

20

Baronkarl thus survived the Nazi period. No one is completely clear on how he did so. Many say that he remained in hiding for a while. Others claim that he simply stayed where and how he was. A homeless man, having just returned from winter vacation in jail, knows a different version: Karl was an inhabitant of the men's shelter back then.

Had, he says, the likes of Baronkarl and him not been officially registered as living someplace, they would have ended up in a concentration camp. And since they were clever, he says, they preferred serving time in the shelter to making lamp shades in the camps, not to mention anything worse. Matzl, for instance, another garbage picker who, back in the good old days, used to let you spit in his mouth for a few cents in front of the gate to St. Anthony's Church, well, the Nazis had barely arrived and they carted Matzl off. And that poor devil hadn't really done anything except march behind the soldiers, salute, etc. In other words, just repeat for them the entire nonsense they had just shown him, but they didn't appreciate that.

Baronkarl, someone else says, was, while still alive, placed under historic preservation. Even the SS-Standartenführer had respect for him. Since his entire life took place in the streets it was impossible to snatch him inconspicuously. Moreover, Baronkarl was able to say things back then that no one else dared to. And he did, in fact, say them.

Once, even though it caused a great stir, they arrested and interrogated him on suspicion of high treason. During the interrogation, however, he freely admitted to having actually said the things they were accusing him of. So why did you say that, man?!, they screamed at him. But Baronkarl simply smiled slightly in return. And said in response: I am a fool, you know!

Supposedly it was also Baronkarl who, in the end, came up with the name Bierleiter Gaukel for Gauleiter Pürkel. And Baronkarl made a joke, which all of Vienna was soon telling, about Pürkel's parting words to the Viennese: I'll return when the lilacs come back in bloom, mark my words! Ever since Gaukel made that promise, Karl supposedly said, the majority of Viennese have been cutting down their lilac bushes. To date, however, it seems they've replanted a large number of them, but Baronkarl, who probably would respond dubiously to the situation and have something caustic to say about it, is dead.

21

In general, they say, Baronkarl got along well with the occupying Soviet soldiers. Since many of them loved music and children they often came to a standstill when he would play his fiddle. To be sure, he, Karl, was no spring chicken any more, and every now and then, while sitting in front of his trash receptacle, he would simply doze off. But he still played his music and made people happy.

Sometimes he would even serenade the Russians. Would play something like "Black Eyes," causing them to laugh and applaud. And if he played "Evening Bells" they would grow sad. They would cry and think of him as a brother.

Only once did he allegedly almost have an argument with one of them, and that went like this: A Russian spoke of the Tolbuchinstrasse, where Baronkarl was supposed to go to pick up a loaf of bread that had been reserved especially for him in the USIA shop. I don't know of any Tolbuchinstrasse, Karl replied. I only know the Laxenburgerstrasse, whose name comes from the fact that it leads to Laxenburger Castle. I don't know any Tolbuchinstrasse.

Look, Towarisch, the Russian replied. From now on the Laxenburgerstrasse is called the Tolbuchinstrasse, named in honor of our glorious Marshall Tolbuchin. Glorious Marshall Tolbuchin led the Red Army in their march on Vienna. And the Red Army brought you freedom.

Freedom, Karl said skeptically. Freedom? If, brother, you mean to say that you got rid of the Nazis for us, then you're right. But no one can *bring* someone freedom. Freedom is something you have inside you. Or not.

Baronkarl died after the war.
He walked out of the pub, went to cross the street,
And was killed and dragged by a car.
Baronkarl was an old man at the time.

All of Favoriten attended his funeral.
Scores of women shed tears.
The priest gave a nice talk.
You could read about Baronkarl in the paper.

But it didn't suit him
To wear a white shirt and tie, they say.
And he could do without
A bank account and a big inheritance, the story goes.

Johnny (3)

And what about hunchback Johnny?

Yesterday I saw a policeman kicking him. He hasn't been around at all today. What's happened to him?

Oh well, the Latin teacher says, hunchback Johnny.

If I'm telling you about Baronkarl, then let me tell you about Baronkarl. Don't distract me.

22

Many say that Baronkarl isn't dead at all, but that he reappears from time to time, here and there. Just yesterday they saw him walking around the district. And, in fact, time and again there are individuals in and around Vienna who are pretty similar to Baronkarl. The actor, for instance, who, speaking the finest theatrical German, allegedly reported every evening to the police station in the Erdberg section of town before he went to sleep under the Stadium Bridge. Or that dialect poet who, dressed in long underwear tied at the knees, was sleeping up until a year ago in the backhoes that are slowly removing the southern parts of the Laaerberg from us.

Many also claim that Baronkarl is hanging out in the Laaerberg. His beard keeps growing until it just can't get any longer. But before they completely level the Laaerberg, he, Karl Báron, will arise and walk.

23

The one who wrote these stories, by the way, supposedly amounted to absolutely nothing. On the trail of Baronkarl, they say, he grew more and more like him with each passing day. At first, as has been said, he still looked pretty reputable. Long-haired, bearded, but certainly well-groomed. But the more time he spent on Baronkarl the more severely he neglected himself. And such an outward transformation is often accompanied by an internal one. In the beginning he merely thought of Baronkarl as an interesting, perhaps even curious, case. But gradually Baronkarl became a role model for him. Or lured him in.

Compulsively, so to speak, he grew to resemble the character he was writing about.

There are, you know, people who spend too much time with the Bible. And one morning they wake up and think they're Jesus.

If he had led a somewhat bourgeois existence prior to his involvement with Baronkarl's story, then there was no chance of that afterwards. Or did it take some time? – Oh well, many involvements, as you know, have long-term effects. He, at any rate, just cast aside the little secure employment he still had. Left his wife and child and moved out of his nice, well-furnished, two-room-plus-kitchen-and-bath apartment into, many say, a cask.

Even if the part about the cask may be exaggerated, he has, as they say, become downwardly mobile. I don't need any of that, he supposedly proclaimed; Baronkarl didn't need any of that either.

He idealized Baronkarl. Baronkarl was a dropout. Baronkarl was a refuser. Baronkarl was the original Yippie.

The people on the Laaerberg didn't take the reporter seriously any more. Sure, when he arrived there with a television crew to make a film about Baronkarl they were impressed. But later, when he appeared with his thinning hair and his thickening beard, his disheveled coat and his baggy pants, all of which were fluttering in the strong wind, they laughed maliciously. Here comes that crazy writer, they would say, and avoid him.

It's unclear where he ended up.

Maybe he drank himself silly. Maybe they committed him to an institution. Maybe both.

They've completely paved over the Laaerberg. The Committee for Beautification did away with anything that didn't fit in.

It's no wonder that, in the course of such actions, someone like him would disappear.

Translated by Craig Decker

FELIX MITTERER 1981

Inventory

A plastic font for holy water, with a relief depicting Saint Dominic. A box for firewood; upon it, two bottles of dish detergent; a small plastic bucket for table scraps; a dirty plate; a spoon; a pot with leftover rice pudding. A stoneware saltcellar decorated with flowers. An electric stove, which can also burn wood; a steamer upon it; hanging from a pole on the stove a poker and a dish towel; above the stove a lamp, lit, without a shade; below the stove wood chips for kindling and a pair of high, lined winter shoes. A galvanized washbasin with a faucet for cold water; above it a mirror, partially clouded on the edges, and bathroom supplies; on a nail beside them two tattered hand towels. A brown wall hanging, depicting a bellowing buck and two does in a glade. A refrigerator; upon it, an empty wine bottle; a half-empty bottle of raspberry juice; a pot; several glasses. A niche in devotion to the Virgin Mary with a wooden Madonna; to the right of it a smaller, white plastic Mary shining in the darkness; in the black base an eye, looking into it towards the light you can see a tiny slide of Maria Taferl, a place of pilgrimage. A window with floral curtains, drawn shut. A radio; a white floral lace doily upon it, upon that a candle with a molded three-dimensional image depicting two inhabitants of the desert riding camels. A record player from the postwar period; three dusty albums upon it, their titles: This is Tyrol; Musical Greetings from Tyrol; The Merry Boys of Oberkrain. A niche in devotion to the Lord's passion and suffering with a crucifix; a few branches of catkin behind it; a small bouquet of everlastings below it; to the left and right two small plastic angels, also serving as candleholders. A print with the inscription: *Don't cause this marriage any grief, our time together is much too brief.* A wrought-iron wall clock with ornamental hands. A framed photograph, showing a serious-looking young man in a German *Wehrmacht* uniform standing in front of a doorway chalked with the initials of the Magi. A framed memorial card with a photograph of a stern-looking old woman whose hair is braided on top of her head, the text: *In Christian memory of our beloved mother, grandmother, and great grandmother, Frau Katharina Sailer, house owner in Zell am Ziller, who, after a long and serious illness and having received last rites, died on September 3, 1970 at the age of eighty-four. May she rest in peace. Children, I must leave you, / Your father I must meet. / You, too, will know life's trials / And moments bittersweet. / Trust in the heavenly Father, / Gather in His light, / He will reunite us / In heaven ever bright.* An additional framed memorial card with a photograph of a friendly-looking old man with a white mustache, the text: *In Christian memory of my beloved husband, our good father and foster father, Herr Michael Kogler, who, after a long and serious illness and having received last rites, died on November 10, 1976 at the age of eighty-two. Our time with you was all too brief. / God called you to eternal peace, / The bonds of suffering He did release.* A framed certificate of honor; the text: *Certificate of honor for Herr Michael Kogler, Kirchberg Community Band. The State Association of Tyrolean Brass Bands has informed the State Government of your more than sixty-year membership in a brass band. In thankful recognition of your long-standing public service on behalf of our homeland. (Signed) Wallnöfer, Head of the Tyrolean State Government. Innsbruck, November 22, 1970.* A framed photograph, showing a friendly-looking boy of about five, wearing lederhosen and a little Tyrolean hat. A calendar featuring paintings by handicapped artists; displaying the week of March 20-26, 1978 and a picture of a chick with Easter eggs and flowers. A bench built into the corner with a red plastic cover; stacked in the corner embroidered pillows. A table with a red-and-white checked plastic tablecloth; upon it: a bowl with bananas and oranges; an opened glasses case; The Kitzbühel Gazette – the weekly paper for the Kitzbühel region, from Saturday, March 25, 1978; above the table a lamp, off, with a blue floral glass shade. Two chairs with cushions. A window with floral curtains, drawn shut; on the windowsill: a bottle of plant food; a deck of cards; a package of bird food; a container of bird powder – insecticide. A brown chest; upon it: five potted plants; a cage with two ornamental Japanese birds, one of which is almost featherless. A sideboard; on the top half: a sugar bowl; a coffee canister; a box of filters; room deodorizer; a bottle with steeping arnica blossoms; on the bottom half: a floral breadbox; knitting needles and yarn; a pair of gray wool mittens; a jar of metholated rub; a liniment for aching joints; a dozen vials of pills and tinctures; a white plastic container for dentures; a package of fast acting, two-phase denture cleaner; The Tyrolean Daily News from Saturday, March 25, 1978; Rupertus – the journal of the Archdiocese of Salzburg, from Palm Sunday,

March 19, 1978; an issue of SPARE TIME – The Big Magazine for Women, from March 9, 1978, cover picture: Farah Diba, text: *Marvelous Color Pictures – Farah Diba in India / Unbelievable: Defenseless Cat Threatened with Murder / Poor Margaret – Is Roddy Just Using Her? / Fashion: Return of the Petticoat*; an issue of SPARE TIME from June 24, 1976, cover picture: King Carl XVI Gustav of Sweden and Silvia Sommerlath, daughter of a middle-class German family, text: *The Latest Story! – The Wedding of the Century!*; three romance novels, their titles: *On the Trail of the Poacher (Hearts as Hard as Rocks), Tragedy of an Ibex (A Passion for Hunting Destroys a Life), The Secret of the Beautiful Doctor's Wife (Will She Confide in Dr. Frank?)*; two crossword puzzle magazines; a crossword dictionary; a brochure for a bus trip; a mail-order department store catalogue; the catalogue of a mail-order florist. Wedged between the glass and the frame of the upper half of the sideboard: a postcard of twilight in the ALAM-KUH-TAKAHT-E-SULEIMAN range (15,880 ft.), Central Elbrus, Iran; stamp imprint: *With thanks to all of our sponsors, friends, and supporters and with hearty greetings from our field of operations, Iran tour 1975* – two signatures; several cards with Easter greetings, for example: *Wishing you a blessed Easter with all our love, the Klotz family. Thank you for the card. We wish you a speedy recovery. – How are you doing with the wood? Were you able to split it? Not much new with us. Siegfried has started building a house and Seppi is getting married, so we'll be alone again. But that's how it is for everyone. – Maybe I'll come to visit. Love, Traudl . . . from Kathi. I can well understand that you miss Michael. It's no different for me since my Robert passed away. But your husband suffered so, now he's at peace. But it's hard when you don't have anyone any more, I know. Love, – . . . Wishing you much joy and peace, love, Sylvia. Now we're in the middle of spring cleaning and on Thursday I have to go to the rectory to clean the chalices. Many greetings*; also wedged there: a bus schedule; the completed entry form for a grocery store contest, the prizes: three coffee sets; part of a postal money order from the insurance agency for workers' pensions, dated March 1, 1978, in the amount of 3,029.20 Austrian Schillings. A black-and-white television set, turned on, the name of the program: The Best of Music is Trump – Highlights From Your Television Request Concert, hosted by Peter Frankenfeld; featuring performances of the following songs: *Springtime in Vienna; Today the Angels are Vacationing in Vienna; Vienna, Vienna, City of My Dreams; The Tennessee Waltz; Bonanza; When the Sun Shines in Texas; It*

Should Rain Red Roses for Me; *This Thing Just Doesn't Work Without Men*; *Darling, My Heart Sends You Greetings*; *A Night in Monte Carlo*; *As Beautiful as Today*; *Show Me the Place in the Sun*; *Climb Aboard the Ship of Love*; *All of Paris is Dreaming of Love*; *That's the Magic of Paris*; *This is the Parisian Tango*; *Here's a Man*; *The Little Pub*; *It's Best in Bed*; *Powidltaschkerln from Beautiful Czechoslovakia*; *Back When Bohemia Was Still Part of Austria*; *Last Night I Danced in My Dreams*; *With a Bit of Luck*; *That's the Way it is With Me*; *Happy is He Who Can Forget What Can't be Changed*.

Translated by Craig Decker

ELISABETH REICHART

1992

The Sunday Roast

It began and had no ending on the ritualized Sundays, after dinner, after the women had gone into the kitchen with the dishes, while the uncles, grandfathers, and fathers stayed at the table with the children . . .

it began after the women had cleared the table, the coffee had been served, the wait for a pipe, chewing tobacco, cigar had ended, after they lit those tobacco products and their saliva became brown . . .

it began, the hunt of the men after the lost years which could not be lost, which were the best years of their lives, confessions in the good room that was open to its owners only on Sunday, nowhere else these words, locked up all week long, like pressure cookers that boiled over on a regular basis . . .

it began or had never ended in the fifties, in a village in Austria, in the good room, Sundays, that the men complained without end and kept alive their yearning for what was their youth, which for them had become one with the great murdering. It had left behind its traces, although they didn't pursue these traces, only those of comradeship, the trenches, narrow escapes, furloughs from the front, the unfulfilled hope that life would always mean this almost unbearable suspense. It was the war that had become their measure for a future they wanted no part of . . .

it began with opening their treasure chest, as they tugged and pulled out the few adventures that had to fill up time – that whore, who leaves you, alone, with your semen spilled for nothing . . .

it began with the war that wasn't over in their heads, that they had believed in as they would believe in nothing again, only one escape from this disappointment, to jump Sundays into the years before it, never into the years after it. What a shallow replacement to be called the "reconstruction generation." Naturally they had reconstructed, lent a hand where it was necessary, but how much more exciting the destruction had been. Compared to the war years, the reconstruction years were dog years, not worth mentioning . . .

it began in the years after, which just happened to be our childhood years, but they certainly couldn't be bothered about that too, about these brats who sat with them, seven of us, seven children with no experience and no idea of the war. What will become of them – nothing came of us, although everything came of us . . .

it began with the sentence: If you don't work you don't eat either, which was applied to each of us children by turns or jointly, which banned us from the dinner table into the corner, where we had nothing of the roast – it had to be a roast on Sundays – just the smell . . .

it began with the other sentence, that once, one single time in life, work was fun, when they had foreign workers and concentration camp inmates to order about and to whom they could relegate the dirty work. Ever since then life was pain and trouble, and it really wasn't worth it anymore . . .

it began in the late sixties when they finally had guest workers to order about again, but they didn't call them "guest workers." The old word is good enough. This was something they could be happy about and laugh about at the beer table, something they could brag about to others . . .

it began with the end of their wisdom, with their warning: Just don't ever attract attention to yourself. Do that and you're lost. In such sentences they betrayed their knowledge, their fear betrayed them, they betrayed their children so as to cherish the war that had eavesdropped on their nights. The murderers shadowed their steps . . .

it began with the secret thoughts, with the fact that curiosity had deserted their bodies and taken questions with it, questions which, if encountered again in their children, only roused them to prohibitions or cynicism. The present had the size of a Sunday roast, and over afternoon coffee the future was spilled with scorn and alcohol into their insatiable stomachs, unfilled by the emptiness into which they had strayed . . .

it began during dinner, while serving the Sunday roast, the nice big pieces for the men, the smaller gristly ones for the women, a few scraps or not even that for the children who served the heroes returning home and the heroines who never left home as the dung heap, right in the middle of the good room, without possibility for escape . . .

it began in the morning; it began in the evening and knew no day of rest; the war was continued, and it had no end, no end . . .

Translated by Linda C. DeMeritt

ELISABETH REICHART   1992

How Far is Mauthausen?

It is now three o'clock.

I have one more hour for myself. They're coming in an hour: Herr Pichler and Frau Worm.

Herr Pichler called me and asked me for an interview. He didn't immediately say what he wanted to learn from me. I thought perhaps it was a mistake. Wanted to believe it was a mistake. And had to think that it wasn't very long ago that I was arranging interviews with women resistance fighters.

"But you do come from this region . . ."

Behind every hill another hill, gentle hills, but the stone: granite, barren soil, part-time farmers, commuters, harsh climate, the Danube, the Gusen, the rushing stream, cold water, forest, then nothing but forest, fruit trees lining the paths and as boundary markers between the fields, windfalls, plums, poppy seed suckers, a big old walnut tree, a stone wall with ferns, the biggest ferns of the finest green, small towns, scattered farms, village inns.

". . . You must have a lot to say about Mauthausen."

One hill, this one hill, only it.

Herr Pichler also used the word *home*. "But this is your home" – or something like that. My answer, an immediate no. Herr Pichler presumed a mix-up. "But you do come from this region." Yes. That satisfied him.

As early as the first grade we snickered at this word: *homeland*. – Just one indication that it must have started early, the mistrust, of this word. Snickering – no words. Perhaps my home is silence. Which could be cracked. By any little thing. And a child heard the sparse sentences and heard the suspended sentences and hears and hears . . .

It was a mistake to say yes.

They're doing their job. Like I did my job. A call. An appointment. The prepared questionnaire and beyond that questions, questions. How many interviews will they need for their broadcast? This one with me is one of many for them. I, on the other hand, close my books and pull the piece of paper from the typewriter and sit there and stare blankly into space.

A broadcast about the concentration camps in Austria. (In my thoughts I correct Herr Pichler: It should be called a broadcast about the concentration camp Mauthausen and its satellite camps: fifty of them. Sometimes, when I look for a place on the road map of Austria, the other names disappear, and only Mauthausen remains, and fifty lines spread out from it – Austria is covered by Mauthausen.)

I imagine how Herr Pichler and Frau Worm will go through the narrow kitchen into my study, how I will offer them something to drink, how they will try to be relaxed, perhaps want to chat about our common friend who told them of me, laugh, joke . . . And I will smile along, tense, and light one cigarette after the next.

Not until much later does it occur to me that I not only come from this region, but that I also worked in Mauthausen. I had forgotten about my time working in Mauthausen.

For a year and a half I guided school classes through the former concentration camp Mauthausen.

That was four years ago.

Herr Pichler called me the day before yesterday. Since his call I am again in Mauthausen.

I quit my job in Mauthausen when I noticed that you can get used to anything – I can get used to anything.

Once – and it was the last time that I tried to talk about this job, it was in a car, after a long day's work, I was tired and so was my colleague – I justified my quitting with precisely these words, dismayed at myself at the same time. I sat next to myself and watched me speak and was angered by my ready-made sentence. Then we spoke about something else.

I didn't think about it again. Not about the sentence and not about the anger.

And now two strangers are coming, and they want to know what Mauthausen means to me, though born after the war. I am afraid of the ready-made sentences. Of the old sentences. I am afraid that this experience did not change during the time of forgetting.

They'll be here soon.

It's a rainy day.

The rainy days in Mauthausen. The sound of the rain on the barracks roof. The wet clothing. The breathing in the room. I hoped that the cold and rain would help the schoolchildren imagine the life of the inmates.

During the time I worked in Mauthausen I wanted to talk about my daily experiences. Some experiences became everyday experiences. Like the sentence: "Boy, the gas chamber is so small." And the disappointment in the face. The friends who dismissed it. Including the historians of the left. They knew all that already. (From behind their desks?) So I was the only one who hadn't known it? The only one for whom the difference between working at a desk and working in the place where the crimes were committed was critical?

Perhaps I just didn't know how to talk about it. I remember one evening at a friend's house, yes, I had to search for words, was hesitant. This was after a schoolgirl had run out of the gas chamber. "I can't stand it," she had cried repeatedly. From some others the names: "show-off," "silly goose," "stupid cow." Then another child said this sentence about her: "She still thinks that her grandparents were gassed for no reason."

Everyone had heard such sentences before. Terrible, yes. Even more terrible when they come from the young. But on the other hand, no wonder. Hadn't I reacted similarly?

So it's just that other place, yet this *just* was once a border, and no other border had ever been stronger.

Until today.

This difference is always there.

I think I was lonely during that time. Silence all around, once laboriously overcome, now I quickly learned it again.

I'm nervous. They'll be here in ten, fifteen minutes.

Depending on how punctual they are.

My first reaction on the telephone was: "I have nothing more to say about that. It's all in the book."

"Just give it a try, please. Nothing is lost if it comes to nothing."

No, nothing is lost. Besides a certain working atmosphere for a completely different topic, nothing is lost.

My thoughts remain in Mauthausen – perhaps it is good after all that I accepted the interview because of this one new realization: How much I was fixated at that time on Mauthausen.

I told these doubts to my boyfriend, who thought that it was arrogance on my part to maintain that I had nothing to say. I could only laugh. And in this laughter I recognized the uncertainty of the women I had interviewed for my book about resistance to fascism. Many had hesitated to agree to an interview. I understand them better now. But the difference between my imagination and their reality still exists.

These two poles in my work at that time – on the one hand my research on resistance to fascism, on the other, my job in the former concentration camp . . .

The sound of Maria's steps in the room next door. At night. She couldn't sleep. I lived with her for several days. During the day we held long discussions about her resistance and her imprisonment in the concentration camp for women at Ravensbrück.

Not many women in Mauthausen. (Not many? The first were four Yugoslavs. They were shot together with forty-six men on the occasion of Hitler's birthday, April 20, 1942. At the end of April 1945, the inmate number 3077 was assigned to a woman. Not until September 9, 1944, did women receive their own numerical series. Each number was distributed just once. But not all women received an inmate number. They were in the main camp as well as in the following satellite camps: Gusen, Hirtenberg, Lenzing, Mittersill, St. Lamprecht, and Amstetten.)

The brothel in Mauthausen. (In June of 1941, Himmler and Pohl visited the concentration camp. At that time Himmler is said to have decided to build a brothel in the main camp and the satellite camp Gusen. The inmates were to build it in their free time. In June of 1942 the one in Mauthausen was finished; in November, the one in Gusen. In the brothels there were ten women each.) Maria knew a woman who, like all the others, was sent from Ravensbrück to Mauthausen. Into the brothel. Who didn't leave the brothel alive.

Maria's sleeplessness and her refusal later to do an additional interview. – I was disappointed. Maria said at that time on the phone: "You still can't begin to imagine how immense this swamp is. You're just a survivor. But you mustn't think of this. Otherwise you aren't even that any more."

Nonetheless, she looked back for several days.

The gray walls, the gray inspection grounds, and that small step from the word *gray* to the word *grave*, and sometimes this place lies beyond time, because the color that appears next to the gray stone table, it can no longer be seen there: gold. The gold teeth.

The quarry – a terrible thought: A stranger comes from the lower road into the quarry, sees the two ponds, stops and thinks, what a nice place for a rest. I have often asked myself if the schoolchildren have enough imagination to think the grass away, to erase all color from their sight and see inmates scuffling with each other for every single blade of grass growing from between the stones. I say goodbye to the schoolchildren. Sometimes the buses wait in the quarry below. I go back up the death stairs alone. I hold a bill for fifty schillings in my hand. A teacher from an agricultural school pressed it into my hand and smiled affably. A girl's class collected money, and the class representative gave me a handful of coins and thanked me on behalf of the class.

Why does that occur to me now?

I was ashamed.

As if every act in this place were a special act.

And it is.

Yes.

It's so.

The shame then to receive money. To be paid anything at all for this job. Even though I had the job in part because I needed money to be able to live, to be able to study.

But just in part.

I had a weekly rhythm.

One week I worked in Mauthausen.

One week I worked on the resistance.

My work on the resistance was not made easier by this interruption.

My work in Mauthausen, however, was. Without this interruption it would have been impossible for me.

Is this thought right?

It would not have been possible in any case for so long.

The first weeks I worked in Mauthausen I lost eight kilograms. Then came the holidays. I could eat nothing there. And in the evening I was too exhausted. At that time I picked up the habit of living off chocolate. It was the only thing that didn't make me sick.

Something else lost its everyday familiarity for me during this time: soap. No information, no report had the same effect as repeating the sentence daily about producing soap from human bones. I was unable to pick up a bar of soap without thinking that people used the word *Judenseife* and thought nothing of it. Today this is merely a memory. Reaching for soap today has become a natural act once again.

The doorbell's ringing. They are very punctual.

Herr Pichler and Frau Worm were here an hour.

Frau Worm said scarcely anything. Frau Worm ran the tape recorder.

He had few questions. Mostly he spoke about the three of us.

I'm tired. It's difficult to do justice to the questions, not to give sweeping answers when the questions posed are sweeping: "Do you think that people today still suppress the past so strongly?"

I am tempted to answer with yes. Studies, statistics – there's proof after all. Then I thought of a school friend I just happened to meet in Mauthausen. She was from the region, and she claimed that no one knew. Together we climbed the hill behind Mauthausen and saw that almost everything could be seen. And I saw that she was capable of seeing.

Herr Pichler forgot his cigarettes. What am I going to do with this pack of cigarettes now? It's almost full.

How difficult it is for me to answer someone who already knows all the answers.

I'm cold.

My fingers are clammy. Sticky. Cold sweat makes them sticky. They don't come off the keys as easily as normal.

I don't want to get up yet again and wash them.

I get up after all. Cut myself a piece of bread. Spread butter on the bread. Place some sausage on top. Make myself a cup of tea to go along with it. The tea warms me. The bread tastes good.

Frau Worm told me briefly that she had been a teacher and had quit after two years. She was incapable of fitting the mold which the schoolchildren expected: those who reward and those who punish. By the age of ten the children already knew that their interests didn't matter; they didn't matter; the only thing that mattered was obedience. She hadn't succeeded in awakening their interest.

No interest in the process of becoming, in the past.

And she wonders where these young people will take root.

She told me that after I had told her about the helpless teacher. A teacher from Linz with a secondary school class from Spallerhof, a part of Linz. A few boys from this class approached me on the path from the museum to the quarry and wanted to hear my name again. If one of them had spelled it correctly. They were friendly with their questions. Stayed friendly with the following sentences: What for? So that they can lock me up. Because the likes of me had to be locked up. They already had a long list of others like me. They would visit the camp frequently. So that they knew how it worked, could put it into operation. Once it got that far. The teacher, who overheard these sentences, raised his shoulders with regret. He knew about it. Later he said to me that he had had to learn to accept the fact that he could not change them. He only hoped that these boys would not succeed in – I think he said – contaminating others.

Perhaps I stopped working in Mauthausen because I saw my own helplessness.

Could I awaken interest in just one schoolboy or girl? In just one? And if so would the interest be strong enough for outside this place? And what direction would it take?

The silent majority in every class. Without reaction. As if Mauthausen were only history.

How far is Mauthausen?

So this job is meaningless? – For whom? – For the teachers who come to Mauthausen with their classes? For the schoolchildren? For you? For your colleagues?

I began this job after a colleague had left. Some colleagues are still there. A persistent question: How can some colleagues bear this job so much longer? What is different for them? Once I asked Helmut. "How can you stand it year after year?" He found it ridiculous that I quit because a sentence like "Here is where the gas flowed in" might have become a natural sentence. Yes, he found me ridiculous. And that wasn't all: "You failed. This job, like every job, must be done with distance." Distance. Would it be possible for me to distance myself from it? Distance from what? From the place? From the question: How was it possible? From those gassed? From the murderers? From the heirs of the murderers? From similar places in other countries today? And where is the border between distance and indifference? And would the distance be able to see the indifference?

At that time Helmut aspired to the administrator's post. In the meantime the administrator retired. Helmut is now the administrator. Helmut has a family. I have no family. Does that explain things?

The words *you failed* remain. But I will not accept them. They go hand in hand with two other words: *token guilt.*

Is this work meaningless for the Austrian state which, after all, finances it?

Herr Pichler said, "We're just beginning to commemorate the anniversary of liberation. By next spring not a soul will want to hear anything more about it."

Translated by Linda C. DeMeritt

DORON RABINOVICI

1994

The Right Nose

Amos unexpectedly came upon a crowd that had been fomenting in the pedestrian zone, a throng of predominantly older women and men who had gathered there to shed their loneliness and act familiarly towards one another, setting off small gaseous explosions of annoyance that soon evaporated. Amos Getreider slipped into those emanations of arrogance. For the time being, he thought he could saunter through them without getting involved, could amuse himself in unabashed nonchalance. A conceited smile was on his lips.

Yet another political event had just taken place on that spot. The mass had already disintegrated into several clusters of people when sounds of discontent filtered into the general harmony and protests grew louder. A few people had tried to distribute leaflets addressing objectionable issues. But the angry crowd had wrested the pamphlets from their hands, and somewhere a placard had been wrested from the hands of a counterdemonstrator and smashed on his head. There he stood, holding his head in a daze – his glasses were on the ground – and the police were on the scene writing down his personal data. He anxiously felt his skull and realized it was bleeding. He didn't answer the inspector who wanted to take him to task; he just looked impassively at the blood in the palm of his right hand and felt the pain with his left. Two men in uniform suddenly twisted his arm behind his back while their superior continued to interrogate him. But the man didn't understand, perhaps because, as a foreigner, he could only comprehend the language when it was spoken slowly and the regional dialect was completely unfamiliar to him, or perhaps because that stout gentleman who had been thrashing him was now screaming loudly at the policemen, demanding they arrest the counterdemonstrator. The stranger glanced around in confusion, startled loudly as his arm was pulled up, and put up resistance when they took him into custody and jammed him into the police van.

In those days, the otherwise so consensual silence, the conspiratorial stillness among the populace, had been undone, and what had struck the basic chord, the good form of the society, had, over the years, degenerated into discord. People had congregated there today to drown out the unheard-of. Their voices, however, betrayed what they sought to cover up.

Amos, who merely wanted to stroll through the tumult, was soon sucked into the conversations. For most of them, the passing of the past was of utmost concern, for a few others, it was the immortality of the crimes. A short man yelled at Amos, "If you all don't like it here, then you should move to Israel – or New York."

"New York is more fun," Professor Rubinstein of Columbia University supposedly said weeks later with regard to V., when he asked Amos one day whether he wanted to stay here – in this city, in this country. "After graduation I want to live in Israel," Amos suddenly – and to his own amazement – replied. "New York is more fun," Aron Rubinstein repeated in response, and even drawled the German translation of the phrase with an American accent.

For weeks now, Professor Rubinstein's black-haired daughter, Susi, had been sitting next to Amos at school. His mother was charmed by the girl from Brooklyn and had invited the American family to their Seder. The Rubinsteins were neither traditional nor sentimental, yet relished the challah, kreplach soup, gefilte fish, and the rest of the meal as well. To be sure, they didn't understand any of the elder Getreider's prayers, but were extremely enthusiastic about the Hebrew songs and all of the other folklore.

Susi spent the few months in which her father was supposed to hold lectures in V. with Amos, whom she wanted to win even more, who meant even more to her, the closer she came to returning to America, and even though, the morning after the banquet, his mother had said, "Such a beautiful girl," Amos was crazy about Susi as well.

In school, which she only planned to attend for four months, she cared so little about her grades that even the performance of her neighbor Amos – who had never been a diligent pupil – hopelessly deteriorated. She tried to see Amos as often as possible so that, as she stressed, she could learn to speak German. Perhaps that lonely, curly-haired American girl was hoping to find her reflection in him, that pale and fidgety youth.

Professor Aron Rubinstein said, "New York is more fun." When Amos wanted to contradict and defend the state that had been founded in response to Jewish suffering, the Professor maintained: "I love Israel. It's a self-purifying process for us. All of the racist, narrow-minded Jews in Brooklyn who hate blacks go to Israel so they can hate Arabs for even better reasons. I love Israel. It's a self-purifying process for us. New York is more fun."

"We don't hate the Jews," an older gentleman with a white beard emphasized from the middle of the crowd and then smiled pensively. He spoke loudly so that he could be heard amidst the general excitement, but had remained calm. He wanted the principal theme of the gathering to sound again, over and above the din. He ignored the crowd's shrill attacks against a young woman (a critic), avenged insults with cutting glances, and calmly waved off all polemics. He spoke very slowly: "We don't hate the Jews. But the Jews, you see, the Jews hate us, perhaps even with good reason. I'd probably hate us too. But we must put an end to all of this hate once and for all."

A counterdemonstrator interrupted him. The older gentleman drew his arms back wide and, pronouncing his words very clearly, responded, "But excuse me, miss." He folded his hands contentedly on his pot belly and continued: "We don't hate the Jews. That's just a big campaign. Fear creating a calamitous alliance with hate. Which fear, you ask?" he anticipated her question and, raising his index finger, declared: "The fear of losing power. Which hate? Well, what do you think?"

For the time being he didn't provide an answer, but as the young woman still hadn't understood, he explained: "Old Testament vengeance. An eye for an eye. A tooth for a tooth." His eyes were considerably dilated, and all of a sudden he was completely quiet.

Now she understood what he had meant, what he had talked about – and against. He kindly rebuffed her brief objections, "Listen, miss, we actually like all races." As others nodded in approval, the man with the beard and the curly white hair continued: "It's so nice that our world is colorful. Its colorfulness just has to be comprehended as a whole, the same way that all colors combine to make white light. Wouldn't it be idiotic if blue and yellow hated each other, or red and green? Well, it's just as idiotic for us to hate the Jews and vice versa."

His final words had silenced the critic, but the old man, a master of harmony, suddenly felt himself subject to overeager agreement. His appeal was amplified by revelations about a certain individual, a politician, a Jew.

He immediately placated the impassioned gentleman: "Yes, we even have to love him. He's not our enemy, hate is." "Which hate?" the young woman asked indignantly. But he continued:

"Yes, and we have to overcome their hate. There's only one way to do so. We have to love the Jews for as long as it takes them to stop hating us. No matter how long it takes."

Amos's mother grew hoarse whenever she spoke about such things. She said: "I want you to hit him. Do you hear?"

She would wake him in the morning with a loud singsong. His father would implore her, "Not so loud. The neighbors." His mother, however, would continue to warble. If she then bellowed at him because he still hadn't gotten out of bed, his father would plead, "Not so loud. The neighbors." Then he would calm Amos down, "Don't make your mama angry. Get out of bed."

She wore her hair up, in tightly pulled abundance. Thus she sternly looked down upon Amos. Thus she smiled at him. Thus she looked at her son, her little boy, who precociously tried to make jokes early on, who asked, "Papa, am I funny?," to whom his father replied, "Yes, you're very funny," and whom she, in contrast, would reproach with kisses, "You're a clown," and who, though only nine years old, sought to educate her politically, who asked her, "Mama am I smart?," whom she kissed, and then sighed, "You're a clown."

By the time he was four, he had picked up the habit of scanning his opposition. "No, we appessst! We appessst!" the little one made up, and when his father told him that he was mispronouncing the word, he shouted to his mother, "No, we protessst." – "The word is appest," the dark-haired woman assured him in response. "Protest! Protest!" he suddenly roared. "No, appest. Appest," she smiled at him as she tied his shoes. "Protest! Protest!" he chuckled back. She, however, snortingly insisted: "Appessst! Appessst! Appessst!" Then they giggled and toddled their way down the staircase.

She screamed herself hoarse: "The next time, I want you to hit him. Do you hear?" During recess, his classmate Helmut told him they had forgotten him at Mauthausen. Amos responded by taking him to task, by discussing, as has been his practice since turning nine, the matter with him, by trying to explain.

"I want you – do you hear? – to hit people like that the next time. Discuss, schmiscuss. Forget about that. If anyone ever says anything like that to you again, I want you to hit him till he bleeds. Do you hear? Until he bleeds! It doesn't matter to me if you come home bleeding as well. I'll take care of your wounds. But you should kick him and scratch him so hard that his blood flows, that his clothes rip, that his parents ask him who did that, that they

complain to the principal about you. Do you hear? I want them to
go see the principal, and then I'll come to school and tell them I
instructed you to do so. Don't worry, I will take it upon myself. Do
you understand?" she screamed. Papa unsuspectingly walked into
the kitchen, saw Amos sitting alone with his head bowed down,
and said, "Do as your mama says. She's suffered enough already."

Amos, however, didn't want to fight. He trusted the power of
his words, the skill of his speech. He had never tried to content
himself with any kind of dialect, with any kind of jargon, with
anything other than standard speech, for fear that he wouldn't be
able to have a good command of the local accent. He also wanted
to be sure that he was in accord with written language.
When he spoke Hebrew he was a different person. His voice
and his expression seemed especially brilliant then, as though his
timbre in that southerly, summery language of the sea sounded
metallic. That idiom rang forth from deep within him and, moving
within that language, he felt as secure as if he were behind tinted
windows, as if he were armed with sunglasses, as if he were
leaning against an olive tree, a blade of grass between his teeth.
Something within him believed that Hebrew would grant him
access to a more exclusive circle, one that had nothing to do with
V., nothing to do with school, nothing to do with his non-Jewish
and his Jewish friends, and didn't even have anything to do with
the devout individuals he sometimes saw moving about the streets
in their dark clothes. No matter how uniquely packaged they all
appeared to be, Amos, in Hebrew, felt he belonged to a prouder
version, to an elegantly bound luxury issue from among the Jewish
assortment.

Peter Bach suddenly appeared from amidst the crowd. That
wiry adolescent bent down to the older man with the white beard
and said: "What's that supposed to mean, the Jews? The Jews, you
declare, hate us. We should love the Jews. The Jews. All of them?"
Peter, a gangly giant of a boy, had been standing behind slight
Amos. A smile flashed between the two classmates, while a short
gentleman wearing a brown hat and a black suit started snarling
agitatedly.

Neither Peter nor Amos had gone directly home from school
that day, nor had they, as they otherwise always did, proceeded
together with Georg Rinser towards the subway. The hundred and
fifty meters from that neo-Gothic building to the station, which

Georg – who always came too late – covered every morning in a few seconds, took the three friends at least a half hour in the afternoon. Actually, Peter Bach just accompanied the duo, whose craziness amused him and whose pranks he gladly let happen. Amos and Georg, in turn, enviously had to acknowledge Peter's lead in amorous affairs, and Amos even asked him for advice when he thought about Susi Rubinstein and when his parents were going away for a few days and his apartment would be available for a late rendezvous with Susi.

Peter Bach said to the squat little man with the hat: "Listen, what you're saying is anti-Semitic." The little man, however, just groaned, "I'm not an anti-Semite. I just can't stand Jews." – "But that's exactly what anti-Semitism is," Peter declared, and was then rebuked by a fat adult, "And what of it? You need to be more tolerant, young man. That gentleman is entitled to his opinion."

Amos: the name was a sign. The mere mention of the name generated sufficient material for an extended conversation. Thus, it was pointless for him to think about denying his origin. On the contrary, he learned to enjoy disconcerting other people by virtue of his exoticism. His stance on the issue was impressive, yet it turned into a pose, a production, as his standing upright had little to do with backbone, and he always had to be sure of his parents' support.
"Our little Amos really knows how to talk," Peter maintained, and Georg, putting his arm around Amos's shoulder, added: "And how. He never stops. He never listens. He prefers listening to himself most of all." Amos smiled. At home, he told his mother, "Peter says I know how to talk, and Georg says he's right." She, however, just looked sternly and sighed: "You are and always will be a clown."

A few people were still standing in separate little groups on the square. Conversations droned on, increased in intensity once again, hailed forth and flared up, as though the downtown square, not far from the cathedral, had been hurled. All of a sudden a swirl of pigeons flapped their wings. The birds circled densely above the crowd and flew off in the shape of an arrow.
An elderly woman, wearing a dark dress and white lace gloves that extended as far as the second joint on her finger, thus exposing her finger tips, and who had stuck her umbrella under her arm, had pushed her way to the front of the fracas. She wore her blue-gray

hair under a little hat, which was held in place by a pin. She whirled her hands through the air in excitement, reminding Amos of the hasty movements of Flemish lace makers. With an array of gestures, she seemed to be spinning away, as she worked herself up in the nasal sounds of a choice and class-conscious accent.

In the course of the discussion Amos had talked himself hoarse, and now contradicted in a sharp staccato.

"How dare you say I'm an anti-Semite," the woman exclaimed. Amos: "What you're saying is anti-Semitic." – "But," the woman smiled peevishly, "you can smell anti-Semites." She placed particular emphasis on the word "smell" and turned up her nose. Amos inquired in a kind and cheerful tone: "And Jews, no doubt, as well?" The woman paused both her hands and her mouth for a moment and then spoke pensively, "Yes, Jews, no doubt, as well."

The crowd breathed heavily, perhaps because some of them realized that the elderly woman had given herself away, perhaps because others were amused by the statement, resembling a dirty, illicit joke, made by a man in his mid-fifties, who leaned forward and announced: "I beg your pardon. That's not true. You cannot smell the Jews. Except for the Polish ones."

Peter seized up, but Amos Getreider just said softly: "My mother is a Polish Jew."

All was quiet for a moment, then a man hastily took hold of the seventeen-year-old's hand and said, "Oh, I'm very sorry."

Shaking his head, Amos could no longer keep himself from bursting out laughing.

The conversation had taken its course. Amos looked up at the monument to the plague, towering above the pedestrian zone. The monument had been erected as a memorial to the Black Death. It was a prayer of stone thanksgiving from all whom the epidemic had spared.

During the final decades of the seventeenth century, the epidemic was circulating through large parts of Europe once again, mingling among the people and infecting thousands. The disease divided the people into those considered to be on the side of life and those on the side of death, who had already contracted the illness and could hardly hope for recovery. Those stricken by the plague were cast out. Their clothes were burned. Their corpses were buried in mass graves. Only their money, their coins, were saved from extermination. They had to continue circulating in spite of the epidemic.

National borders were closed and, ever since those days, can only be crossed with certificates of health. It was the task of the military and the government to banish the disease. The Jewish people, who have been accused of poisoning the wells ever since the Middle Ages, had already been expelled from the city years beforehand.

Amos looked at the monument to the plague. Dark figures in old, traditional dress were passing by it. The black swarm crossed the square where, shortly before, the event had taken place and the crowd had blaringly condensed.

Peter Bach followed his friend's gaze and suddenly gasped: "Anti-Semitism is inexcusable, of course. But whenever I see orthodox Jews I have to wonder why they insist on segregating themselves. They don't have to go around looking like that. And besides, how come they only accept people who are circumcised? On some level, you can understand how resentments arise. I mean, they're not very clever, not even as far as politics are concerned. Those men, for example . . . "

That was precisely the moment in which a long-standing friendship as well as Peter's nose were broken.

That right hook was intended to change Peter's face conspicuously. The classic linearity which had distinguished his olfactory organ up until that point was crushed and bent. Amos, however, didn't need to worry about the problems this incident caused at school; his mother, of course, attended to them. With a single blow Amos had become the hero of his family.

Translated by Craig Decker

Explanatory Notes

Ingeborg Bachmann, "Sightseeing in an Old City"

p. 10   *Danubius Fountain* – Created by Johann Meixner, the fountain is located on the Albertinaplatz in Vienna's First District. It was originally part of a complex of fountains that was partially destroyed in World War II.

Liberation of the Spring Fountain – Created in 1903 by Josef Heu, the fountain depicts two male figures attempting to lift a stone.

City Park – The park was opened in 1862. It consists of twenty-two-and-a-half acres located just off the Ring that encircles downtown Vienna.

the most famous water in the world – Words appearing in italics in "Sightseeing in an Old City" are in English in the original German text.

Karlskirche – At the height of Vienna's plague epidemic in 1713, Emperor Karl VI vowed that he would build a church dedicated to Charles Borromeo, a patron saint of the plague. Designed by Johann Bernard Fischer von Erlach and completed by his son, the Karlskirche, an eclectic masterpiece of Baroque architecture, was built from 1714-37.

National Library – Located on the Josephsplatz in the First District, the Austrian National Library is housed in a magnificent Baroque building designed by Johann Bernhard Fischer von Erlach and completed by his son Joseph Emanuel. It was built 1723-26.

the mountain face of St. Martin's – ("die Martinswand") A 1,113-meter-high wall of rock on the southern slope of the Hechenberg in Tyrol. Emperor Maximilan I (1459-1519) purportedly got lost there while hunting for chamois at the end of the fifteenth century.

Archduke Charles – (1771-1847) The third son of Emperor Leopold II, Archduke Charles was famous for his early-nineteenth-century reforms of the imperial army. In 1809 he defeated Napoleon at the Battle of Aspern. A statue of him on horseback stands on Vienna's Heldenplatz.

the monument commemorating the plague – The "Pestsäule" or Plague Pillar, which stands at the center of the Graben (part of downtown Vienna's pedestrian zone), was commissioned by Emperor Leopold I in 1679 in thanksgiving for the end of a plague epidemic that cost 30,000 lives. The current column, which stands seventy feet tall, was completed in 1693.

Leopold I – (1640-1705) The son of Emperor Ferdinand III, he ruled from 1658-1705.

State Opera House – One of the world's leading opera houses, the Vienna State Opera was designed in the French Early Renaissance style by August von Siccardsburg and Eduard von der Müll and built on the Ring from 1861-69. It suffered heavy damage during World War II and was rebuilt from 1946-55.

Burgtheater – Built on the Ring in 1874 to replace the old Hoftheater, the Burgtheater, considered to be one of the most prestigious stages in the German-speaking world, was designed in Baroque style by Gottfried Semper and Carl von Hasenauer. The theater caught fire and burned down in 1945, reopening in 1955 with a performance of Franz Grillparzer's *König Ottokars Glück und Ende*.

p. 11   *University of Vienna* – The University on the Ring, completed in 1884, was designed in Renaissance style by Heinrich Ferstel.

Votive Church – Built in 1856 to commemorate a failed assassination attempt on Emperor Franz Joseph, the church was designed by Heinrich von Ferstel.

the first turkish danger – Vienna was besieged by the Turks in 1529. The second Turkish siege occurred in 1683.

Kipfel – The Austrian (and Bavarian) term for a croissant.

Stephansdom – Construction of St. Stephen's Cathedral, the symbol of the city, began in the twelfth century. The cathedral's spire is 450 feet high. The roof was destroyed by fire in the final days of World War II. Postwar reconstruction and restoration, begun in 1948, lasted until 1962.

Pummerin Bell – The current bell was cast in 1951 and has been hanging in the North Tower of St. Stephen's Cathedral since 1957. It is ten feet in diameter and weighs twenty tons.

giant ferris wheel – The "Riesenrad," located in the Prater amusement park, was built in 1896 by Walter B. Basset for the World Exhibition. It was destroyed during the Second World War, but was rebuilt and back in operation by 1946. The wheel is 200 feet in diameter and revolves at a speed of about three-feet per second.

Lainzer Tiergarten Park – Once the hunting reserve of Emperor Joseph II, the Lainzer Wildlife Park stretches over some ten square miles. The area was opened to the public in 1923, and has been a nature preserve since 1941.

Schönbrunn Palace – Built over the course of the eighteenth century, Schönbrunn was the grandiose summer residence of the Habsburgs.

"to my peoples!" – So began Kaiser Franz Joseph's declaration of war in 1914.

Grinzing – Located in Vienna's Nineteenth District, the suburb of Grinzing is known for its wine production and its "Heuriger," wine taverns. Nowadays, the area's quaint and narrow streets are frequently overrun with tour busses.

Romy Schneider – The actress (1938-82), born as Rosemarie Magdalena Albach in Vienna, made her international breakthrough by playing Empress Elisabeth ("Sissi") in a trilogy of Sissi films in the mid-1950s. Sissi, the wife of Emperor Franz Joseph, was born in 1837 in Munich and murdered in Geneva in 1898.

Madeira – Emperor Karl I, who abdicated in 1918, is buried at Funchal in Madeira.

Prater – A former imperial hunting ground that was opened to the public in 1766, the Prater is a park of some 3,200 acres located in Vienna's Second District between the Danube and the Danube Canal. The park consists of two distinct parts: the smaller "Wurstel" or "Volksprater" – an amusement park containing rides (including the giant ferris wheel), games, and restaurants – and the much larger "green Prater," an expanse of meadows, ponds, and wooded areas.

Crown Prince Rudolf – (1859-89) The eldest son of Emperor Franz Joseph, Crown Prince Rudolf committed double suicide with his seventeen-year-old mistress, Baroness Maria Vetsera, on January 30, 1889, at the imperial hunting lodge in Mayerling.

p. 12   *Madame Catherine Deveuve* – A French actress born in 1943, she played Maria Vetsera in the 1968 film *Mayerling.*

Gypsy barons, Csardas princesses, beggar-students, bird-peddlers – These are all characters in famous Viennese operettas.

"Tales from the Vienna Woods" – "G'schichten aus dem Wiener Wald," a waltz composed by Johann Strauss (1825-1899) in 1868.

"Vienna Life" – "Wiener Blut," a waltz composed by Strauss in 1872; it is also the title of his last operetta (1899).

"Vienna, City of My Dreams!" – "Wien, Wien, nur du allein," a popular Viennese folk song.

p. 13   *Kaiserschmarrn* – A cut-up pancake served with raisins and powdered sugar that is a typically Austrian (and Bavarian) dish.

Kapuziner Church and *Kapuzinergruft* – Dedicated to Our Lady of the Angels, the church was founded by Empress Anna in 1618. Beneath the church is the Habsburg family vault, where 138 members of the House lie buried. Since 1633, virtually all of the Austrian Emperors have been buried here.

Arthur Schnitzler, "Lieutenant Gustl"

p. 29   *Traviata* – La Traviata, "The Fallen Woman," opera by Giuseppe Verdi, premiered in 1853.

p. 31   *Sans Gêne – Madame Sans-Gêne* (Madame Carefree), a comedy by Victorien Sardou and Emile Moreau (1894).

the Ring – Vienna's grand Ring boulevard ("Ringstrasse"), which encircles the center of the city, was built in the second half of the nineteenth century on former military grounds. Two-and-a-half miles long and 185 feet wide, the Ring is the location of such representative buildings as the Parliament, the City Hall, the University, the Burgtheater, and the State Opera House.

p. 38   *Aspern bridge* – Spanning the Danube Canal, the bridge was built in 1863 as a chain bridge. The original bridge was demolished in 1913, and not replaced until 1920.

Kagran – Lying northeast of the center of Vienna and located in the Twenty-Second District, this area was first incorporated into the city in 1904.

Ronacher – Built in 1887 in Vienna's First District, the Ronacher was the first German-language variety theater.

p. 39   *Przemsyl* – At the turn of the century, Przemsyl was located in the Crownland of Galicia. In 1900, it had a population of 46,350.

Sambor – Located close to Przemsyl, Sambor is a manufacturing town. In 1900, its population was 17,350.

p. 40   *Prater* – See the entry for "Prater" on p. 205.

p. 42   *Graz* – A city in southeastern Austria, Graz is the capital of the province of Styria.

p. 45   *Lohengrin* – Opera by Richard Wagner, premiered in 1859.

p. 46   *North Railroad Station* – Vienna's first railroad station, it was built in 1838. Renovated and enlarged in 1859-65, it became one of the most splendid stations in Europe.

Tegetthoff monument – Close to the Prater, the Tegetthoff monument commemorates Rear Admiral Wilhelm von Tegetthoff's 1866 victory over the Italians at the Battle of Lissa.

p. 50   *When we were down there in '78* – The 1878 Treaty of Berlin gave Austria-Hungary the right to occupy and administer Bosnia and Herzegovina.

Volksgarten – Laid out in 1819-23 and extended in 1862, this "People's Park" is located off the Ring.

Joseph Roth, "The Bust of the Emperor"

p. 55   *Przemysl* – See the entry for "Przemysl" on p. 207.

Brody – The Galician town in which Joseph Roth was born.

p. 56   *Hungarian Banat* – Part of the "population politics" of the Habsburg Empire included sending German-speakers to settle this area in Southern Hungary.

Theresianische Akademie – Founded by Empress Maria Theresia in 1746 to educate future civil servants and military personnel, the school was known as one of the finest in Austria.

p. 57   *Gymnasium* – Secondary school.

p. 59   *Ruthenian* – From Ruthenia, a region south of the Carpathian Mountains. The region is currently part of the Ukraine.

p. 60   *Grillparzer* – The dramatist, poet, and prose writer Franz Grillparzer (1791-1872) is considered by many to be the "father of Austrian literature."

p. 65   *the crown of St. Stephen* – Kaiser Karl, who became Emperor in 1916, was the last to wear the crown.

p. 66   *Kapuzinergruft* – See the entry for "Kapuzinergruft on p. 206. *Die Kapuzinergruft* is also the title of Roth's 1938 novel representing Austria from the final years of the Habsburg monarchy until the Anschluss.

p. 69   *Rittmeister* – cavalry captain.

Robert Musil, "The Blackbird"

p. 79   *South Tyrol* – At the end of World War I, Italian troops occupied South Tyrol. Postwar settlements gave the area to Italy, and 220,000 German-speaking Tyroleans came under Italian rule.

Ödön von Horváth, "Crossing the Border"

p. 89   *Voralberg* – Austria's westernmost province, Voralberg borders on Germany, Liechtenstein, and Switzerland.

p. 90   *Seefeld* – Tyrolean town (population 2,751) just northwest of Innsbruck.

Zugspitze – A mountain in the Bavarian Alps on the border with Austria, it is the highest point in Germany.

Martin's Cliff – See the entry for "St. Martin's" on p. 203.

golden roof – Built in 1497-1500 and located in the center of Innsbruck, the golden roof consists of 2,738 fire-gilded copper shingles and commemorates the marriage of Maximilian I and Bianca.

p. 91   *Kufstein* – Dubbed the "Pearl of Tyrol," Kufstein lies in the Inn Valley very close to the border with Germany.

the new Italian border – See the entry for "South Tyrol" on this page.

Hofrat – "Hofrat" is an honorary term in Austria. It can also be used as a slang expression to connote a slow, bureaucratic person.

Gauleiter – District leader.

Heimwehr – A paramilitary organization founded in November 1918 by various groups on the right, the Heimwehr increasingly fought against the Social Democrats and their paramilitary organization, the "Republikanischer Schutzbund." The Heimwehr was disbanded in 1936.

Mount Isel – In the vicinity of Innsbruck, this locale is famous for the freedom fights that took place there in 1809 under the direction of Andreas Hofer (1767-1810), a Tyrolean patriot who was executed on orders from Napoleon.

Halsmann – In September 1928, Max Halsmann died while hiking in the Zillertal Alps. His son Philipp (born in 1905) was accused of murdering his father and sentenced to ten years in prison. A new hearing was held in 1929. Despite repeated assertions of his innocence, the son was sentenced to a four-year term.

p. 92   *Vienna's red government* – The institution of large-scale social welfare programs – including the building of extensive municipal housing projects – characterized the city's "red" government during the interwar period.

Styrian – From the southeastern Austrian province of Styria.

In hoc signo vinces! – By this sign you will conquer!

ad maiorem gloriam – to the greater glory

p. 93   *I.G. Farben* – The largest chemical firm in Germany, it came to symbolize the partnership between big business and the state in the Nazi war economy.

Ingeborg Bachmann, "Youth in an Austrian Town"

p. 95   *K* – Klagenfurt, the city of Bachmann's birth, is located in the province of Carinthia, close to the Slovenian border.

Ulrichsberg – An isolated mountain, 1,015 meters high, located north of Klagenfurt.

p. 97   *Rosental* – Lowlands along the Drava River, located approximately 270 miles south of Klagenfurt.

p. 99   *Seven Years' War* – 1756-63.

Thirty Years' War – 1618-48.

Romance in a Minor Key – Directed by Helmut Kautner, this

1943 film is based on a novella by Guy de Maupassant. Set in Paris at the end of the nineteenth century, the film depicts a woman who dreams of a more vibrant life. The film was nearly banned by Goebbels for seeming too defeatist.

Glan – A tributary of the Gurk River, the Glan flows through Klagenfurt, ending shortly past the city.

I. Bachmann, "Among Murderers and Madmen"

p. 101 *Inner Town* – Vienna's First District.

p. 102 *black Friday* – While this term conjures up the stock market crash in the United States, it was also on a Friday that Hitler's troops marched into Vienna in 1938.

p. 103 *Ju 52* – First built in 1930, there were a total of 5,000 Junkers Ju 52 airplanes (nicknamed "Aunt Ju") produced. The majority of them were used by the Nazi Luftwaffe to transport troops.

Voronezh – Large industrial Russian city 360 miles south of Moscow.

General Manstein – Having served the German military on both the Western and Eastern fronts in World War I and II, Manstein (1887-1973) secured the entire Crimea (with the exception of Sevastopol) in fall 1941. During the winter of 1942, he successfully withstood a Soviet counteroffensive.

Burgenland – Austria's easternmost province, the area was part of Hungary until World War I. The area was ceded to Austria in the Treaty of St. Germain.

Gumpoldskirchen – A small village south of Vienna known for its wine production.

Veldes – German name for Bled, a town in the Julian Alps in northwest Slovenia (current population 11,113).

p. 105 *Tagblatt* – A Viennese daily founded in 1867.

feuilleton – The term can apply to the section of a newspaper roughly equivalent to the Arts section as well as to individual essays appearing there. The *feuilleton* can serve as an important forum for intellectual exchange.

Gestapo – The Nazi terrorist police force ("Geheime Staatspolizei") whose primary mission was to identify enemies of the state.

p. 108 *Battle of the Isonzo* – In total, Austro-Hungarian and Italian forces fought four battles along the sixty-mile-long Isonzo Front in 1915: the first from June 23-July 7; the second from July 18-Aug. 3; the third from Oct. 18-Nov. 3; and the final battle from Nov. 10-Dec. 2.

Kleiner Pal – An Alpine battlefield where Austro-Hungarian and Italian soldiers fought during World War I.

p. 109 *Hötzendorf* – Franz Conrad von Hötzendorf (1852-1925), whose many military positions included Chief of Staff of the Austro-Hungarian Army.

p. 110 *"Old Comrades reunion"* – To this day, Austrian veterans of World War II continue to reunite to "reminisce" about the war. Such gatherings expose the contradiction between the party-sanctioned veterans' reunions and the state-sanctioned myth of Austrian innocence in World War II.

Narvik – On April 9, 1940, the Nazis launched a seafront attack on Norway and, with the aid of ground troops, took control of Narvik. Later the next month Allied forces attacked and liberated Narvik, resulting in the Nazis' first military defeat in World War II. The Allied victory did not last long, however, as Nazi troops reinvaded Narvik and remained there until the end of the war.

p. 113 *the Dollfuss period* – The Austro-fascist dictatorship ("Ständestaat") of Engelbert Dollfuss began in 1933. Dollfuss himself was killed a year later during an unsuccessful Nazi putsch. Austro-fascism lasted until the Anschluss with Nazi Germany in 1938.

p. 115 *Graz* – See the entry for "Graz" on p. 207.

p. 116 *Ring Streets* – See the entry for the "Ring" on p. 207.

p. 117 *Monte Cassino* – The Battle of Monte Cassino was actually four separate battles fought Jan.-May 1944. The Allies were ultimately victorious, and the breakthrough at Cassino enabled Allied troops to go on to capture Rome.

Thomas Bernhard, "The Italian"

p. 120 *Silvaplana* – Located in the Upper Engadine Lake District in Switzerland (population 900), Silvaplana lies 1,815 meters above sea level.

Fiesole – A town of 15,000 inhabitants nine kilometers from Florence.

Zimmerwald – The International Socialist Conference of September 1915 was held in Zimmerwald. The group Zimmerwald Left, founded on Lenin's initiative, emerged from this meeting.

Karl Liebknecht – One of the leaders of the revolutionary Spartacus League, Liebknecht (1871-1919) was executed during the 1919 uprising in Berlin.

Caltanisetta, Enna, Agrient, Palermo, and *Cefalù* – Towns in Sicily.

p. 123 *Pavese* – Cesare Pavese (1908-50), novelist, poet, and translator, was a major figure in postwar Italian literature. He fled from the fascists and was subsequently imprisoned. Pavese committed suicide in 1950.

Ungaretti – Giuseppe Ungaretti (1888-1970), poet, critic, and translator, he inaugurated poetic Hermeticism.

Lampedusa – Giuseppe di Lampedusa (1896-1957) is best known for his novel *The Leopard* (1958) which depicts the demise of aristocratic society and the unification of Italy.

Campanella – Tommaso Campanella (1568-1639), Italian Renaissaance philosopher and writer, best known for his utopian work *The City of the Sun* (1623).

Mazzini – Giuseppe Mazzini (1805-72), Italian patriot and revolutionary.

Modigliani – Amedo Modigliani (1884-1920), Italian painter and sculptor.

p. 126 *the Chartist movement in England* – The Chartist movement (1838-50) sought to improve the economic and social conditions of the industrial working classes through political reforms.

Spartacus League – The Spartacus League, which was to become the Communist Party of Germany in 1919, was led by Karl Liebknecht and Rosa Luxemburg.

Rosa Luxemburg – Born in Poland, Luxemburg (1871-1919) came to Berlin in 1898. Like Liebknecht, she was shot during the 1919 Berlin uprising. Her body was thrown into the Landwehr Canal and not discovered until months afterward.

Klara Zetkin – A prominent figure in the German and international workers' movement, Zetkin (1857-1933) was a founding member of the German Communist Party and in 1921 became a member of the Executive Committee of the Communist International.

Thomas Bernhard, "Crimes of an Innsbruck Merchant's Son"

p. 132 *Melk* – Located on the Danube in the Wachau, Melk (population 5,139) is dominated by a Baroque monastery towering from a hill above the town.

Ybbs – Located in the province of Lower Austria, Ybbs (population 5,770) lies on the south bank of the Danube.

p. 133 *Natters* – The village of Natters (population 1,788) lies south of Innsbruck.

Barbara Frischmuth, "Oh, My Dear Augustine"

p. 137 *Augustine* – Legendary Viennese street singer, bagpiper, and extemporaneous poet (1645-85). In 1679, he supposedly fell drunk into a pit filled with victims of the plague, without ever contracting the disease himself. The popular folk song "Oh, My Dear Augustine" ("Ach du lieber Augustin") commemorates him.

Landstrasse – Vienna's Third District, the area was incorporated into the city in 1850.

Erdberg – Once an autonomous village and then a suburb of Vienna, Erdberg has been a section of Vienna's Third District since 1850.

Kronen-Zeitung – The largest-selling newspaper in Austria, its tone is sensationalistic and its political stance extremely conservative.

p. 138 *Team Austria* – Founded in 1911 as the "Viennese Amateur Sport Club."

Vienna team – Founded in 1898 as the "First Viennese Workers' Soccer Club."

Rochus Church – Built in 1642 and located in Vienna's Third District.

Bonatus – Johannes de Bone (born 1168), his relics were brought to the church from Rome in 1754.

St. Peter's Church – Located in Vienna's First District, the church's Baroque ornamentation was completed in 1733.

p. 139 *Ringstrasse* – See the entry for the "Ring" on p. 207.

p. 140 *Stadthalle* – Built in the 1950s and located in the Fifteenth District, the Stadthalle serves as a venue for large musical and sporting events as well as conventions.

p. 142 *Danube Canal* – The southern branch of the Danube in Vienna, it has been known as the Danube Canal since 1686. Approximately ten miles long, it was expanded in the nineteenth century to prevent flooding.

Prater – See the entry for "Prater" on p. 205.

p. 143 *Biedermeier* – The period from 1815-48, the term connotes an apolitical retreat into the private sphere.

p. 146 *just like the river that doesn't flow through it* – It is the Danube Canal – and not the Danube River – that actually flows through Vienna.

Barbara Frischmuth, "A Neighbor of Mine and Musil's"

p. 147 *Musil* – See the entry for Robert Musil on p. 209.

Agathe and Ulrich – Ulrich is the title character in Musil's *The Man Without Qualities*; Agathe is his sister, with whom he has an affair.

a complementary Austrian flag – The Austrian flag consists of three stripes, two red and one white.

St. Gotthard – Swiss mountain range in the Lepontine Alps.

p. 148 *Prater* – See the entry for "Prater" on p. 205.

Café Zartl – Café located in Vienna's Third District.

Weltwoche – A weekly Swiss newspaper published in Zurich; since May 2002 it has been appearing as a magazine.

Frankfurter Allgemeine Zeitung – Daily German newspaper published in Frankfurt.

Spiegel – A weekly German news magazine published in Hamburg.

the National Library – See the entry for the "National Library" on p. 203.

p. 150 *Wroclaw* – The chief city of Silesia in southwest Poland (population 514,400).

Peter Henisch, "Baronkarl"

p. 151 *Favoriten* – In 1874, the area of Favoriten was separated from the Fourth District to become the Tenth. During the second half of the nineteenth century it developed into a predominantly industrial and working-class area. Currently Vienna's most densely populated district, Favoriten has historically had a substantial immigrant population – in the nineteenth century they were mainly Czech immigrants, and more recently Turks, Serbs, and Croats.

p. 161 *Favoriten as film locale* – Favoriten played an important role in the early development of the Austrian film industry. Many silent films were shot in the district.

Augustine – See the entry for "Augustine" on p. 214.

p. 162 *Till Eulenspiegel* – The title character of a popular sixteenth-century book (1510-11), Till is a country rogue who is forever making fools of the city bourgeoisie by literally carrying out the tasks they set for him.

Viennese Action Artist – The Viennese Action Artists ("Wiener Aktionisten") combined visual, musical, and literary arts (and frequently the senses of taste and smell) to create works and happenings intended to confront and provoke a conservative and Catholic postwar Austrian public seeking to avoid conflict. Their first major event was *Zock* in Vienna (1967). Important members of the group include Günter Brus, Otto Mühl, Hermann Nitsch, and Rudolf Schwarzkogler.

p. 176 *USIA shop* – Initially ISIWA ("Uprawlenje Sowjetskim Imuschestworm w Awstrij," "Administration of Soviet Assets in Austria"), the agency administered industrial and agricultural enterprises considered to be former German assets in the Soviet zone of occupation and also ran a series of shops.

Towarisch – A common form of address among Soviets, "Towarisch" is Russian for "comrade."

p. 180 *Erdberg* – See the entry for Erdberg on p. 300.

Stadium Bridge – Bridge spanning the Danube Canal in the Erdberg section of the city.

Felix Mitterer, "Inventory"

p. 182 *Maria Taferl* – Located in Lower Austria, the village of Maria Taferl (population 811) is visited annually by 250,000-300,000 pilgrims. The Baroque pilgrimage church, located on a terrace high above the Danube Valley, was built 1660-1710.

initials of the Magi – According to Tyrolean tradition, the initials of the Three Wise Men chalked above the doorway will bring blessings to the house and its residents.

p. 183 *Zell am Ziller* – The main settlement in the central Ziller Valley in Tyrol, Zell am Ziller has a population of 1,802.

Kirchberg – Tyrolean village (population 4,092) located west of Kitzbühel.

p. 184 *Farah Diba* – Wife of the former Shah of Iran.

p. 185 *Powidltaschkerln* – A dessert dumpling.

Elisabeth Reichart, "How Far is Mauthausen?"

p. 188 *the Gusen* – Northern tributary of the Danube east of Linz.

p. 191 *Ravensbrück* – The only major Nazi concentration camp solely for women, Ravensbrück was located in Northern Germany near Fürstenberg.

Gusen – In Upper Austria.

Hirtenberg – In Lower Austria, south of Bad Vöslau.

Lenzing – In Upper Austria, north of the Attersee.

Mittersill – In the province of Salzburg.

St. Lamprecht – In the province of Styria.

Amstetten – In the Alpine foothills of Lower Austria.

Himmler – Heinrich Himmler (1900-45), *Reichsführer SS*, built up the Nazi system of institutional control and terror, including the concentration camps. Arrested by the British in May 1945, he committed suicide by swallowing poison.

Pohl – Oswald Pohl (1892-1951), S*S-Obergruppenführer*, was the chief financial administrator of the SS. He obediently carried out Himmler's orders to annihilate concentration camp inmates through hard work. He was captured in 1946, tried, and sentenced to death.

the quarry – The quarry, where prisoners were forced to work, was located below the camp.

p. 192   *the death stairs* – A long and extremely steep set of narrow stone stairs leading from the camp to the quarry below. Emaciated prisoners were forced to carry heavy stones up and down the stairs. They frequently lost their footing, which often resulted in multiple deaths.

Judenseife – Literally, "Jew's soap."

Doron Rabinovici, "The Right Nose"

p. 193   *Mauthausen* – See E. Reichart, "How Far is Mauthausen?"

p. 201   *You cannot smell the Jews.* – The original German sentence, "Die Juden kann man nicht riechen," contains a double-meaning that cannot be rendered in a single English sentence. Literally, the sentence means, "You cannot smell the Jews," while figuratively it can mean, "People cannot stand the Jews."

the monument to the plague – See the entry for "the monument commemorating the plague" on p. 203.

p. 202   *poisoning the wells* – The German noun "Brunnenvergiftung" can mean both "poisoning the wells" and "vicious (political) calumny."

About the Authors

INGEBORG BACHMANN was born in Klagenfurt, Carinthia in 1926. She studied philosophy, psychology, and German literature in Graz, Innsbruck, and Vienna, completing a dissertation on Martin Heidegger. During the 1950s, Bachmann worked for the radio station "Rot-Weiß-Rot" and also served as the Rome correspondent for the *Westdeutsche Allgemeine Zeitung*. Her first poetry and prose publications appeared in 1946 in Austrian newspapers and literary journals, and she became well known as a result of her 1952 reading for the "Gruppe 47," a prominent group of post-World War II authors. Bachmann moved permanently to Rome in 1966, and died there in 1973 as the result of burns. Bachmann was initially known for her poetry, which was at first received in largely existentialist terms. More recently, critics have devoted increased attention to her prose, and the trend has been toward a more historically grounded reading of her work. Virtually all of Bachmann's work is available in English translation, including the short story collections *The Thirtieth Year* and *Three Paths to the Lake*, and the novel *Malina*.

"Sightseeing in an Old City" first appeared in the literary journal *Text + Kritik* in 1971; "Youth in an Austrian Town" and "Among Murderers and Madmen" were both published in *Das dreißigste Jahr*, a collection of short stories that appeared in 1961.

THOMAS BERNHARD was born in Heerlen, Holland in 1931, and grew up in and around Salzburg, often in the company of his maternal grandfather. In 1949 he contracted an incurable lung disease, and spent the following two years in sanitoria. Bernhard studied singing and acting at Salzburg's Mozarteum, graduating in 1957. That same year he published his first volume of poetry, *Auf der Erde und in der Hölle*. His first novel, *Frost*, appeared in 1963. Bernhard's tragi-comic view of life, death, and pain is often presented in the form of seemingly endless monologues. His plays and prose are marked by unrelenting and – for some – exaggerated tirades against everything Austrian. As a result, Bernhard's work and public persona were frequently the cause of scandals and even lawsuits. Bernhard died in 1989, and in his will he expressly prohibited the subsequent publication and performance of his works in Austria until the expiration of the copyright. Virtually all of Bernhard's work is available in English translation, including the novels *The Loser*, *Extinction*, and *Old Masters*, as well as his multivolume autobiography *Gathering Evidence*.

"The Italian" appeared in *An der Baumgrenze*, a collection of short stories published in 1969; "Crimes of an Innsbruck Merchant's Son" appeared in *Prosa*, a collection of short texts published in 1967.

BARBARA FRISCHMUTH was born in 1941 in Altaussee, Styria. She studied translation in Graz as well as Oriental languages and literatures in Vienna. In 1962, she became a member of the "Forum Stadtpark," an important avant-garde literary group based in Graz. Her first novel, *Die Klosterschule* (1968), depicts, in formally innovative ways, life in a Catholic boarding school for girls. Frischmuth has subsequently published many novels, short stories, and children's books, including: *Amoralisches Kinderklapper* (1969); *Haschen nach Wind* (1974); *Die Schrift des Freundes* (1998); *Die Entschlüsselung* (2001); and the trilogy *Die Mystifikationen der Sophie Silber* (1976), *Amy oder Die Metamorphose* (1978), and *Kai und die Liebe zu den Modellen* (1979). An academically certified translator, Frischmuth has translated prose, poetry, and plays from Hungarian and English into German. Three texts of hers are available in English translation: *The Convent School*, *The Shadow Disppears in the Sun*, and *Chasing After the Wind*.

"Oh, My Dear Augustine" and "A Neighbor of Mine and Musil's" appeared in *Traumgrenze*, a volume of short stories published in 1983.

PETER HENISCH was born in Vienna in 1943. He studied German literature, philosophy, history, and psychology at the University of Vienna, and began a dissertation on utopia in the works of Ernst Bloch. In 1969, Henisch was one of the founders of the literary periodical *Wespennest*. His first novel, *Hamlet bleibt*, appeared in 1971. He has since published numerous novels, plays, and poems, whose subjects include: his own father, a highly decorated photographer in the Third Reich (*Die kleine Figur meines Vaters*, 1975; revised and republished in 1980 and again in 1987; in 2003 a new edition appeared containing some of his father's photographs); the Austrian student movement (*Der Mai ist vorbei*, 1978); Jim Morrison (*Morrisons Versteck*, 1991; revised and republished in 2001); and the historical and rhetorical controversies surrounding the "Waldheim Affair" (*Steins*

Paranoia, 1988). The title character of Henisch's most recent novel, *Schwarzer Peter* (2000), is the son of a Viennese streetcar conductor and an African-American GI. To date, a volume of poetry and two prose texts, *Negatives of My Father* and *Stone's Paranoia*, have been translated into English.

"Baronkarl" is one of three stories comprising Henisch's *Vagabundengeschichten* (1980). Additional stories about Baronkarl and his surroundings can be found in Henisch's *Vom Baronkarl: Peripheriegeschichten und andere Prosa* (1972) and *Baronkarl: Alte und neue Peripheriegeschichten* (1992).

HUGO VON HOFMANNSTHAL was born in Vienna in 1874. He studied at the University of Vienna, receiving a doctorate in Romance languages and literature. While still a high-school student, Hofmannsthal was a published and highly acclaimed poet, with many of his poems appearing under the pseudonym Loris. He soon stopped writing poetry, however, and devoted his literary energies to other genres, in particular drama and opera libretti. Hofmannsthal's collaboration with Richard Strauss resulted in such operas as *Elektra* (1903), *Der Rosenkavalier* (1911), and *Die Frau ohne Schatten* (1919). Hofmannsthal's "Ein Brief" (1902), also known as "Der Lord Chandos Brief," is considered a paradigmatic text of modernist language critique. Hofmannsthal was one of the initiators of the Salzburger Festspiele, and his drama *Jedermann* (1911) has been performed annually in Salzburg since 1920. Hofmannsthal died in 1929 in Rodaun, close to Vienna. Virtually all of his fiction is available in English translation.

"The Tale of the 672nd Night" was first published in 1895 in three installments in the Viennese weekly *Die Zeit.*

ÖDÖN VON HORVÁTH was born in 1901 in Susak (currently Rijeka) on the Adriatic coast. The son of a civil servant in the Hungarian Ministry of Trade, Horváth spent his youth in Belgrade, Budapest, Munich, Preßburg (Bratislava), and Vienna. He began to study theater at the University of Munich, but decided shortly thereafter to cease his university studies and move to Berlin. Horváth is best known for his plays – including *Geschichten aus dem Wiener Wald* (1931), *Kasimir und Karoline* (1932), and *Glaube Liebe Hoffnung* (1936) – which contributed significantly to the rejuvenation of the "Volksstück" (popular drama) tradition during the interwar period. His first novel, *Der ewige Spießer*, appeared in 1930, followed by two novels written in exile, *Jugend ohne Gott* (1937) and *Ein Kind unserer Zeit* (1938). Horváth had made plans to emigrate to the United States when, in 1938, he was killed by a falling branch on the Champs-Elysées in Paris. Upon his death, his works were virtually forgotten, but they experienced a widespread rediscovery in the late 1960s and early 1970s. His plays now belong to the standard repertoire of the German-speaking theater. Most of his plays as well as his prose have appeared in English translation.

"Crossing the Border," which arose as preparatory work for *Der ewige Spießer*, appeared in *Von Spießern, Kleinbürgern und Angestellten*, an anthology of Horváth's short prose published in 1971.

FELIX MITTERER was born in 1948 in Achenkirch, Tyrol, and grew up in the Tyrolean towns of Kitzbühel and Kirchberg. He began a teacher's training course in Innsbruck, and then went on to work for ten years at the customs office in the Tyrolean capital. Known primarily as a dramatist in the tradition of the "Volksstück" (popular drama), Mitterer has written many plays, film scripts, and radio plays in which the effects of National Socialism and the explosive growth of tourism in Tyrol play significant roles. He has also acted in many plays, including the lead role in his drama "Kein Platz für Idioten." Since the mid-nineties, Mitterer has been living in Ireland. Two collections of his plays are available in English translation: *Siberia and Other Plays* and *The Wild Woman and Other Plays*.

"Inventory" appeared in *An den Rand des Dorfes*, a collection of short stories published in 1981.

ROBERT MUSIL was born in 1880 in Klagenfurt, Carinthia. The son of an upper-middle-class civil servant, Musil initially studied mechanical engineering in Brünn. After working at the Technical University in Stuttgart, Musil went to Berlin, where he studied philosophy and psychology and completed a dissertation on Ernst Mach. Working as a librarian in Vienna until the outbreak of World War I, he served as an officer and edited a military newspaper during the war. Musil spent most of the interwar period in Berlin, and when the Nazis came to power he returned to Vienna, where he stayed until the Anschluss. In 1938 he emigrated to Switzerland, and died in Geneva in 1942. Shortly after his death, *The London Times* called Musil "the most significant German-language novelist of the first half of the twentieth century as well as the era's least known author." Virtually all of Musil's prose is available in English, including recent translations of his novels *The*

Confusions of Young Törless and the monumental *The Man Without Qualities*.

"The Blackbird" appeared in *Nachlaß zu Lebzeiten*, a collection of prose texts published in 1936.

DORON RABINOVICI was born in Tel Aviv in 1961 and moved with his family to Vienna in 1964. He studied medicine, psychology, ethnology, and history at the University of Vienna. In 1991 he began a dissertation on Vienna's Jewish Council from 1938 to 1945, a study that subsequently appeared as *Instanzen der Ohnmacht* (1999). To date, Rabinovici has published a collection of short stories, *Papirnik* (1994); a novel, *Suche nach M.* (1997); and a volume of literary and political essays, *Credo und Credit* (2001). Austro-Jewish history and culture play a significant role in his work as a writer of fiction and history. Rabinovici has also co-edited two important volumes addressing the contemporary political situation in Austria: *Österreich: Berichte aus Quarantanien* (2000) and *Republik der Courage: Wider der Verhaiderung* (2000). *The Search for M* is available in English translation.

"The Right Nose" appeared in *Papirnik*.

ELISABETH REICHART was born in 1953 in Steyregg, Upper Austria. She studied history and German literature in Salzburg and Vienna, and received her doctorate for a dissertation on resistance to National Socialism in the Salzkammergut. Her first novel, *Februarschatten* (1984), examines Austria's Nazi past and the dynamics of memory and repression by way of a mother-daughter relationship, while her second novel, *Komm über den See* (1988), explores the female resistance movement in Austria. Violence, especially violence against women, plays an important role in Reichart's works. *Das vergessene Lächeln der Amaterasu* (1998), which takes place in large part in Japan, is her most recent novel. *February Shadows* and *La Valse and Foreign* are available in English translation.

"The Sunday Roast" and "How Far is Mauthausen?" both appeared in *La Valse*, a collection of short stories published in 1992.

JOSEPH ROTH was born in 1894 in the Galician city of Brody (currently in the Ukraine). He studied German literature and philosophy in Lemberg (Lvov) and Vienna. During the First World War, Roth served as an officer in the Austro-Hungarian army, and in 1918 began a career as a journalist, first in Vienna and then in Berlin. When the Nazis came to power in 1933, Roth went into exile in Paris, where he died, impoverished, in 1939. Most of Roth's novels and short stories evoke the lost world of the Habsburg Empire. Virtually all of Roth's work is available in English translation, including his major novels *The Emperor's Tomb*, *The Radetzky March*, and *Job*, and the recently translated *The Collected Stories of Joseph Roth*.

"The Bust of the Emperor" was first published in French translation in 1934; the original German version appeared in installments in the *Pariser Tageszeitung* in 1935.

ARTHUR SCHNITZLER was born in Vienna in 1862. The son of a professor of medicine, Schnitzler studied medicine as well, becoming a specialist in nervous disorders. He had a particular interest in psychology, and Freud referred to Schnitzler as his alter ego. In 1890, Schnitzler joined the group of "Jung-Wien" authors centered around Hermann Bahr. The premiere of Schnitzler's drama *Liebelei* in 1895 at Vienna's Burgtheater brought him great success, but his subsequent plays and prose works frequently resulted in scandal. The moral and sexual hypocrisy of the Austrian bourgeoisie and the country's growing anti-Semitism figure prominently in Schnitzler's texts. Schnitzler died in Vienna in 1931. Virtually all of his work is available in English translation.

"Lieutenant Gustl" first appeared in 1900 in Vienna's *Neue Freie Presse*. On account of the text's portrayal of the military, Schnitzler was stripped of his officer's title.

Austria in the Twentieth Century

A Chronology

1888   First Party Congress of the Social Democrats is held in Hainfeld.

1892   Founding of the Christian Social Workers' Club (later to become the Christian Social Party) in Vienna.

1896   Election reforms; all male citizens now have the right to vote.

1897   "Badeni Crisis," occasioned by statutes introduced by Prime Minister Kasimir Count Badeni requiring all federal civil servants in Bohemia and Moravia to prove their bilingualism (German and Czech) within four years. Following substantial rioting by German nationalists against the multi-ethnic empire, the statutes are eventually rescinded.

Women admitted to the university.

Karl Lueger becomes Mayor of Vienna, holding that office until his death in 1910.

Founding of the Secession, a group of modernist artists in Vienna whose members include Gustav Klimt.

1908   Annexation of Bosnia and Herzegovina.

1914   Assassination of Archduke Franz Ferdinand, heir to the Austrian throne, and his wife in Sarajevo.

One moth later, Austria-Hungary declares war on Serbia.

World War I begins.

1916   Emperor Franz Joseph dies, ending his sixty-eight-year reign. Karl the First ascends to the throne.

1917   Passage of the Wartime Enabling Act.

1918   Extensive strikes by industrial workers; calls for an end to the war.

Collapse of the Habsburg Empire in October.

Drafting of a provisional constitution for German-Austria.

Cease-fire agreement between Austria-Hungary and the Entente in November.

Kaiser Karl renounces the throne, ending over 600 years of Habsburg rule in Austria.

The Republic of German-Austria is proclaimed by the Provisional National Assembly.

1918-19 Women granted the right to vote.

1919   The imperial family leaves Austria for Switzerland.

Passage of anti-Habsburg laws and abolition of the aristocracy in Austria.

Repeal of the death penalty.

In April and June, Communist uprisings in Vienna.

Signing of the Treaty of St. Germain in September. Its stipulations include prohibiting the name "German-Austria" – the state is to be called the "Republic of Austria" – and prohibiting an Austrian Anschluss with Germany.

1920   Founding Convention of the Pan-Germanic Party ("Großdeutsche Volkspartei").

National Assembly ratifies the constitution of the First Austrian Republic.

Founding of the Salzburg Festival.

1921-22   Hyperinflation.

1925   The Austrian Schilling becomes the national currency.

1927   In the Burgenland village of Schattendorf, members of a veterans' club fire upon members and supporters of the Republican Defense Corps ("Republikanischer Schutzbund," the paramilitary organization of the Social Democrats founded in 1923), killing two persons and wounding five others. Six months later in Vienna, the Palace of Justice is set on fire to protest the acquittal of the accused in the Schattendorf trial.

1931   Collapse of the Credit-Anstalt.

1933   Parliament is disbanded.

The Austro-fascist dictatorship of Engelbert Dollfuss begins. Dollfuss advocates a "social, Christian, German state of Austria organized on a corporate basis with strong authoritarian leadership."

The Republican Defense Corps is outlawed. Shortly thereafter, the Communist Party is outlawed.

In spring, Nazi Germany imposes a "Tausend-marksperre"; all Germans traveling to Austria must pay 1,000 Marks. In retaliation, the Nazi Party is outlawed in Austria.

1934   Civil war breaks out in Austria, lasting less than one week. Vienna and Linz are the major sites of conflict.

The Social Democratic Party is outlawed.

A new corporative constitution is introduced.

Unsuccessful Nazi putsch, during which Dollfuss is murdered. Kurt Schuschnigg becomes Austrian Chancellor.

1936   July Agreement between Austria and Germany. Germany recognizes Austria's sovereignty. Concessions are made to the National Socialists in Austria, and Nazi Germany abolishes the "Tausendmarksperre."

Dissolution of the Heimwehr, a paramilitary organization of the right.

1938   Hitler and Schuschnigg meet in February in Berchtesgaden.

On March 11, Nazi Germany issues an ultimatum to Austria. Schuschnigg calls off a planned plebiscite regarding annexation by Nazi Germany. Schuschnigg resigns and the Nazi Arthur Seyß-Inquart becomes Austrian Chancellor. On March 12, German troops march into Austria. Not a single shot is fired.

On March 15, a massive demonstration in support of the Nazi regime is held on Vienna's Heldenplatz. Hitler delivers his "Heim ins Reich" speech there, proclaiming Austria as the newest bastion of the German Reich.

In April, a plebiscite is held concerning the Anschluss. One month later, Austria is divided into seven administrative "Gaus" and the territory is renamed "Ostmark."

On November 9-10, the "Reichskristallnacht" (the "Night of Broken Glass") occurs.

1939   The Nazi army attacks Poland.

World War II begins.

1941   The deportation of Jews begins.

1943   Air raid attacks on Austrian cities begin.

The Moscow Declaration, identifying Austria as the "first victim" of Nazi aggression, is issued by the

Allies. The notion of "first victim" will come to play a central role in constructing Austrian national identity during the postwar period.

1945   In March, the Red Army reaches Austrian territory.

In April, the Austrian Socialist Party (SPÖ) and the Austrian People's Party (ÖVP, successor to the Christian Socials) are founded.

The Proclamation of Austrian Independence is issued by the provisional government.

The German Reich surrenders in May.

The Allies occupy Austria, dividing the country (and the city of Vienna) into four zones of occupation.

The Allied Commission recognizes Austria's Provisional Government, headed by Karl Renner, in October. In November, the first federal elections of the Second Austrian Republic are held.

Prohibition of the National Socialist Party.

1947   Austria is included in the Marshall Plan.

Currency reform.

1949   Founding of the Union of Independents (VdU), consisting largely of former nationalist and Nazi groups.

1955   After frequently stalled negotiations, the Austrian State Treaty (expressly not called a peace treaty) is signed on May 15, establishing the country's independence and the withdrawal of all occupying troops on the condition that Austria remain politically neutral.

Austria joins the United Nations.

The Austrian Freedom Party (FPÖ) is founded.

1966   End of the "Grand Coalition" between the Austrian Socialist and People's parties.

1986   Kurt Waldheim, former Secretary General of the United Nations, runs as the People's Party candidate for Austria's presidency. As Waldheim's wartime activities in the German Wehrmacht – and his postwar suppression of those activities – receive increased attention in the national and international press, the presidential election gives rise to the first widespread discussion of Austria's fascist past. Waldheim wins a run-off election and assumes the presidency, but his six-year term is marked by considerable domestic and international controversy.

1995   Austria enters the European Union.

1998   Austria assumes the six-month presidency of the European Union.

1999   The Austrian Freedom Party, with its charismatic, radical-right leader Jörg Haider, makes tremendous gains in federal elections.

2000   The Austrian People's Party enters into a coalition with the Freedom Party, causing great protest in Austria and the imposition of sanctions by the European Union.

Ariadne Press
Studies

ARIADNE PRESS

http://ariadnepress.com; http://www.onb.ac.at/biblos/engl.htm
270 Goins Court, Riverside, CA 92507
Tel: 951 684 9202; fax: 951 779 0449
email: ariadnepress@aol.com

Recent Studies

Ingeborg Bachmann's Telling Stories:
Fairy Tale Beginnings and
Holocaust Endings
By Kirsten Krick-Aigner

The Fiction of the I:
Contemporary Austrian Writers
and Autobiography
Edited by Nicholas J. Meyerhofer

Postwar Austrian Theater:
Text and Performance
Edited by Linda C. DeMeritt and
Margarete Lamb-Faffelberger

After Postmodernism:
Austrian Literature and Film
in Transition
Edited by Willy Riemer

Balancing Acts:
Textual Strategies of Peter Henisch
Edited by Craig Decker

Barbara Frischmuth in
Contemporary Context
Edited by Renate Posthofen

Modern Austrian Prose:
Interpretations and Insights
Edited by Paul F. Dvorak

Critical Essays
on Julian Schutting
Edited by Harriet Murphy

The Writer's Place:
Heimito von Doderer
and the Alsergrund
District of Vienna
By Engelbert Pfeiffer
Translated and Expanded
with an Afterword
By Vincent Kling

Austria in Literature
Edited by Donald G. Daviau

Stefan Zweig
An International Bibliography
Addendum I
By Randolf J. Klawiter